Integrating
Library Use Skills
into the General Education
Curriculum

Forthcoming topics in *The Reference Librarian* series:

Published:

Integrating Library Use Skills into the General Education Curriculum

Edited by
Maureen Pastine and Bill Katz

The Haworth Press
New York • London

Integrating Library Use Skills into the General Education Curriculum has also been published as *The Reference Librarian*, Number 24.

The Haworth Press, Inc., 10 Alice Street, Binghamton, NY 13904-1580
EUROSPAN/Haworth, 3 Henrietta Street, London WC2E 8LU England

Library of Congress Cataloging-in-Publication Data

Integrating library use skills into the general education curriculum / edited by Maureen Pastine and Bill Katz.
    p. cm.
"Has also been published as the Reference librarian, number 24" — T.p. verso.
Includes bibliographies.
ISBN 0-86656-841-7
    1. Libraries, University and college — Reference services. 2. Bibliography — Methodology — Study and teaching (Higher) 3. Research — Methodology — Study and teaching (Higher) 4. College students — Library orientation. 5. Libraries and education. 6. Libraries and students. I. Pastine, Maureen. II. Katz, William A., 1924- .
Z711.2.I54 1989
025.5'677 — dc19   89-31193
                                                                 CIP

Integrating Library Use Skills into the General Education Curriculum

CONTENTS

PART III: LIBRARY SKILLS IN A COMMUNITY COLLEGE

Building Alliances: General Education and Library Skills in a Community College   **57**
Susan Griswold Blandy

PART IV: LIBRARY SKILLS IN COLLEGES AND UNIVERSITIES

University Approval of Library Research Skills as Part of the General Education Curriculum Requirements   **75**
Judy Reynolds

The View from Square One: Librarian and Teaching Faculty Collaboration on a New Interdisciplinary Course in World Civilizations   **87**
Paula Elliot

ABOUT THE EDITORS

Maureen Pastine, MLS, is Director of Libraries at Washington State University. She has published articles on bibliographic instruction in recent books and professional journals and has given several presentations on this topic at professional association meetings. She has taught graduate library school courses at San Jose State University and The University of Illinois at Urbana-Champaign. Former Chair of the ACRL, Bibliographic Instruction Section, Ms. Pastine is currently serving on an ACRL Task Force on Librarians as Instructors and on the ALA Library Instruction Round Table's Long Range Planning Committee.

Bill Katz, editor of *The Reference Librarian*, is internationally known as one of the leading specialists in reference work today. In addition to the two-volume *Introduction to Reference Work*, he is the author of *Magazines for Libraries* and *Reference and Online Services: A Handbook*. Past editor of *RQ*, the journal of the Reference and Adult Services Division of the American Library Association, Bill Katz currently edits a magazine column in *Library Journal*. He is also the editor of a new Haworth journal, *The Acquisitions Librarian*.

Introduction

"Integrating Library Use Skills into the General Education Curriculum" is a collection of articles written by many of those who have been active participants in planning and administering user education programs and/or who have served as instruction librarians for many years.

This volume in *The Reference Librarian* series is intended as a forum for further discussion on some of the major ideas underlying integration of library use skills and research methodologies into general education programs and curricular reform. It should be noted at the outset that the compiler of this issue has not limited "general education" to the lower division coursework requirements of an academic institution. Instead, the premise of the compiler is that a library user education program, in order to be effective, must be designed to build on basic library use skills through a progressively sophisticated program that is fully integrated into course curriculum at all levels, from the freshman year to graduation and beyond.

As May Brotman reported at a recent American Library Association Instruction in the Use of Libraries Committee, an effective user education program requires

> a comprehensive research framework for determining the role of library use instruction in the educational process. To be effective, the framework should be designed by librarians from all types of libraries and by [other] educators. To be viable, it must be a cooperative project involving librarians from all types of libraries, educators involved with the development of critical thinking skills, and educational researchers.

This volume focuses on integration of library user education into the general education curriculum of academic institutions. It is not meant to cover all issues but, instead, to provide some thought-provoking concerns and to describe some recent examples of library user education activities on which others can build and develop stronger, more integrative programs.

In recent years there has been a renewed emphasis on general education curricular reform. The institution in which I am employed, Washington State University, has begun a massive revamping of its general education philosophy and in redirection of the general education university requirements. It has received grant funding for a pilot World Civilizations Course (described in this volume in articles by Paula Elliot and Alice Spitzer). It has established a General Education Commission and an All University Writing Committee, both of which are made up of members of the instructional faculty, the administration (including ex-officio seats for the Director of Libraries on both groups), and student representatives — undergraduate and graduate. The new general education curricula will require writing-intensive assignments and integrated library course-related assignments whenever possible. A three-tiered course framework if approved, will require general education courses from the freshman through the senior year, with writing placement and proficiency examinations prior to graduation, along with other assessment methodologies. The plan is not a smorgasbord approach to general education courses, but a carefully planned, limited selection of course requirements to ensure a common body of knowledge in the sciences, social sciences, and humanities, and the development of critical thinking and reasoning skills, basic mathematical skills, an understanding of the interdisciplinary nature of knowledge, awareness of cultural diversity, and the ability to use libraries and new technologies effectively and efficiently for life-long learning.

Dr. Patricia Breivik comments, in the introductory chapter, on the national concerns for quality education and the need for librarians to take a more aggressive role in the search for excellence and in establishing learning priorities, particularly as these relate to information literacy and/or resource-based learning. All of us have seen the proliferation of local, state, and national conferences, institutes, workshops, and seminars from the American Association of Higher Education's national conference in March of 1988 on ''The Highest Calling: Teaching to Rebuild a Nation'' to the University of South

Carolina's annual regional conferences on "The Freshmen Year Experience." Most of us have read some, if not all, of the many reports, journal articles, and books on the subject, many mentioned by a number of contributors to this issue. They include such titles as *A Nation at Risk: The Imperative for Education Reform*; Carnegie Foundation's Special Report, *Higher Education and the American Resurgence*; Ernest L. Boyer's report, *College: The Undergraduate Experience in America; Alliance for Excellence: Librarians Respond to a Nation at Risk*; the American Council on Education's Report, *General Education Requirements in the Humanities*; the Office of Scholarly Communication and Technology of the American Council of Learned Societies' survey results on scholars' views on publications, computers, and libraries published in the summer of 1986 in *Scholarly Communication*; and best sellers, such as Alan Bloom's *The Closing of the American Mind*, or other fascinating titles such as Arthur N. Applebee et al., *Learning to Be Literate in America: Reading, Writing, and Reasoning* (Princeton, Educational Testing Service, March 1987). Although some of these books, articles, and reports touch on the need for improved library use skills, few address the role of the library in development of critical reasoning skills, access to and evaluation of information sources, and building on basic library skills to develop more advanced search techniques and a greater understanding of the nature and structure of knowledge for life-long learning outside of the classroom. Libraries must plan a much greater role in the teaching/learning/research process if we truly expect our leaders of the future to be information-literate and oriented to the growth and development of knowledge. It is hoped that the following articles will provide some thought on where our weaknesses exist in fully integrating library user education into the curricula and some ideas on revamping and enhancing existing programs of library instruction to ensure a balanced effort in reaching all levels of higher education with library instruction not just the traditionally served undergraduate student.

Maureen Pastine

PART I: GENERAL

Politics for Closing the Gap

Patricia Senn Breivik

SUMMARY. Despite the realities of the Information Society, national concerns for quality education in America have largely ignored libraries. The major cause of this neglect is the lack of perception among most educational leaders that library personnel and resources both have something to offer in the search for excellence and that librarians are committed to serving their institutions' learning priorities. To rectify this situation will require informed and aggressive leadership by librarians. Nonetheless, concerns raised by some educational leaders call for reforms that have strong implications for the instructional role of libraries. Resource-based learning can make a major contribution to preparing students for lifelong learning, active citizenship and risk taking. A number of recent, current and projected activities and publications are described. These can offer a good foundation for librarians wishing to promote information literacy and/or resource-based learning.

In 1983, the publishing of *A Nation at Risk*[1] heralded the beginning of the current educational reform movement. In *A Nation at Risk* and in the reports which followed, one thing became clear: the educational establishment and its leaders saw no role for librarians

Patricia Senn Breivik is Director, Auraria Library, 11th at Lawrence Street, Denver, CO 80204.

5

or libraries in issues related to quality education. At best, a few made passing reference to libraries and laboratories as places other than classrooms where learning might take place. At worst, one questioned the ability and commitment of librarians to move beyond the owning, cataloging and lending of books.[2]

This oversight is difficult to understand given the nature of some of the major concerns which have been raised. First, issues covered in many of the reports make it clear that the writers are not unaware, at least in some aspects, of the information society in which this and all future generations will exist. In particular there is a great deal of concern for the fragmentation of research and learning which is occurring due to the increasing abundance of information. It then seems ironic that libraries, which are the primary access point to information in all disciplines and which provide a framework for the interrelation of the literature of the diverse fields, should be so absent from their thinking.

Second, the nature of the learning reforms, which run as a thread through many of the reports, would seem — at least to librarians — to cry out for the involvement of librarians and learning resources. The reports call for active learning that prepares students for life-long learning, active citizenship and risk taking. It would seem almost self-evident that one good way to accomplish this would be for classroom faculty to build their courses around the existing literature of their fields rather than on lectures and textbooks. A more active learning experience could be provided by placing students in the position of using the same books, journals, videotapes and on-line databases for their class assignments that will be available to them for learning after they graduate. Through resource-based learning, students could master the information retrieval and evaluation skills that will be useful for learning throughout their lives. They could become information literate.

The same skills are important for active citizenship. As U.S. Representative Major R. Owens wrote:

> Information literacy is needed to guarantee the survival of democratic institutions. All men are created equal but voters with information resources are in a position to make more intelligent decisions than citizens who are information illiterates.

The application of information resources to the process of decision-making to fulfill civic responsibilities is a vital necessity.[3]

Good information retrieval and evaluation skills also can facilitate the development of risk takers. The more pertinent information one has to factor into solving a particular problem, the greater the likelihood of the solution being an appropriate one. In this manner risk taking becomes less "risky" and therefore a less threatening endeavor for people to undertake.

Librarians are good at pointing out the reluctance of faculty to change their teaching styles, and it would be a nice "out" if librarians could be the good guys in white hats currently held back by the black-hatted classroom faculty. Faculty attitudes are important, but they cannot be blamed for the lack of attention given to libraries in the reports, because the authors of these reports are calling for changes in faculty attitudes and teaching styles. The problem is that, even among those educators committed to change, there is little or no understanding that libraries have any contribution to make to learning besides their traditional warehouse role.

Much of the blame for this lack of awareness must lie within our profession — indeed, with us as individual librarians. Despite all that we have to offer within the search for educational excellence, we seem to have successfully managed to keep it a secret. Certainly it is not our intent. The whole library instruction movement and even this volume of *The Reference Librarian* is dedicated to the concept of "selling" library instruction and getting it integrated into the mainstream of the educational experiences of students.

Perhaps librarians have been too isolated over the years. This is not the first time that educators have called for more active learning. For example, a study conducted by the Association of American Colleges published in 1940 discussed the criticisms of the traditional form of American college teaching and urged that, in place of specific assignments and set lectures, students should be directed to the literature of the subject with the professor becoming an aid in the acquiring and understanding of this knowledge rather than its source and final end.[4] Within the literature of our field there is no indication that librarians responded to this report with any new initiatives. There was the library college movement, but its flavor was always more one of control by librarians than librarians seeking to support the educational agenda of others. Even our current terms of bibliographic and library instruction reinforce the perception of something which stands alone from the curriculum and that is useful only within libraries. Yet, for years our better programs have focused on search strategies which lead to needed information, whether housed in a library or elsewhere.

The result of this isolation — or self-centeredness — is manifested in another way, which has had an incalculable effect on the national visibility of libraries. The current rating system of libraries based on quantitative measures has produced an informally acknowledged academic library elite made up of a few directors of the very large Association of Research Libraries (ARL). These are the people most likely to be sought for insights into librarianship by people concerned with national academic issues, and there does not appear to be any equivalent elite for school or public libraries. The irony of this elite, which the profession has allowed to exist unchallenged, is that it is a most inappropriate representation for addressing the issues of concern to the writers of the reform reports.

Just as the largest and most prestigious universities are seldom known for innovation in instruction or quality undergraduate education, their libraries seldom provide models of innovative or even user friendly service and instructional support. This situation, in fact, should be expected, i.e., a library should reflect the personality and commitments of its institution. A problem only occurs when the interests and concerns of these very few, very large research libraries are represented as being those of academic libraries as a whole. When this happens, the overriding concerns for bibliographic control and preservation seem to be the preoccupation of all, and these concerns are far out of sync with national priorities, such as more active learning and the recruitment and retention of minorities.

In this mismatching of concerns, the impression has also been given that the priorities of libraries interfere with the ability of libraries to provide information systems that will meet users' needs. The following statement appeared in the Carnegie Foundation Special Report, *Higher Education and the American Resurgence*.

Library personnel, while now fully competent to handle the library automation that has taken place, have neither the education nor the emotional commitment to prepare for the shift in outlook required to change from owning, cataloging, and lending, to becoming electronic data sleuths ready to link a student or faculty member to someone else's data bank. Moreover, the time has come for information specialists to learn more about the needs of libraries.[5]

Frank Newman, President of the Education Commission of the States, authored the above. Since then he has considerably revised his assessment of libraries and librarians as evidenced by his editorial in the July/August issue of *Change*.[6] The shame is that, when writing the above, he had believed that the agenda of a few research libraries was representative of all. On the other hand, Ernest L. Boyer's report, *College: The Undergraduate Experience in America*, was based on the baccalaureate sector of higher education and included visits to twenty-nine colleges and universities. Boyer's report states, "At a college of quality there is a wide range of learning resources that enrich and extend classroom instruction and encourage students to become independent, self-directed learners."[7] Boyer's wider exposure to libraries provided a far more positive attitude toward libraries and their importance to education than Newman's initial more narrow perspective. Somehow a new message must be consistently and effectively sent out from libraries of all sizes and types. Instead of placing the emphasis on library problems, librarians need to emphasize how they can help solve the problems of others. They need to make it clear that the agendas of school and academic libraries are the same as those of their institutions, that libraries do have much to offer in the addressing of identified educational priorities, and that library personnel and resources can be strong tools of empowerment for achieving those priorities.

Failure to effectively communicate such a message can be attributed in part to the reluctance of most librarians to be risk takers. Many are far too busy and comfortable within their library circles to venture far out into the wider seas of education and the professions. Few librarians become active in any professional organization that is not library related. Too few do research and publishing; the little that is done seldom focuses on issues of concern to educators; and libraries almost never publish in nonlibrary publications. Recently, for example, in the *Library Instruction Round Table Newsletter* there was a list of publications that would accept articles on library instruction in which only library publications were listed. The seeds for this problem are planted early in their careers, for most library schools focus on libraries in isolation rather than providing any serious consideration of the environments in which libraries exist.

If these comments seem too harsh a condemnation to those librarians reading this volume, they need to be weighed in terms of the problems confronting our country and the long term implication of our collective unwillingness to pay the price of leadership within the larger boundaries of education. Let me cite just two of the realities of concern to the reform writers by way of example.

> Each generation of Americans has outstripped its parents in education, in literacy, and in economic attainment. For the first time in the history of our country, the educational skills of one generation will not surpass, will not equal, will not even approach, those of their parents.[8]

> At stake is more than simply the issue of the health of the American economy. At stake is the fundamental issue of the place of the United States in the world, whether it will define itself as a country moving ahead or as a country drifting into a lesser role. We believe that the United States is gearing up for an economic renewal. Education at all levels is expected to play a role.[9]

To meet the challenges put forward in the reform reports, there have been many recommendations forthcoming about increasing teachers' salaries and creating better working conditions for them. Unfortunately, however, few new solutions have been forthcoming regarding how learning experiences should be changed. Initial responses called for longer school days, longer school years and more homework, as if more of what has not been working would work. (Probably the most meaningful outcome to date has been the assessment movement which, while not offering a solution per se, is beginning to hold schools and academic institutions accountable for improvement in student performance. In other words, some governors and legislatures are insisting that schools and colleges be able to document student achievement.)

Given the paucity of possible solutions and the seriousness of the situation to the future of our country and to the quality of American life, it is inexcusable for people to withhold the potential to make a major contribution, or to not be as winsome as possible in presenting their ideas. Librarians need to attractively package the concept of resource-based instruction and develop a strategy for its acceptance which will not fail to gain the attention of educational leaders at local, state and national levels.

The good news is that it is not too late for the potential role of librarians and learning resources to be explored within the reform agenda. Several recent and imminent occurrences are keeping that window of opportunity open.

First and foremost was the publication of Boyer's *College: The Undergraduate Experience in America*, which was published in 1987 under the auspices of the Carnegie Foundation for the Advancement of Teaching and to which I have already referred. The entire report makes a strong case for heavy library use despite the current discouraging statistics that "today, about one out of every four undergraduates spends *no* time in the library during the normal week, and 65 percent use the library four hours *or less* each week."[10] Boyer calls for a closing of the gap between the classroom and the library. He calls for the library to become a central learning resource on the campus and says that to make that possible:

. . . we need, above all, liberally educated librarians, professionals who understand and are interested in undergraduate education, who are involved in educational matters, and who can open the stacks to students, create browsing rooms, reform the reserve book system, help distribute books throughout the campus, and expand holdings in ways that enrich the undergraduate experience.[11]

If these comments do not reflect what librarians are doing on your campus, a good first step might be to have every librarian read

College from cover to cover and set up a series of meetings to discuss implications of the report for your campus.

Another occurrence which can be useful to librarians willing to respond to Boyer's challenge was the holding of the first higher education conference on libraries, jointly sponsored by the University of Colorado and Columbia University in March of 1987. The symposium was planned to address the issue of "Libraries and the Search for Academic Excellence" before *College* was published and when it seemed that no one would be addressing the potential contribution of librarians and library resources toward the problems being identified in the reform reports. The summary of the symposium was published in the July/August issue of *Change*[12] along with a description of four academic libraries which can serve as models for addressing particular reform issues. *Change* has a subscription list of over 60,000 educators, which allowed for a much wider audience for the symposium discussions than would have otherwise been possible. What is also worth noting is the caliber of the national educational leaders who participated—including both Boyer and Newman. The papers prepared for the symposium as well as discussion summaries and recommendations will be published by Scarecrow Press later this year. Meanwhile, the commissioned papers are available through ERIC.[13]

Some outcomes of the symposium are likely to capture national attention for the potential role of libraries in the search for educational excellence. Near the end of the symposium, Ernst Benjamin, President of the American Association of University Professors, committed his organization to work with the Association of College and Research Libraries to set up one or more opportunities for faculty and librarians to further discuss the integrating of libraries into the curriculum. Margaret Chisholm, American Library Association President, has established a Presidential Committee on Information Literacy which is charged:

> To define information literacy within the higher literacies and its importance to student performance, life-long learning and active citizenship; to design one or more models for information literacy development appropriate to formal and informal learning environments, throughout people's lifetimes; and to

determine implications for the continuing education and development of teachers.

The Task Force contains a good representation of both educators and librarians.[14] The presence of the former is designed not only to ensure a document that will target existing educational concerns but also to gain credibility for the outcomes of the deliberations early in 1989. The outcomes of the Committee may also serve as a basis for a conference being planned by the American Association of School Librarians and the National Commission on Libraries and Information Services for the spring of 1989. This conference will also seek to bring educational leaders together with librarians, but it will focus on the K-12 sector.

In addition, a book which is directed at academic officers encouraging them to use their libraries more fully as tools of empowerment for achieving all campus priorities will be published late this year by MacMillan under the auspices of the American Council on Education (ACE). The ACE sponsorship, and the book's co-authorship by the University of Colorado (CU) president and a CU librarian should provide a wider audience among educational leaders than most books on libraries receive.

Such national windows of opportunities, however, will be meaningless unless librarians across the country continue the dialogue at educational and professional meetings, in nonlibrary journals and in their own states and institutions. Such undertakings must take place in terms of the prevailing concerns of those whom librarians are seeking to serve. If the concern is assessment, let librarians discuss information literacy skills as part of the assessment of academic support skills and show how such skills can be assessed. If the concern is writing across the curriculum, let librarians support information literacy across the curriculum and document its benefits. If the concern is student retention, let librarians document how information literacy skills can promote academic survival. If the concern is the recruitment and retention of minorities (a major theme in many of the reform reports), let librarians suggest ways in which library-to-library bridge programs to local schools can be of benefit.

The key to the success of such dialogues is the capturing of sufficient attention of educational leaders. For example, in October of

1987, the New Jersey State Library sponsored a three-day conference entitled, "Library Media Centers in New Jersey: An Educational Imperative." Participation by school systems required attendance by complete teams consisting of a school media specialist, a teacher, a member of the board of education and a top administrator (i.e., either the superintendent or the assistant superintendent). Barbara Weaver, the State Librarian, characterized the outcome of the conference as "a drastic reorientation of thinking about school library media centers and a determination to put changes into effect." Three days of dialogue regarding resource-based learning led to many participants articulating a complete change in attitudes toward the role of school library media centers.

To prepare for such dialogues librarians must, as Boyer suggests, be knowledgeable about education matters and be committed to education as much as to librarianship. It is not enough to efficiently operate a reserve system; librarians need to be out educating teachers as to why reserve systems are not desirable within the concern for active learning—not to mention educating them to how little most reserve materials have been used. Henry Wriston, who was president of Lawrence College in Appleton, Wisconsin (1925-1937) and Brown University (1937-1955) personally fought a war against reserves, firmly believing that "the reserve shelf supplied a fairly accurate index of diminishing expectations on the part of the professor, and concrete evidence that the student was being short-changed in his education."[15] Too few librarians, however, have ever challenged a faculty member to consider that there might be a better way of facilitating student learning than putting a large number of items on reserve.

Taking a greater leadership responsibility in education will require other changes as well. More research is needed. When the mastery of information literacies are planned for inclusion in a core curriculum, librarians could work with faculty to retain examples of bibliographies and term papers that could be contrasted against those produced by students receiving the new instruction. When faculty are willing to switch from a lecture and textbook approach to a resource-based learning approach, librarians could work with them to develop ways to evaluate student satisfaction and performance against those in more traditional courses. If academic survival programs are being set up for high risk students, librarians could include information literacy in some sections but not others, and follow both groups of students throughout their academic programs. In addition, both to gain better research skills and to promote faculty acceptance of librarians not only as team players but as educational leaders, more librarians will need to get doctorates — though not necessarily in librarianship.

We have thrust upon us a call to leadership, a call to help our institutions meet the challenges of quality education for an information society. The question is how we shall respond. Are we willing to respond in terms that are meaningful not only to ourselves but also to our institutions?

Certainly this volume of *The Reference Librarian* should be helpful to those whose response is yes. A number of issues which have emerged from the reform reports are addressed in this publication: bridge building among higher education institutions and between K-12 and colleges, critical thinking skills, writing across the curriculum, core or general education requirements and fostering the academic success of nontraditional students. Articles such as these should help librarians to place their efforts within the framework of school and campus concerns. Then, working together with teachers, the gap between the classroom and the library will be closed.

REFERENCES

1. The National Commission on Excellence in Education, *A Nation at Risk: The Imperative for Education Reform* (Washington, D.C.: National Commission on Excellence in Education, April, 1983).

2. Frank Newman, *Higher Education and the American Resurgence*: (Princeton, N.J., Princeton University Press, 1985), 152.

3. Major R. Owens, "State Government and Libraries," *Library Journal* 101 (1 January 1976): 27.

4. Harvey Branscomb, *Teaching with Books: A Study of College Libraries* (Chicago: Association of American Colleges and the American Library Association, 1940), 63-64.

5. Newman, *Higher Education and the American Resurgence*, 152.

6. Frank Newman, "Adapting Academic Libraries to the Future," *Change* 19 (July/August 1987): 4-5.

7. Ernest L. Boyer, College: *The Undergraduate Experience in America* (New York: Harper & Row, 1987), 160.

8. The National Commission on Excellence in Education, *A Nation at Risk*, 11.

9. Newman, *Higher Education and the American Resurgence*, xiii-xiv.

10. Boyer, *College*, 160.

11. Ibid., 165.

12. Patricia Senn Breivik, "Making the Most of Libraries in the Search for Academic Excellence," *Change* 19 (July/August 1987): 44-52.

13. Patricia Senn Breivik and Robert Wedgeworth, *Libraries and the Search for Academic Excellence*, A National Symposium sponsored by Columbia University and the University of Colorado, New York, 15-17 March 1987 (Bethesda, M.D.: ERIC Document Reproduction Service, ED 284-585, 1987).

14. Members of the American Library Association Presidential Committee on Information Literacy are: Gordon M. Ambach, Executive Director, Council of Chief State School Officers; William L. Bainbridge, President, School Match; Chair—Patricia Senn Breivik, Director, Auraria Library; Rexford Brown, Director, Policy and the Higher Literacies Project, Education Commission of the States; Judith S. Eaton, President, Community College of Philadelphia; David Imig, Executive Director, American Association of Colleges for Teacher Education; Sally Kilgore, Director, Office of Educational Research, U.S. Department of Education; Carol Kuhlthau, Director, Educational Media Services Programs, Rutgers University; Joseph Mika, Director of Graduate Library Science Program, Wayne State University; Richard D. Miller, Executive Director, American Association of School Administrators; Roy D. Miller, Executive Assistant to the Director, Brooklyn Public Library; Sharon J. Rogers, Director of Library, George Washington University; and Robert Wedgeworth, Dean, School of Library Service, Columbia University.

15. Henry W. Wriston, *Academic Procession: Reflections of a College President* (New York: Columbia University Press, 1959), 133.

Staffing for Bibliographic Instruction: Issues and Strategies for New and Expanding Programs

Donna L. McCool

SUMMARY. In planning for new or expanding bibliographic programs, library administrators and instruction librarians must work together to develop strategies for using limited staff resources effectively. Issues related to who should teach, how to develop needed skills, and which instructional methodologies to adopt must be addressed. Organizations in which assumptions and priorities can be examined, and where risk-taking is encouraged, often achieve goals which otherwise might be unobtainable.

The rise of bibliographic instruction in the 1960s and 1970s has been described as a grassroots movement practiced largely by reference librarians, often without the knowledge or support of library administrators.[1] While reference librarians have taken the leadership in bringing bibliographic instruction to its present level of sophistication, there are management concerns associated with instruction programs which must be addressed and resolved through the combined efforts of librarians and library administrators. One such area of concern is staffing.

ISSUES

Dyson found that the most effective instruction programs are those that involve a large number of staff.[2] Attempting to implement a strong BI program while maintaining a full range of other library

---

Donna L. McCool is Assistant Director for Administrative Services, Washington State University Libraries, Pullman, WA 99164-5610.

17

services can be difficult, however. The pressures on one undergraduate library where a few librarians were trying to be all things to all people are described by Kohl. The complexity of the university's academic programs plus the diversity of special needs represented within the student body presented a potential instruction load which appeared to be staggering to overworked librarians.[3]

It is unlikely that most academic libraries can expect a large number of new positions to staff a BI program. While grants can sometimes facilitate the development of innovative new programs, granting agencies normally will not fund on-going program costs. Nor can most libraries expect to receive a significant infusion of new money from university administrators, who are faced with competing demands from throughout the institution for larger shares of the pie. The opinions they hold of bibliographic instruction programs are likely to reflect values, biases, and perceptions held over from their days as faculty members. While there may be occasional exceptions, not many administrators will view the issue as a major area of concern. Or, if the value of BI is understood, it is likely to be considered to fall within the teaching faculties' realm of responsibility. The result is that librarians to staff a BI program must come, in most cases, from within the existing library allocation for personnel.

The problem then becomes one of setting priorities, of making tough choices about what must be given up if staff resources are to be reallocated. Administrators and librarians together must ask:

1. Who should teach? Reference librarians only? Others?
2. How can limited staff resources be used most effectively?
3. Should all librarians participate or just those with special skills?
4. What skills are needed? How can they be developed?
5. How do instructional methodologies impact staffing levels?

These issues, as well as the strategies which libraries have adopted to address them, are the subject of this paper.

WHO SHOULD TEACH?

Perhaps it is natural that reference librarians were the first proponents of formal library instruction programs. Through their interactions with students they have been first-hand observers of the difficulties students experience in using libraries. Because reference librarians understand users' needs as well as library tools and information resources, it is reasonable to center the bibliographic instruction function around the reference department. However, reference librarians already have many demands on their time and increasing the time spent in one activity will mean eliminating, or at least reducing, time spent on something else.

One strategy for creating more time for instruction involves de-emphasizing the information provision function. Librarians spend less time at the reference desk providing one-on-one assistance in order to spend more time teaching. This approach is based on the view that on-demand reference service is labor intensive, reaches relatively few students and does little to strengthen their own information-seeking and processing skills. A better use of the librarian's time, the argument goes, would be to free the librarian to implement instructional programs which would reach more students and teach them skills of value for life-long learning.

As might be expected, the "information versus instruction" debate has generated a large volume of literature, certainly more than can be summarized here. One point which might be made, however, is that every library organization must decide for itself the appropriate balance between information and instruction and what constitutes heavy reference desk duty in one institution may represent a regular workload in another. For example, elsewhere in this volume of *The Reference Librarian*, Miner explains how one large academic library ceased scheduling librarians at reference desks.[4] Instead, each subject specialist was scheduled for 13-14 hours per week to back up para-professionals at the desk. By way of contrast, in this author's institution 13-14 hours per week is considered a typical reference desk assignment. What was achieved in Miner's library was more in-depth help for those referred to the librarian, as well as the time to implement an integrated bibliographic instruction program. Another point which might be made is that replacing librarians with para-professionals does not necessarily save money which then can be used to hire more librarians. In some institutions senior level para-professionals may be paid more than entry-level librarians. Any "savings" comes from a more effective use of the librarian's expertise and time. The real message which comes from this strategy of de-emphasizing information provision, however, is that libraries which create an environment in which assumptions can be examined and priorities realigned, and where risk-taking can be encouraged, often come up with creative ways to achieve a goal which otherwise might be unattainable.

Another strategy for gaining more BI staff is to enlarge the group of librarians who teach. Enlisting the assistance of technical services librarians is one example. As Dykeman points out, no one is more qualified to explain subject headings, call numbers, and cross references than a cataloger. Plus, technical services librarians can often bring strong subject backgrounds to the instructional program. Participation lets them see firsthand how library tools and collections are used, gives them contact with library users and the opportunity to establish credibility, which is valuable when tenure and promotion are considered.[5] Widening the base of participants also counters the elitism which sometimes finds it way into programs in which only a small group is involved. Involving technical services librarians in the BI function also creates an environment where they and the public services librarians can work together on a common project. And, library administrators should not be overlooked. They can benefit from the opportunity to keep reference skills fresh and can gain first-hand knowledge of the constraints and problems experienced by the BI program.

Should all librarians teach? Involvement of many librarians does offer a solution to the problem of obtaining instructors. And as mentioned earlier, other organizational and personal benefits accrue from widespread participation. However, if an individual hates teaching, is not a good teacher or is not supportive of the BI effort, s/he should not be forced to become involved. S/He may undermine the entire effort if his/her negativism spreads to the students s/he teaches and/or to his/her librarian colleagues.

Before leaving the question of who should teach, the potential role of nonlibrarians should be noted. In *Planning the Library In-*

struction Program, Patricia Breivik notes that teachers and graduate students, paraprofessionals, library science students and even volunteers, may have something to contribute.[6] She cites as examples a teaching assistant who grades papers, a library para-professional with a doctoral degree who teaches, a student who teaches newly acquired skills to his peers, and the faculty wife who volunteers to lead orientation tours. By utilizing the skills and talents of others where appropriate, the time of those librarians involved in BI can be stretched further.

SKILL DEVELOPMENT

Initial planning for a new or expanding BI program should include an assessment of the expertise represented within the current staff. Many librarians do not bring prior teaching experience or teacher education backgrounds to an instruction program. What does the current staff know about learning theory, instructional methodologies, testing, and evaluation? Are there special media skills represented? How much grounding in the theoretical concepts of reference do the reference librarians have? Could most of them teach search strategies? What particularly strong subject strengths are represented? How many of the librarians have had prior experience with strong BI programs? What was the nature of that experience? Answers to these and similar questions pinpoint strengths and weaknesses, identify areas for additional training and, perhaps most importantly, assist in defining what the scope of a realistic user education program might be at the present time.

In organizations without widespread experience, the recruitment of an experienced individual to administer the program will help establish a sense of direction. This administrator should be knowledgeable about teaching methodologies; possess personnel management, budget and planning skills; be knowledgeable about measurement and evaluation of library services and programs; be able to recognize and target user groups and meet their needs.[7]

A second key element for the program is establishment of a continuing education program. Where funds for travel and registration are limited, creative strategies for stretching those dollars will be necessary. A series of in-house seminars or workshops featuring leaders in the field will expose all the staff to new ideas for the price of one plane ticket. Tutorials at which librarians can share expertise with colleagues might be tried. And academic institutions represent a concentration of scholars who can be tapped as guest speakers. For example, a university administrator might be asked to discuss trends in higher education, a scientist might explain how information is generated and communicated in his field, a faculty member in the college of education might present a series of workshops on teaching skills. All of these ideas represent strategies for reaching more staff members with a minimum expenditure of funds. It should be remembered, however, that attending a conference or training event away from home where there is an opportunity to interact with other colleagues can be a great energizer and a portion of the continuing education budget should be earmarked for this purpose. Having a traveller share what she learned at a brown bag lunch can spread the enthusiasm.

INSTRUCTIONAL METHODOLOGIES

Staffing is the major cost associated with BI and how best to balance program objectives, instructional methodologies, and staffing levels and skills requires continuing review and feedback. Enormous amounts of staff time can be consumed by activities which have little permanent educational value. One example is extensive use of librarians to conduct tours.

In *Learning the Library* Beaubien and her co-authors present an excellent discussion of the pros and cons of several different instructions modes — printed materials, audio-visual presentations, point-of-use explanations, programmed instruction, single lectures, formal courses and tutorials.[8] Each of these modes makes different demands on staff time and requires different staff skills. While the learning objective will normally be the most important factor in the choice of instructional mode, impact on staff must also be considered. In most cases the challenge will be how to get the most educational impact with available staff, whether that staff is librarians, para-professionals, volunteers, or others.

POLITICAL REALITIES

The politics of gaining support for bibliographic instruction from the academic community is a theme which surfaces throughout this volume of *The Reference Librarian*. To counter the lack of understanding of the full contribution libraries and librarians can make to undergraduate and graduate education, there are calls for librarians to become more active outside the library. Time must be spent talking with faculty, attending departmental faculty meetings, serving on general education and writing committees, in short, becoming more visible and selling the value of libraries and librarians.

The time spent becoming involved in educational activities outside the library should be perceived by librarians and library administrators as a legitimate and important component of a librarian's assignment. The importance of this involvement must be acknowledged in the formal personnel system. For example, these activities should be incorporated into written position descriptions and performance criteria. Methods for assessing the quality of that involvement need to be developed. And finally, the formal reward system should recognize successes in integrating the library more completely into the educational process.

REFERENCES

1. Joseph A. Boisse and Duane Webster, "Looking Ahead: An Administrative View," in *Bibliographic Instruction: The Second Generation*, ed. Constance A. Mellon (Littleton, Colorado, Libraries Unlimited, 1987), 45-52.

2. Allan J. Dyson, "Organizing Undergraduate Library Instruction: The English and American Experience," *The Journal of Academic Librarianship*, 1 (March 1975), 9-13.

3. David F. Kohl, "Large-Scale Bibliographic Instruction — The Illinois Experience," *Research Strategies*, 2(Winter 1984), 6-11.

4. See Afton McGrath Miner, "Impact and Implication of a Library-Use Integrated Education Program," elsewhere in this volume.

5. Amy Dykeman, "Betwixt and Between: Some Thoughts on the Technical Services Librarian Involved in Reference and Bibliographic Instruction," *The Reference Librarian*, 10(Spring/Summer 1984), 233-238.

6. Patricia Senn Breivik, *Planning the Library Instruction Program* (Chicago, American Library Association, 1982), 111-112.

7. Maureen Pastine, "Library Instruction and Reference Service: Administration of a Bibliographic Instruction Program in the Academic Library," *The Reference Librarian,* 10(Spring/Summer 1984), 181-189.

8. Anne K. Beaubien, Sharon A. Hogan and Mary W. George, *Learning the Library: Concepts and Methods for Effective Bibliographic Instruction* (New York, Bowker, 1982), 45.

Structures of Bibliographic Instruction Programs: A Continuum for Planning

Lori Arp
Lizabeth A. Wilson

SUMMARY. Five structures of bibliographic instruction programs have emerged over the past twenty years: orientation; course-related instruction; course-integrated instruction; team teaching; and, separate courses. Defined by the level of cooperation between and among librarians, departmental faculty, and university administrators, the structures can be viewed on a continuum of cooperation when planning and selecting a structure for bibliographic instruction programs. This paper presents the five structures, details the requirements for cooperation, and discusses how the structures can be used to guide the development of bibliographic instruction programs.

Any librarian who has discussed bibliographic instruction (BI) in general education programs with a university administrator or departmental faculty member has more than likely experienced a breakdown in communication. Administrators and departmental faculty are generally aware of the purpose of bibliographic instruction to the extent that they understand that it concerns "teaching students how to use the library." Likewise, administrators and faculty are usually fully conversant with a wide variety of instructional methods given their own teaching experience. When the discussion turns to the structure of BI programs, or the manner in which in-

Lori Arp is Coordinator of Instructional Services, Auraria Library, University of Colorado at Denver, Lawrence at 11th Street, Denver, CO 80204. Lizabeth A. Wilson is Assistant Director for Undergraduate Libraries and Instructional Services, University of Illinois at Urbana-Champaign.

struction can be tied to the curriculum, administrators and faculty are less apt to understand or appreciate the content or structure of BI programs.

It is not surprising that administrators and departmental faculty are unfamiliar with the structures of BI programs. In the BI community itself, practitioners have not been particularly consistent in describing instructional structures. BI terminology is often used indiscriminately within different contexts. In an attempt to define structures of BI programs, particularly as they relate to university curriculums, this paper will discuss the characteristics of instructional structures and provide a continuum for planning BI programs.

STRUCTURES VERSUS TEACHING METHODS

Structures of BI programs are often discussed in the literature in tandem with teaching methods. For purposes of clarification, a teaching method is the manner in which information is presented to students. The literature is particularly rich with reviews of the variety of teaching methods used for bibliographic instruction. Svinicki and Schwartz's *Designing Instruction for Library Users* provides an excellent description and analysis of teaching methods.[1] A teaching method may be a slide-tape production, a videotape, computer-assisted instruction, a lecture, a workbook or a tutorial. The choice of the teaching method, although dependent upon the composition of the targeted group and myriad library factors, is not dependent on interdepartmental and administrative cooperation. The selection of the structure of the BI program is, however, dependent primarily on the level of interdepartmental and administrative cooperation.

STRUCTURES OF BIBLIOGRAPHIC INSTRUCTION PROGRAMS

As the field of bibliographic instruction has matured over the past twenty years, five major structures of bibliographic instruction have emerged. As described in the *Bibliographic Instruction Handbook*[2] and defined generally by practitioners, the options include:

1. ORIENTATION: "Service activities designed to introduce potential users to the services, facilities and organization of a particular library. The primary purpose is to familiarize the user with the library as a system."
2. COURSE-RELATED INSTRUCTION: "Any instruction which provides students in a given course with library and literature use skills necessary to meet the objectives of the course. The instruction may provide students with an understanding of the subject's literature, its structure, and effective methods of accessing it with emphasis on the literature. The instruction occurs with the cooperation and support of the instructor and during class time."
3. COURSE-INTEGRATED INSTRUCTION: "Any instruction which is part of a course's objectives. Instruction is viewed as essential to knowledge of the subject and therefore to successful completion of the course. This integration is usually achieved by discussion between faculty and librarians at time the course is designed."
4. TEAM TEACHING: Instruction which is developed, taught and evaluated by a librarian and departmental faculty member.
5. SEPARATE COURSE: A bibliographic instruction course which is taught by a librarian for credit or no credit and considered a part of the institution's curriculum.

CONTINUUM OF COOPERATION

The five structures are differentiated by the type of cooperation necessary. Four types of institutional cooperation are possible: (1) cooperation between departmental faculty and the library; (2) cooperation between the library and the university administration; (3) cooperation among departmental faculty, the library, and the university administration; and (4) lack of any institutional cooperation. Each of the five structures requires a particular level of cooperation. The continuum of cooperation shown in Diagram 1 places no cooperation at one extreme with total cooperation at the other. The continuum defines the structures in the context of the type of cooperation.

When selecting a structure of a BI program, the librarian must

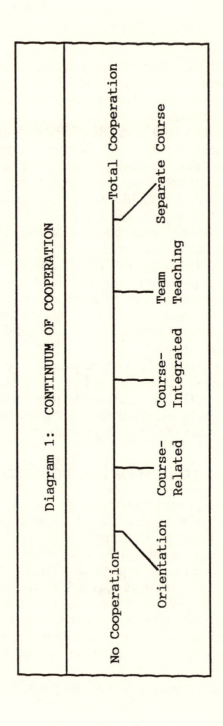

Diagram 1: CONTINUUM OF COOPERATION

No Cooperation — Total Cooperation

Orientation   Course-Related   Course-Integrated   Team Teaching   Separate Course

28

first analyze the political environment, support for the program, and the type of cooperation available. If the library is receiving no support from departmental faculty or the university administration, orientation may be the only viable structure. Course-related instruction, course-integrated instruction, and team teaching all minimally require the cooperation of departmental faculty. In the ideal case, these structures would also enjoy the support of the university administration.[3] However, the administration's support is not absolutely essential for course-integrated, course-related, or team teaching structures.[4] In some cases, if there is friction, ambivalence, or antagonism between the university administration and departmental faculty, these three structures may be the best choices because administrative cooperation need not be overt. Separate courses require university administration support. If departmental faculty are not supportive of the course on at least the level of the university's curriculum committee, it is unlikely that the separate course will continue to flourish, particularly if it is required of all students in a general education program.

Orientation

Many libraries have developed BI programs by first offering tours. No institutional cooperation is required for tours. The tour serves as a public relations tool if conducted with enthusiasm and an awareness of the audience. Obviously, tours must have the support of the targeted audience of students, and hopefully, faculty. Many libraries use new faculty tours as one way of building faculty support for bibliographic instruction. Frequently, the next step in the maturation of BI programs is the introduction of workshops, such as online catalog workshops.[5] Workshops require little if any faculty cooperation, although there must be a willing audience. In order for workshops to be successful, however, effective publicity must reach and motivate the targeted audience.

Course-Related Instruction, Course-Integrated Instruction, and Team Teaching

Of the five structures, course-related, course-integrated, and team teaching require interdepartmental cooperation and faculty support to insure success. The three structures vary in the amount of cooperation required. Course-related instruction, the typical "one-shot" lecture, requires that the departmental faculty view bibliographic instruction as important and the librarian as the expert in bibliographic research. Course-integration and team teaching demand close cooperation between librarians and faculty. Specifically, the three structures vary in the degree to which the librarian controls the following characteristics:

1. the overall objectives of a course;
2. the timeliness of the instruction in relation to the students' information needs;
3. the type of evaluation or grading procedures used to determine success;
4. the development of course design and content; and,
5. the level of cooperation between librarian and faculty.

Diagram 2 examines these three structures and the degree to which each of the characteristics is present, using compliance levels of null, low, medium, and high.

Diagram 2 provides important guidance in planning bibliographic instruction programs. Course-related instruction, course-integrated instruction and team teaching structures require progressively more faculty cooperation. The development of objectives, evaluation techniques, and course design parallel this progression. However, the time of need does not parallel the other parameters in that a course team taught by a librarian and an instructor may or may not occur at the time when the information is most appropriate to the student's academic career. For example, an advanced level course on research techniques which is taken in the last semester of the student's senior year is not ideally timed even though a high degree of cooperation exists between the librarian and departmental faculty. On the other hand, team teaching the research paper where the primary goal is the completion of that one assignment is timed appropriately in relation to the student's short term goals.[6] Less institutional cooperation may be needed to develop a course-integrated approach than team teaching, yet by its very nature, course integra-

Diagram 2: PARAMETERS OF THREE STRUCTURES

STRUCTURE	PARAMETERS				
	1.Objective	2.Timing	3.Evaluation	4.Design	5.Cooperation
1. Course-Related	Low to Medium	Low to Medium	Low	Low to Medium	Low to Medium
2. Course-Integrated	Medium to High	High	Medium to High	Medium to High	Medium to High
3. Team	High	Low to High	High	High	High

31

tion provides a high degree of timeliness in relation to the student's academic assignments.

Separate Courses

Separate courses, the fifth structure, may exist with only the co-operation of the university administration. However, without faculty support, it may be difficult to motivate students to enroll in the course. If the course is for credit and required of all entering students, faculty resentment may result, particularly from those faculty whose departments have tight credit hours due to highly structured degree plans. Ultimately, without some departmental faculty support, most notedly from the university-wide curriculum committee, it is unlikely that separate courses will remain a permanent part of the curriculum except as an elective. With administration and departmental faculty cooperation, credit courses can be successful and popular with students.[7]

In the separate course, librarians have complete control over the development of objectives, evaluation, and course design. If separate courses were added to Diagram 2, it would become apparent that the time of instructional need parameter is erratically addressed. A course taken in the final semester of a student's career may contribute to life-long information needs but it does not necessarily address the student's information needs demanded throughout the four years of undergraduate study. Likewise, students who take a course at the beginning of their college career may not be able to make the cognitive leap necessary to apply the information learned to other classes, never fully grasping the variations in doing bibliographic searching in different disciplines.[8] In addition, by completely controlling objectives, evaluation, and course design, yet maintaining little contact with departmental faculty, the librarian risks losing the cooperation of the faculty and the university administration.

A final but very important consideration to examine when determining a structure for a BI program is the level of cooperation between the library administration and the librarians. Consensus on the structure must be achieved in the library to guard against confusing departmental faculty and university administration with mixed signals. The importance of library administrative support to the success of BI programs has been well documented.[9] Space, staffing, and equipment considerations are important factors in determining the structure, size, and quality of BI programs. If there is strong university administrative support, many of these considerations may be addressed outside of the library.

CONCLUSION

Five major structures for bibliographic instruction have emerged as viable options for practitioners: orientation; course-related instruction; course-integrated instruction; team teaching; and, separate courses. The five structures are distinguished by the level of cooperation required between and among librarians, departmental faculty, and university administrators. In selecting a structure of bibliographic instruction, librarians must first evaluate and analyze the political environment, existing support, and the level of institutional cooperation. Since the five structures are predicated on the type of cooperation, librarians may be limited to particular structures because of the low level or absence of cooperation.

When selecting a structure of bibliographic instruction, librarians must take into consideration several factors and be aware of the limitations and strengths of each. While easily identifiable to departmental faculty and university administration, separate courses may not be the best option given a particular political environment. Additionally, the timeliness of the instruction is an important consideration. Course-integrated instruction requires less cooperation and has a built-in guarantee that information will be provided to the student at the time of need. However, unless course-integration occurs throughout all levels of the curriculum, as in the case of Earlham College,[10] the instruction may only be of short-term value to students. Regardless of the structure used, it is important for the librarian to secure the support of library administrators and library faculty.

As BI programs develop and mature, institutional cooperation often strengthens and expands. As cooperation expands, the library can move from orientation to structures more closely tied to the university's general curriculum.

REFERENCES

1. Marilla D. Svinicki and Barbara A. Schwartz. *Designing Instruction for Library Users: A Practical Guide* (New York: M. Dekker, 1988).

2. Association of College and Research Libraries. Bibliographic Instruction Section. Policy and Planning Committee. *Bibliographic Instruction Handbook* (Chicago: American Library Association, 1979).

3. For discussion of a proven program which enjoys the support of librarians, departmental faculty, and administrators see Evan Ira Farber's "Library Instruction Throughout the Curriculum" in *Educating the Library User*, ed. John Lubans (New York: Bowker, 1974), pp. 145-162.

4. For discussion of programs and research on course-integrated instruction and cooperation issues see Lizabeth A. Wilson and Lori L. Arp's "Large-Scale Bibliographic Instruction—Library Instructor's View—Practical," *Research Strategies* 2 (Winter 1984), pp. 23-32 and Constance A. Mellon's "Process Not Product in Course-Integrated Instruction: A Generic Model for Library Research," *College and Research Libraries* 45 (November 1984), pp. 471-478.

5. Betsy Baker and Brian Nielsen. "Educating the Online Catalog User: Experiences and Plans at Northwestern University Library," *Research Strategies* 1 (Fall 1983), pp. 155-166.

6. Kathleen Kenny and Lori Arp. "Using the *Model Statement of Objectives* in Community College Instruction: A Case Study." In progress.

7. Mignon Adams and Jacquelyn Morris. *Teaching Library Skills for Academic Credit* (Phoenix: Oryx Press, 1985).

8. See David Carlson and Ruth H. Miller's "Librarians and Teaching Faculty: Partners in Bibliographic Instruction," *College and Research Libraries* 45 (November 1984), pp. 483-491 and David F. Kohl and Lizabeth A. Wilson's "Effectiveness of Course-Integrated Bibliographic Instruction in Improving Coursework," *RQ* 27 (Winter 1986), pp. 206-211.

9. For discussions on the importance of library administrative support see Patricia Senn Breivik's *Planning the Library Instruction Program* (Chicago: American Library Association, 1982) and Joseph Boisse's "Library Instruction and the Administration," in *Putting Library Instruction in Its Place*, ed. Carolyn Kirkendall (Ann Arbor, Michigan: Pierian Press, 1978), pp. 1-12.

10. Farber, "Library Instruction Throughout the Curriculum."

PART II:
BRIDGING THE GAP BETWEEN
HIGH SCHOOL AND COLLEGE

Library Use Skills for College-Bound High School Students: A Survey

Mary M. Nofsinger

SUMMARY. Despite national concern with general educational articulation for high school students making the transition to college, little research has been reported in the literature specifically on library use/research skills. This paper summarizes recent literature on this topic from an academic librarian's point of view. In addition, the results of a survey of academic library user education services provided to high school students in Washington State are reported and contrasted to current cooperative efforts in other states. The relevance of library use skills for lifelong learning as well as for college-bound students is emphasized.

Much has been written about the need for improved educational collaboration between secondary schools and their college and uni-

Mary M. Nofsinger is Public Services Librarian at Holland Library, Washington State University, Pullman, WA 99164-5610.

versity counterparts. Prestigious educational organizations, including the Carnegie Commission on Higher Education, the American Association for Higher Education, the National Commission on Excellence in Education, and the Carnegie Foundation for the Advancement of Teaching have issued reports[1] which emphasize the need for increased articulation, or the linkage of student educational experiences along the learning continuum.[2] As a result of these efforts, a coast-to-coast survey reveals a dramatic upsurge in high school-college collaboration,[3] and educational literature contains increasing numerous reports of these educational partnerships.[4,5,6,7]

LIBRARY USE SKILLS AND ARTICULATION

Despite national concern with improving high school-college collaboration, the articulation of library use/research skills is infrequently mentioned in educational literature. For example, Maeroff's special report for the Carnegie Foundation[8] does not mention library use or research skills in its index. After a two-year collaborative effort between school teachers and college faculty, the College Board's report, *Academic Preparation for College*,[9] only mentions libraries once — buried in fine print under the basic academic competency of studying. Indirectly, the necessity for high school students learning library use skills may be inferred from a specific writing skill listed: "the ability to gather information from primary and secondary sources; to write a report using this research; to quote, paraphrase, and summarize accurately; and to cite sources properly."[10]

However, librarians have also expressed concern with excellence in education and in promotion of lifelong learning for all citizens. In collaboration with the Department of Education, the Libraries and a Learning Society project was launched. Leaders in the library and information science community held seminars to examine how academic libraries, public libraries, library science training institutions, and school library media centers could promote a "learning society." Recommendations were published,[11] including the promotion of linkages between library and community resources and the teaching of effective use of information sources in elementary and secondary school curriculum.

SURVEY OF LIBRARY SCIENCE LITERATURE

Articulation of library use/research skills for college-bound students is a relatively obscure topic in the professional literature. A few early articles have documented the situation for academic librarians:

> Those who work with library orientation and bibliographic instruction programs involving college freshmen are well aware that the problem of continuity between high school and colleges deserves more attention than it gets . . . learning is a lifelong process, and both high school and college programs contribute in valuable ways at different stages of a student's development.[12]

> Most instructors simply assume that college students know how to use a library. . . . That this assumption is contrary to fact is well known to every academic librarian who has ever worked at a public service point. . . . Most students enter higher education virtually without any inkling of how to use a library. . . . The only effective way to insure that students will gain a working knowledge of libraries adequate to their needs is to start early in the educational process . . .[13]

Several models of school/college library cooperative programs have already been identified and described.[14] Recent literature reveals a variety of additional programs.

University of Akron, Ohio/Garfield High School

During the 1980-81 school year, seventy-four seniors at the high school participated in an ESEA Title IV-C Teacher Grant Program, "Elimination of Academic Library Research Shock." The objectives of this program were to introduce high school seniors (a) to an academic library environment, (b) to general and specialized reference sources, and (c) to techniques of research strategy and writing prior to graduation.[15] Students from the Advanced Placement English and Problems of Democracy classes, who were mostly college-bound, were pre- and post-tested to ascertain their knowledge of library organization and resources.

The high school librarian presented information on the card catalog and general reference sources. A professor in library sciences then visited the classes to discuss special reference sources in various disciplines which would be available in the academic library. Working closely with teachers of each class, the seniors visited the University of Akron Library where librarians and other University representatives presented a panel discussion on the importance of library research skills. Finally, research papers were researched and written for the classes.[16]

As a result of the grant, a color videotape cassette summarizing the program and a slide-tape program comparing the secondary and academic library resources/services was prepared. In addition, a library research guide, *Elimination of Academic Library Research Shock; a Freshman's Library Survival Booklet*, was published.[17] After the students completed one year of college course work, a survey was planned to evaluate the impact of the program on their success and failures in using academic libraries.

State University of New York, Albany

Academic librarians launched their Bridging the Gap program to provide instruction to college-bound students from New York State high schools, the source of 90 percent of SUNY Albany's freshman enrollment.[18] To arrange for class visits, teachers or administrators must make advance arrangements with the SUNY Library. The school librarian is also asked to accompany the group for follow-up and reinforcement learning. Prior to arrival, a library skills pre-test is sent to the high school and administered before students view a slide-tape which orients them to the academic library. Previsit library skills knowledge is encouraged; study packets are available.[19]

When a class arrives, a lecture and tour is provided. Immediately afterwards, students are expected to work in the library, either on a research paper or on some other well-planned assignment. After the field trip, a post-test is provided to be administered by the high school. Data on the tests is reported back to the schools so staff and administration can evaluate program effectiveness. Feedback from participants has been extremely positive. One teacher did a longitudinal study, following her former senior English students to see how valuable the library research unit was in helping them adjust to college. Over 70 percent found the experience valuable.[20]

Virginia Polytechnic Institute and State University

Funded in 1985 by an LSCA, Title III grant via the Virginia State Library, a cooperative program to teach library skills to college-bound high school students in twenty-six southwestern Virginia counties is being implemented.[21] The grant proposal will address two main problem areas. First, library skills needed by college-bound students will be identified. Secondly, high school librarians and teachers will be trained to teach these fundamental library skills needed. Instructional aids are being written and a videotape is being filmed in an academic library.

Plans are being made to establish a clearinghouse at the Virginia Tech Library where teaching packets and the videotapes would be housed. Scheduling of training sessions would also be implemented through the clearinghouse. It is envisioned that basic skills as well as concepts of authorship, classification, etc. will be taught. It is hoped that teaching fundamental library skills in secondary schools will enable academic librarians to devote more efforts to evaluating and managing information.

Winthrop College, South Carolina

Since 1982, the Winthrop College Library has offered several outreach programs for advanced placement (honors) students in local high schools.[22] After consulting with area teachers and school librarians, guidelines were established. Prior to a class visit, secondary teachers are requested to have students take a self-guided tape tour to physically orient them to the library. Later, orientation sessions and library assignments are scheduled by academic librarians at nonpeak library usage periods. After orientation, students receive ID cards and have the same library services as college students, except for the circulation of books.

In addition to library skills instruction, a one-week clinic for prospective college freshmen includes a session on library research materials and how to access information. Also, a Summer Camp for Academic Development is offered annually. For three weeks, classes are offered in a variety of subjects including study skills and library research. Finally, an "academic library experience" has been established for gifted fifth and sixth grade students who need enrichment activities and advanced level assignments.

University of Vermont, Burlington

Academic library orientation workshops are conducted by the University of Vermont to acquaint college-bound high school seniors with the resources available in an academic library.[23] Announcements are sent to all high school librarians in the state, and publicity appears in the state library association newsletter as well as in the state media association's publication. Half-day visitation sessions include an orientation tour, an explanation of the card catalog and LC subject headings, procedures for locating periodical articles and government documents, and usage of the microforms area. In the reference area, individual written exercises are assigned; librarians correct the assignment sheets and give students immediate feedback. Participating students and teachers complete written evaluations which are used to monitor the program's effectiveness.

William Rainey Harper College, Illinois/ Arlington High School/Arlington Heights Memorial (Public) Library

After receiving LSCA Title III funding in 1983, a six-step, sequential library research strategy to teach college-bound junior and senior high school students was developed.[24] First, teachers and librarians were trained in the library research strategy. Then, a high school class in expository writing and a community college class in English served as the test group while two other similar classes served as the control group. The test group was taught the research strategy for their topics: (1) Begin with general encyclopedias, (2) Use subject encyclopedias, (3) Use specific reference tools (almanacs, yearbooks, etc.), (4) Use periodical indexes, (5) Check abstracts and citation indexes as guides to scholarly literature, and (6) Consult the card catalog and book collection on the topic.

The project was evaluated in several ways. Students had kept logs of their work to show how they accumulated a bibliography. Instructors evaluated student performance. Also, students were given a questionnaire designed to assess their sense of the utility of the research strategy. It was found that the strategy helped give students a better understanding of their topic and helped them narrow it to a workable size. The control group had more difficulty with locating appropriate information on their topics. Overall, the cooperative project was deemed promising for general application.

State University of New York, Plattsburgh

For the past several years, the library at SUNY Plattsburgh has a five-week library skills course for college-bound students who are educationally disadvantaged.[25] Designed and taught by library faculty, the course focuses on fundamental concepts and skills. After each class presentation, worksheet assignments are distributed and completed during the class period. Worksheets are graded, discussed in class, and returned to students. Instructors evaluate their students on assignments and class participation. An evaluative questionnaire at the conclusion of the course revealed that students judged the course to be, overall, a successful experience for them.

WASHINGTON STATE: A SURVEY

This is a report on the results of a 1986 survey sent to all academic libraries in Washington State. The survey's purpose was to assess the extent of library user services provided by academic libraries to classes of high school students. It was designed to determine how library user instruction was requested, the methods of user education most used, the types of instructional materials used, estimates of type and quantity of high school class visits, academic library policies on class visits, the types of staff who provided instruction, evaluative measures used, and basic library skills considered most important for college-bound students. Finally, plans for future user education instruction of high school classes were assessed.

Methodology

Initially, the survey questionnaire was drafted, pre-tested with selected academic libraries in the local area, and then revised to incorporate suggestions. Next, the *American Library Association Directory* was used to identify all academic libraries, both public and private, in the state: two-year community colleges, four-year colleges, and universities. Finally, the questionnaire and a letter were sent to the director/administrator of each academic library. The letter explained the purpose of the survey, stressed the importance of responding, and emphasized that individual institutional data would be kept confidential. A month after the initial mailing, a follow-up letter and questionnaire were sent to those institutions which had not yet responded. Of the forty-nine institutions surveyed (see Table 1), forty-four libraries responded for a return rate of 90 percent.

Findings

User Education Provided to High School Classes

Of the academic libraries which responded to the survey, approximately one-third (34%) provided user education for high school classes. The percentage breakdown for each type of library was 20

TABLE 1

ACADEMIC LIBRARIES SURVEYED IN WASHINGTON STATE

Total	Community Colleges	Colleges	Universities
49 Libraries	n=26	n=11	n=12
Survey Return Rate 90%	96%	73%	92%
44 Libraries	n=25	n=8	n=11

percent of community colleges, 62 percent of colleges, and 45 percent of universities (see Table 2). The remaining two-thirds of academic libraries (66%) did *not* provide user education to high school classes. In regard to making arrangements for instruction for high school classes (see Table 3), the survey revealed that most academic library instruction (93%) was provided *after* being requested by high school personnel. None of the responding libraries, at their own initiative, had made any attempt to contact high schools to offer user instruction to classes. In addition, only one-fourth of the libraries surveyed (27%) would allow their librarians to visit high schools to present information about library resources. It appears that academic library outreach efforts were minimal at the time of the survey.

TABLE 2

USER EDUCATION PROVIDED TO HIGH SCHOOL CLASSES

Academic Libraries n=44	Total	Community Colleges	Colleges	Universities
Provided User Education	34% n=15	20% n=5	62% n=5	45% n=5
Did NOT Provide User Education	66% n=29	80% n=20	38% n=3	55% n=6

TABLE 3

APPROACHING ACADEMIC LIBRARY PROVIDERS
OF USER EDUCATION FOR HIGH SCHOOL CLASSES

Provided instruction to high school classes, upon request of high school personnel	93%
Initiated contacts with high school classes (outreach)	0%
Librarian(s) will visit high school classes upon request	27%

User Instruction Methods

Among the variety of methods used by the academic libraries surveyed (see Table 4), two activities were predominantly used. Conducted tours were prevalent in all three types (87%) of libraries. This finding supports statements by others that the traditional library tour is still the most popular technique for orienting students to a library.[26] The next most popular instructional method, usually used in conjunction with a conducted tour, was a librarian lecture on subject resources. It is interesting to compare the usage breakdown for a subject lecture at the three types of institutions: only 20 percent at community college libraries, but 60 percent at college libraries and 100 percent at university libraries.

These results might be explained by the fact that universities and colleges are more research-oriented, and usually have larger library collections. Librarians in larger institutions tend to provide more subject-specific user instruction to meet the needs of professors and students in advanced-level courses. As for the remaining instructional methods, none were used except by university librarians.

Usage of Print and Nonprint Materials

In analyzing the type of printed materials used for user education, it was found that lists of library resources i.e., bibliographies, subject handouts, etc. were most heavily used by university (100%) and college (40%) libraries (see Table 5). University libraries also frequently used library handbooks (80%) and self-guided tour sheets (60%). In contrast, community college libraries (40%) used library handbooks predominantly. One explanation for the different usage patterns could be that university libraries, having larger numbers of users, also need more types of materials to meet diverse demands.

As for nonprint materials, authorities have long touted the advantages of using audiovisuals for presentations.[27] However, the survey revealed that few academic libraries in Washington State reported usage of these materials with high school classes (see Table 6). The popularity of using printed materials instead of nonprint is probably due to cheaper production costs and/or lack of availability of appropriate commercially-produced materials.

TABLE 4

INSTRUCTION METHODS FOR USER EDUCATION OF HIGH SCHOOL CLASSES

	Total	Community Colleges	Colleges	Universities
Conducted Tours	87%	80%	100%	80%
Lecture on Subject Resources	60%	20%	60%	100%
Class Assignment Lectures	13%	0	0	40%
Self-Guided Tours	13%	0	0	40%
Formal Course	6%	0	0	20%
General Workbooks	0	0	0	0
Term Paper Counseling	0	0	0	0

TABLE 5

USAGE OF PRINT MATERIALS FOR HIGH SCHOOL CLASSES

	Total	Community Colleges	Colleges	Universities
Lists of Library Resources	53%	20%	40%	100%
Library Handbook	47%	40%	20%	80%
Self-Guided Tour Sheets	20%	0	0	60%
Library Pathfinders (short subject guides)	20%	20%	20%	20%
Class Assignment Sheets	7%	0	0	20%

Quantity and Type of High School Class Visits

Most of the institutions surveyed were only able to "estimate" quantities of high school classes visiting annually (see Table 7). In regard to total numbers of students in those classes, estimates ranged from 25 to 400 with universities serving larger quantities of students. In analyzing the class levels of visiting students, institutions predominantly served seniors (93%) and juniors (80%). Of

TABLE 6

USAGE OF NON-PRINT MATERIALS FOR HIGH SCHOOL CLASSES

	Total	Community Colleges	Colleges	Universities
Slide-Tape Presentations	13%	20%	20%	0
Slides	6%	0	20%	0
Videotape/TV	6%	0	20%	0
Films	6%	0	20%	0
Audio Tapes/Cassettes	6%	0	20%	0
Computer Aided Instruction	0	0	0	0
Transparencies	0	0	0	0
Graphic Displays	13%	0	20%	20%

those classes visiting, most (73%) were English classes. The remaining classes were from a variety of disciplines.

Academic Library Policies on Class Visits

According to the survey, most academic institutions had two important policies for high school class visits: (a) Fines were levied on high school students (80%) just like other users (see Table 8), and (b) An adult leader had to accompany the class (73%). Differences also appeared in regard to student borrowing privileges with universities and colleges much more restrictive than community college libraries. In addition, 60% of university libraries placed some type of restriction on the time a class could visit. Reasons varied for different restrictions, depending on available staffing levels, peaks in academic workloads, the needs of primary clientele, and other factors.

Providers of User Education
for High School Classes

Of the libraries responding, 100 percent used reference librarians, 7 percent used technical service librarians, and 13 percent used paraprofessional or support staff for user education of high school

TABLE 7

ESTIMATED NUMBER AND TYPE OF HIGH SCHOOL CLASS VISITS

	Total	Community Colleges	Colleges	Universities
Number of Classes Visiting Annually for Instruction	Unknown	Ranged from 0-5	Ranged from 1-10	Ranged from 6-20
Total Number of Students in Annual High School Class Visits	Unknown	Ranged from 25-75	Ranged from 20-200	Ranged from 96-400
Level of Classes				
Seniors	93%	80%	100%	100%
Juniors	80%	60%	80%	100%
Sophomores	33%	20%	20%	60%
Freshmen	33%	20%	20%	60%
Types of Classes				
English	73%	80%	80%	60%
History	47%	40%	40%	60%
Others (Honors, College Preparatory, Vocational/ Career, Social Studies)	60%	60%	60%	60%

47

TABLE 8

ACADEMIC LIBRARY POLICY ON HIGH SCHOOL CLASS VISITS

	Total	Community Colleges	Colleges	Universities
Fines Were Applicable	80%	80%	80%	80%
Adult Leader Had to Accompany Class	73%	60%	60%	100%
Each Student Had Borrowing Privileges	53%	100%	20%	40%
Restrictions on Time of Class Visit, etc.	47%	40%	40%	60%
Only Adult Leader Could Borrow Materials	27%	0	40%	40%

classes (see Table 9). Librarians were assisted by staff, depending on the circumstances. Most of the providers (67%) participated voluntarily, although assigned participation was required at times (27%). The only other major difference revealed by the survey was that only one person in most community college libraries (80%) was predominantly responsible for user education while in most university libraries (80%), several people participated (see Table 10).

Evaluative Measures

Evaluation is often considered vital for making decisions, measuring effectiveness, and determining changes needed. "Champions of instruction, as well as critics and neutral observers, have urged practitioners to evaluate their programs, or researchers to develop better methods of evaluation for others to use."[28] Unfortunately, the survey revealed that none of the libraries surveyed had formally evaluated their user education efforts via pre-tests and/or post-tests of students' performance. The predominant methods of evaluation used were surveying adult leader responses (40%) and informal feedback (47%) (see Table 11).

TABLE 9

PROVIDERS OF USER EDUCATION FOR HIGH SCHOOL CLASSES

	Total	Community Colleges	Colleges	Universities
Reference Librarian(s)	100%	100%	100%	100%
Technical Service Librarians	7%	20%	0	0
Paraprofessional/Support Staff	13%	0	20%	20%

TABLE 10

LIBRARY STAFF PARTICIPATION IN USER EDUCATION

	*Total	Community Colleges	Colleges	Universities
Participation was Voluntary	67%	40%	80%	80%
Participation was Assigned	27%	20%	20%	40%
Only One Person Participated	53%	80%	40%	40%
Several People Participated	53%	20%	60%	80%

*Totals exceed 100% since options were not exclusive.

TABLE 11

MEASURES USED TO EVALUATE USER EDUCATION EFFECTIVENESS

	Total	Community Colleges	Colleges	Universities
Pre-test of Student Skills	0	0	0	0
Post-test of Student Skills	0	0	0	0
Survey of Adult Leader Response	40%	20%	40%	60%
Informal Feedback	47%	20%	20%	60%
Survey of Student Response to Library Visit	7%	20%	0	0

Basic Library Skills/Competencies

Librarians from the responding institutions were asked to indicate which basic library skills/competencies were most important, in their opinion, and to estimate which of these skills "average entering" students possessed (see Table 12). Analysis showed that librarians considered all fourteen skills/competencies to be important (52% or higher). However, librarians estimated that only half of the entering students could perform *five* of these fourteen basic skills. Thus, approximately two-thirds of the skills (64%) were not being achieved by the average student. There appears to be a clear need for more user education in minimum library skills/competencies for high school students.

Future Plans

Overall, the survey did not reveal any major plans by academic libraries to increase user education services to high school students (see Table 13). Approximately half of the libraries surveyed (55%) plan to continue their current level of service (80% of these currently provide user education to high school classes). Approximately one-third (36%) of the libraries had no specific plans for future service or did not respond to the questionnaire. Only a small group (9%) planned to expand services for high school classes. However, none of the academic libraries surveyed planned to decrease services.

RECOMMENDATIONS FOR INCREASING ARTICULATION OF LIBRARY SKILLS

Based on the results of the Washington State survey and related library science literature, the following recommendations are suggested for improving the articulation of library use/research skills for college-bound students:

TABLE 12

BASIC SKILLS/COMPETENCIES NEEDED IN ACADEMIC LIBRARIES

	Librarians Considered Important	Entering Students Could
Recognize basic library terms (call number, book stacks, citation, etc.)	98%	77%
Understand the concept of an index (what it does)	98%	59%
Use library catalogs to find materials by author, title, or subject	93%	80%
Understand call numbers so that materials can be retrieved from the shelves	91%	57%
Interpret the information given in a periodical index citation	89%	39%
Use basic reference sources such as subject dictionaries, encyclopedias, almanacs, etc.	84%	61%
Interpret the information in a bibliographic record	82%	23%
Develop a search strategy using library resources	70%	7%
Recognize different types of citations (book, periodical, government document, etc.)	68%	16%
Evaluate information	64%	14%
Distinguish between scholarly and popular literature	57%	5%
Distinguish between primary and secondary sources	57%	7%
Recognize different ways of alphabetizing	55%	16%
Understand the concept of subject hierarchies	52%	14%

TABLE 13

ACADEMIC LIBRARIES' FUTURE PLANS FOR USER EDUCATION
OF HIGH SCHOOL CLASSES

	Total n=44	Community Colleges n=25	Colleges n=8	Universities n=11
Maintain Current Services:	55%	52%	62%	55%
Offers User Education		(80%)	(80%)	(80%)
Does NOT Offer User				
Education		(45%)	(33%)	(33%)
Decrease Services	0	0	0	0
Develop New Services	9%	12%	0	9%
No Plans for Future Services				
or No Response	36%	36%	38%	36%

1. Improve communication among school, academic, and public librarians by holding joint inservice workshops, sharing newsletter mailing lists, and/or journal articles, and holding more concurrent meetings of professional associations.[29]
2. Support academic librarian outreach activities for college-bound students, including high school visitations, discussions with high school librarians and teachers, and development of cooperative library skills programs.
3. Develop state guidelines for cooperative programs of library skills/information literacy, and develop statements of minimum library competencies for high school and college graduates.[30]
4. Encourage school librarians to teach a sequential program of library/media skills, including search strategy and the transfer value of information/research skills. Facilitate visitations to nearby college and university libraries by school librarians and college-bound students.
5. Include library/information literacy instruction in teacher preparatory curricula, offer both undergraduate and graduate academic library research methods courses, and offer inservice programs to academic faculty who have not yet received the needed preparation for incorporating library skills in their courses.[31]
6. Encourage classroom teachers to integrate literature searching/information finding skills into basic courses. Emphasize the need for lifelong learning skills to meet the challenges of a rapidly changing society.

CONCLUSION

Despite increased concern with educational collaboration, a coordinated, nationwide effort to promote articulation of library use/research skills for college-bound students has not yet been implemented. Some states, however, are developing standards for library skills programs in the elementary and secondary schools.[32] If these statewide standards were implemented uniformly in school districts, college-bound students could be expected to have learned basic library skills. At the present time, however, most library skills programs tend to be local in nature.

REFERENCES

1. The Carnegie Commission on Higher Education, *Continuity and Discontinuity: Higher Education and the Schools* (Highstown, N.J.: McGraw-Hill, 1973); American Association for Higher Education, "High School/College Partnerships," *Current Issues in Higher Education Annual Series 1* (1981); National Commission on Excellence in Education, *A Nation at Risk* (Washington, D.C.: U.S. Government Printing Office, 1983); Ernest L. Boyer, *High School: A Report on Secondary Education in America*, Carnegie Foundation for the Advancement of Teaching (New York: Harper & Row, 1983).

2. Joseph Menacker, *From School to College: Articulation and Transfer* (Washington, D.C.: American Council on Education, 1975), p. 1.

3. Gene I. Maeroff, *School and College: Partnerships in Education*, The Carnegie Foundation for the Advancement of Teaching (Lawrenceville, N.J.: Princeton University Press, 1983).

4. Jerrald R. Shive, "School and University Partnerships: Meeting Common Needs," *Improving College and University Teaching* 32 (Summer 1984): 119-122.

5. Leslie L. Huling, Judith A. Richardson, and Shirley M. Hord, "Three Projects Show How University/School Partnerships Can Improve Effectiveness," *NASSP Bulletin* 67 (October 1983): 54-59.

6. Franklin P. Wilbur, "School-College Partnerships: Building Effective Models for Collaboration," *NASSP Bulletin* 68 (October 1984): 34-49.

7. Hechinger, Fred M., "School-College Collaboration—An Essential to Improved Public Education," *NASSP Bulletin* 68 (October 1984): 69-79.

8. Maeroff, p. 79-83.

9. The College Board, *Academic Preparation for College: What Students Need to Know and Be Able to Do* (New York: The College Board, 1983), p. 10.

10. The College Board, p. 8.

11. *Alliance for Excellence: Librarians Respond to A Nation at Risk* (Washington, D.C.: U.S. Department of Education, 1984).

12. Lennart Pearson, "The High School Library and the College-Bound Student," *The South Carolina Librarian* 24 (Fall 1980): 11-13.

13. Dennis W. Dickinson, "Library Literacy: Who? When? Where?" *Library Journal* 106 (April 15, 1981): 853-854.

14. Barbara E. Kemp, Mary M. Nofsinger, and Alice M. Spitzer, "Building a Bridge: Articulation Programs for Bibliographic Instruction," *College and Research Libraries* 47 (September 1986): 470-474.

15. Juanita Buddy, "If Only I had Known . . ."*Ohio Media Spectrum* 33 (July 1981): 8.

16. Juanita Buddy, "Orientation to the University Library—The Missing Link," *NASSP Bulletin* 66 (December 1982): 100.

17. Akron Public Schools, *Elimination of Academic Library Research Shock; A Freshman's Library Survival Booklet* (Akron, Ohio: Akron Public Schools, 1981). Available from Project LOEX, Ypsilanti, Mich.

18. Jacquelyn Gavryck, "Information Research Skills: Sharing the Burden," *Wilson Library Bulletin* 60 (May 1986): 23.

19. Mary V. Ratzer, *Information Retrieval and University Level Research* (Bethesda, Md.: ERIC Document Reproduction Service, ED 266 782, 1986).

20. Ratzer, p. 24-25.

21. Donald J. Kenney and Linda J. Wilson, "Developing a Partnership in Library Instruction," *College and Research Libraries News* 47 (May 1986): 321-322.

22. Nancy M. Davidson, "Innovative Bibliographic Instruction: Developing Outreach Programs In an Academic Library," *The South Carolina Librarian* 29 (Spring 1985): 19-20.

23. Lorraine A. Jean, *Introducing the College-Bound Student to the Academic Library: A Case Study* (Bethesda, Md.: ERIC Document Reproduction Service, ED 200 236, 1981).

24. Eileen Dubin and Shari Kilgust Hetzke, "New Research Strategy for Library Use: Community Interlibrary Cooperation Grant," *Community & Junior College Libraries* 3 (Summer 1985): 33-37.

25. Topsy N. Smalley, *Library Skills Course for EOP Students* (Bethesda, Md.: ERIC Document Reproduction Service, ED 202 459, 1980).

26. George R. Jaramillo, "Educating the Library User: A Survey of Academic Libraries in Colorado," *Colorado Libraries* 9 (June 1983): 18.

27. Anne F. Roberts, *Library Instruction for Librarians* (Littleton, Colo.: Libraries Unlimited, Inc., 1982), p. 44.

28. Richard Hume Werking, "Evaluating Bibliographic Education: A Review and Critique," *Library Trends* 29 (Summer 1980): 153.

29. The Task Force on Library Instruction: High School to College, "Primed for Success," *Ohio Library Association Bulletin* 56 (October 1986): 29.

30. The Task Force on Library Instruction, p. 30-31.

31. The Task Force on Library Instruction, p. 31.

32. Some examples: Frederick R. Reenstjerna, "Developing Statewide Library Instruction Standards: Rationale and Preliminary Steps," in *Teaching Library Use Competence: Bridging the Gap from High School to College*, ed. by Carolyn A. Kirkendall (Ann Arbor, Mich.: Pierian Press, 1982), pp. 87-107; Gavryck, p. 23; The Task Force on Library Instruction, p. 29-30.

PART III:
LIBRARY SKILLS
IN A COMMUNITY COLLEGE

Building Alliances:
General Education and Library Skills
in a Community College

Susan Griswold Blandy

SUMMARY. College librarians are convinced that using the library is an essential part of a college education, a conviction not necessarily shared by faculty. Integrating library research into courses can be especially difficult at community colleges where faculty have heavy course loads and the curricula are very practical. However, at Hudson Valley Community College, library skills are now part of the College Objectives as well as the English Composition syllabus. Library assignments occur in most general education courses and are the means for adding general education concepts to courses in technology, sciences, business, etc. The librarians have found that by building alliances with the faculty, they can take advantage of opportunities to build library skills into the curricula.

Susan Griswold Blandy is Public Services Librarian, Learning Resources Center, Hudson Valley Community College, Troy, NY 12180.

57

The debate over what is an educated person continually simmers just below the surface at a community college. Faced with the task of taking students with wildly varying academic abilities and covering the highly pragmatic course material in two years, faculty could be content with simply turning out employable graduates. Our faculty carry a heavy work load—up to five classes, up to 150 student contact hours per semester, and moonlighting or consulting encouraged as a way of staying current in one's field. The idea of grading 150 ten-page research papers sets one to figuring out the mathematics of time spent and weekends lost. But there is a lively and nagging sense that for many students this is all the college they get and if they ever are going to see their career in a larger context, if they ever are going to grapple with concepts such as values in technology, cultural bias in criminal justice, or the ownership of information, then the introduction to cross-disciplinary and critical thinking, the exposure to professional literature has to happen here, and now. "General Education" as the term is used at Hudson Valley Community College (HVCC) does refer to the required English and social sciences classes, but more often refers to those ideas and issues that all citizens must deal with.

Over the years, by carefully recognizing and creating opportunities, the librarians at HVCC have developed a strong relationship with the faculty and a strong program of library skills in a variety of courses. These assignments are intended to help the student better understand course concepts, but they are also a powerful way of adding general education concepts—connectedness—to a course while training students in self-education skills. Library assignments are created and survive for very practical reasons, nurtured by the enthusiasm of the staff. While the exact circumstances that led to the current program are unique to HVCC, there are general concepts at work that other librarians should find useful.

HVCC PROGRAMS

According to the requirements of the State University of New York system, most HVCC students must take two semesters of English Composition and one semester of a social science elective. These are the courses known in some colleges as the General Education courses. Class size ranges from 20-33 students; in Fall 1987 approximately 3000+ students were in English Composition and 3500 in social science classes, classes taught throughout the day and offered at local shopping centers and high schools as well as on campus. For more than ten years the English Composition courses included library skills in the syllabus with faculty members working out their own approach. Ten to fifteen faculty regularly brought all their classes to the LRC for formal bibliographic instruction while other faculty used LRC prepared handouts in the classroom and brought classes to the library for "research hours." Some faculty felt their students needed so much remedial work that library work was a frill. This past year in response to concerns about transfer students, the *Recommended Library Skills and Competencies for Graduates of Community Colleges in New York State*[1] was prepared by the SUNYLA (State University of New York Library Association) Bibliographic Competencies Task Force (in which we have a member) and were approved by the SUNY Two-Year Colleges Head Librarians group. Accordingly, the HVCC librarians and English Department faculty incorporated these skills into a revised English Comp. syllabus so that, while the faculty retain control of the teaching mode, everyone is working to the same competencies over the two semesters.

Library research is also an integral part of the liberal arts courses with various combinations of research assignments, bibliographic instruction and handouts used in courses such as Economics, Sociology, Psychology, Technical Writing, Short Story, and Western Civilization. In addition, because of a campus-wide commitment to educating the whole person, and because of the requirements of accrediting agencies, all credit courses are supposed to have a library component. Some departments — such as Nursing — require library use in every course without exception, but most library assignments are the result of collaboration between the liaison librarian and faculty member, individualizing the assignment to the demands of the content, the faculty member's approach, and student skills and background. Various combinations of assignments (not necessarily term papers), bibliographies and research guides, and 10-50 minute bibliographic instruction (BI) packages have been used in classes as diverse as Electrical Construction and Maintenance, Police and Community, American Art, Early Childhood Education, Thermodynamics, Personnel Administration, Data Processing, Biology for Non-Science Majors, and many others.

Since 1982 the college objectives listed in the college catalog have read

> . . . 3. To acquire the ability to use a library/learning resources center effectively;
> . . . 6. To obtain a foundation of knowledge and culture to provide a basis for life-long learning.[2]

The commitment to these objectives shows up not only in coursework, but in other areas. The School of Liberal Arts and Sciences provides a year-long program of cultural events including gallery, jazz, poetry readings, modern dance, theatre and chamber music. Other departments sponsor cross-disciplinary public forums such as the recent one on AIDS sponsored by the Mortuary Science Dept. Courses approved by the Curriculum Committee must include an LRC impact statement; several of the annual Faculty Workshop Days have included General Education seminars; a committee is investigating General Education as part of various proposals for an Honors Degree; the General Education Committee has sponsored several one-credit open enrollment courses including one based on local cultural opportunities; and the one credit Library Research course has had a successful run as a general education course required of all mortuary science students, the justification being that the social and health context of funeral directing changes so frequently, our graduates must be able to locate information in these areas.

SUSTAINING PROGRAMS: PRACTICAL REALITIES

We have been defining and implementing general education concepts at HVCC for more than ten years, as a pragmatic response to the needs of both students and faculty. The original impetus was partly external. The College was affected by national trends, including the debate over the role of the humanities and the need for a core curriculum in college programs. The earlier C. P. Snow discussion of the two cultures and Alfred North Whitehead's *Aims of*

Education were part of the debate. Harvard University's well-publicized restructuring of required courses was closely followed as well as other colleges' redefinition of degree distribution requirements. Because HVCC has transfer agreements with many four-year schools, we needed to make sure our transfer degree programs carefully paralleled these schools' first two years. In order for the highly visible transfer programs at HVCC to continue to attract students, we had to be able to guarantee that the full two years of courses would indeed transfer. Philosophically there was also much discussion of the role of liberal arts in programs that were so technical and skills-oriented that they amounted to apprenticeships. In the maturing community college philosophy the linkage between disciplines was valued, translating into a search for ways to put the skills — Accounting, Machine Design, etc. — into a social, psychological and political context, linking the career to the world at large. The College administration has strongly supported efforts to teach critical thinking skills, to link curricula, and to promote skills for lifelong learning.

Our ruminations were aided by a spate of publications that are still worth reviewing: *The Humanities in American Life*, the Rockefeller Foundation's Commission on the Humanities report (1980); *The Humanities and Sciences in Two Year Colleges* prepared by the Center for the Study of Community Colleges; the American Association of Community and Junior Colleges' *Strengthening Humanities in Community Colleges*; and *Advancing the Liberal Arts* from the Jossey-Bass series *New Directions for Community Colleges* (see bibliography). A core group also used Ronald Havelock's gracious and practical *The Change Agent's Guide to Innovation in Education*. Through all this, various librarians were actively involved in the discussions, on committees and over coffee, in the hallways, at the reference desk, serving as resource people often before groups realized there were resources to be had.

MIDDLE STATES

This process was made sharply practical by the reaccreditation of the College in 1984 by the Middle States Association of Colleges and Schools. Their pamphlet *Characteristics of Excellence in Higher*

Education became the bible of the self-study process. The following statements stared at us from the pages:

> [An institution must] require . . . some work in general education and liberal arts or related areas.[3]
>
> . . . The centrality of a library/learning resources center in the educational mission . . . must be supported by more than lip service. . . . Faculty and library staff need to work closely together in planning the development and employment of the library/learning resources center to achieve their educational objectives. . . . The level of excellence in the professional staff is measurable in part to the extent that they are active participants in teaching and learning.[4]

In other words, one of the things that distinguishes a college course from a high school course is independent library research. The College, of course, also has to meet the requirements of the State University system, and various HVCC curricula are accredited by professional associations which carry the same message. Specifying library assignments in course syllabi became an essential part of maintaining accreditation.

INTERNAL PRACTICALITIES

The internal practicalities are just as compelling on a day-to-day basis, and unless the LRC-classroom alliance works for the faculty members and students, the assignments demonstrated for accreditation will wither away. Library assignments make sense to faculty because they fulfill a need. We are all aware of faculty who use media in class as a way of reducing preparation/teaching time, and yet we cannot object when the media program is in fact well-chosen and introduced. Bibliographic instruction that meets the students' need to know how to research an assignment is legitimate use of classtime but it also may free the regular faculty for such activities as conference attendance and religious observances. Because the librarians have faculty status it is consistent with campus practice that they be called upon to cover a class, and it can be perceived as a welcome opportunity.

Pedagogically, a library assignment gives the students a chance to work at their own pace, in contrast to the hour exam, and to work essentially with a contract with the professor, with an understanding of how much and what quality of work is required. Library assignments reach both the weak and strong students, giving the less able student a chance to manipulate unfamiliar concepts (including library research) and challenging the bright student to go off on an independent tangent, each student working within his/her own learning style. By introducing students to the professional literature in their field we help them to learn independently, to know how to keep up with developments in rapidly changing fields. Whether they are, for instance, Human Services or Technology students, they graduate with skills that will become obsolete. Professional reading and the research experience in methods for staying current make them more employable.

Our students, no matter what their age, tend to arrive for their first semester with limited experience, limited curiosity, and very limited time (most are trying to work half- to full-time). Library assignments, especially at HVCC with its emphasis on extended reference attention, help build the students' self-confidence. Libraries, many students thought, were for the other guys; we introduce them to the practicalities of libraries for their careers, including the handbooks and professional references they may need on the job.

The College's commitment to training for life-long learning means that library assignments emphasize both content and skills, applying general concepts learned in class to specific topics, analyzing reports and research, building on the students' skills and rules orientation to guide them to a more free-wheeling response to the subject matter. A library assignment with a broad choice of topics helps build student enthusiasm for a course as they are introduced to scholarly articles, the current "hot topics," the controversies, the methodology. A well-designed assignment is not difficult for a professor to grade because its requirements are carefully spelled out.

Several professors are working with the concept "writing across the curriculum" that is based on the realization that you cannot write about what you do not understand, but trying to write about a concept helps you understand it. Asking students to research a topic and write about it, if only abstracting an article, gives them experience in writing within their career field. The required English Composition and social sciences courses are not segregated by curriculum; nursing, construction technology, insurance and liberal arts students will all be mixed in together. Consequently there is no "Economics for Business Majors," no "English for Chemists" and the library assignment becomes a vital means of giving each student a chance to apply common concepts to a particular field. It also gives faculty a chance to assign exposure to general cultural education, as when one English professor asked students to pick a part of the U.S. Constitution they didn't understand, research it, and prepare a limited essay.

This close alliance between professors and librarians has direct, practical impact on the collection. At a time of curtailed budgets the available money is spent to support anticipated library use. The library is not a research collection in the university library sense, and the collections directly service curricular needs. The LRC liaison program is therefore involved with selection, evaluation and utilization of the collection.

HISTORY OF THE PROGRAMS

Twenty years ago when the new HVCC library building was in the planning stages, the trustees understood that a "real" college has to have a library and they saw its public relations value, instructing the architect to design something for the front lawn of the campus that would look good on a postcard. They also understood that for the liberal arts, business and community services divisions the Learning Resources Center was in many ways the equivalent of a laboratory; consequently the LRC received excellent support for building the collections. It was the job of the librarians and media specialists to get those collections used. Soon after we moved into the new building each professional staff member was assigned a liaison area, a department/subject concentration to some extent based on each person's enthusiasms or training. We also began a bibliographic instruction program coordinated with English Composition. Some of our faculty felt their courses were already too full or too technical to be able to add a library component. Other faculty had had little personal experience with college library research and saw only that it meant more papers to grade. Still other faculty had no idea that there were useful alternatives to a term paper. The librarians were activists. They wangled invitations to present LRC resources at department meetings, they talked to faculty over coffee and during office hours, they served on all-campus committees and as faculty union officers. They ran new faculty teas, brown bag lunch talks featuring their faculty, department orientations and open houses, orientations for secretaries and term paper workshops. They reviewed course outlines and textbooks when possible and tried to act as ombudsmen for the professors to the LRC. Faculty were not only invited to suggest new materials, they were sent book reviews and included in media previewing, collection evaluation and withdrawal decisions. On a regular basis lists of relevant magazines and media were distributed to each department and the librarians were involved in the professional accreditation process.

And always: enthusiasm, conversation, follow-through, resource highlighting. When students came to the reference desk with an assignment they were struggling to complete, we would try to visit that professor and suggest library handouts and instruction to make the work easier and the resulting projects more interesting. Because of active support from the LRC administrators we were able to spend adequate time researching and preparing sample assignments so that when a faculty member agreed to try our ideas, we were ready to make it a successful venture. The hardest part was accepting that after several semesters even the best idea wears thin and the faculty member is ready to try something else.

Meanwhile the librarians were also involved in presenting public programming, including an annual Poetry Forum and an Art and Technology seminar series. As equals of the classroom faculty they were invited to seminars in international education, health sciences, insurance, data processing, etc. The one-credit information course, Bibliography and Research, was added to the curriculum. The LRC was a regular participant in recruiting open houses and a stop on campus tours.

GENERAL EDUCATION COMMITTEE

By the time of the Middle States Reaccreditation self-study in 1982-83, the LRC could make a strong case for staff and collection involvement in instruction; indeed the author was a member of the self-study team. The Middle States report praised the LRC but concluded that general education was weak, that the coursework was too singlemindedly devoted to technologies and skills. The Liberal Arts Dean who was also in charge of the self-study immediately set up a General Education Committee. The author, who had spent years talking to faculty about honors programs, ethics courses, library collections, international education, energy conservation, industrial archeology and curriculum reform, had her bluff called and was asked to chair the committee with responsibility for designing open-structured general education one-credit courses that would be approved by the Curriculum Committee before the end of the semester (6 weeks). She had already arranged for the College to offer crafts for credit at the local Arts Council, so the format was somewhat established. Three main concepts were accepted for later implementation: first, cross-disciplinary courses could be taught out of more than one department; second, an open structure for a one-credit course would allow us to plug in a campus lecture or seminar series so that attendees could get credit (and the college get FTEs); and third, the development of one-credit cross-disciplinary courses was encouraged and not considered "course proliferation." Faculty were to be encouraged, especially through the evening division, to teach their special enthusiasms. This program continues to have active administrative support.

The author, as an advocate of internationalizing the curriculum and educating our students about the rest of the world, had discovered how easy it was to infiltrate the curricula. It was a matter of knowing the issues, facts and resources, and using international examples when examples were needed. The content was graspable by all levels of students, cut across curricula, and made courses more vivid. That the issues were in the news was a bonus. It was not necessary to take positions on controversial issues but rather to present concepts that had implications that could be discussed and researched. If it was this easy to increase international awareness, what could be accomplished with a whole range of general education concepts, or what E. D. Hirsch calls cultural literacy?

The members of the General Education Committee, both in meetings and in casual conversation with other faculty, have been asking: what *do* we mean by General Education? Does the required social science elective have to carry the whole burden of creating an educated person? Do we mean cultural activities on campus if the students don't attend? Are we talking about optional term papers? An honors program? Do we want to emphasize the connectedness between disciplines? Do we want to encourage the faculty to share their enthusiasm for the multi-dimensions of their craft?

How directed should the general education experience be, extra credit for the few or required of all when so many students already feel an enormous tension between job, school, social life, career, technologies and the sense of being too tired and ineffective to make any real difference in the world? Are we limiting general education to explaining context to the technologies, or are we also explaining technical implications to the other students? Where does the time come from to add material, redesign a course, assign and correct research? One conclusion was that General Education concepts extend the boundaries of a course or curriculum and that they should be used to help the student learn critical thinking. With that, we are back to the role of the liaison librarians who use library assignments to build those general education, analytical and research skills into the coursework.

Planning the Assignment

Packets of sample course materials from colleges around the country have been available from the ACRL Bibliographic Instruction Liaison Project, but, while these have given us ideas and assurance, our best work is done in collaboration with the faculty. Over time we have developed generic services we can offer, including in-class instruction, workshops, reference area visits by the class, and handouts. The teaching and handouts are tailored to the particular course and include the suggested research sequence for that assignment, periodicals lists, index lists with instructions for locating periodicals, other bibliographies and lists of reference tools, media lists, the Library of Congress classification and relevant subject pages from the "Red Book." The research process is backed up by the Learning Assistance Center which offers tutoring in assembling the report. We do not prepare "Pathfinders" or "Jackdaws" or specific bibliographies for these assignments unless the faculty member wishes to limit the sources.

Assignment Design Process

The assignment design process, once mastered, moves very quickly. First, the liaison librarian must know the collection, not every book, but the subject strengths and weaknesses. If 90 students are working on similar assignments can the collection (and equipment) accommodate them? Sometimes something as simple as extending the time available to finish the work or requiring the work to be turned in in sub-units can spread the students out enough to make a small collection or not enough equipment work out to be adequate. The librarian especially needs to know the reference tools and the regional periodical support. Students do not have six weeks to wait for articles to come from miles away, and are often willing to travel to other local libraries. The librarian should work through the proposed assignment, testing it against the reality if the library is used by students for the first time.

Armed with this background the librarian then engages the faculty member's attention (unless that person has already appeared on the doorstep). This process is person-to-person, but as formal or informal as will produce the desired results: a library assignment. Some faculty require wooing, educating them slowly to the library resources their students are missing out on; others are actively looking for ways to deal with the diversity among their students or for ways to get students to cover independently those concepts the syllabus doesn't have time for. The librarian elicits faculty attitudes toward library assignments and toward the college LRC. It is pointless to hand over a lovingly created assignment to someone who is apathetic, or, worse, had a rotten personal library experience. Many successful alliances have started with very brief assignments that students could complete in two hours and the faculty grade in 3-5 minutes.

Faculty may need advice on alternatives to research papers, and, more important, they need advice on topics to assign and how to grade the results. When the faculty are clear about how they will grade the results, they then understand what they expect students to do in the library, what they expect them to do with the results. The faculty can then write up clear instructions specifying the steps of the assignment and how it will be graded. These instruction sheets are especially valuable at the reference desk when students arrive confused and unsettled, often slightly antagonistic, and, in the case of a community college student, perhaps bearing the emotional load of not doing well at library work in high school. Clear sequential instructions help everyone. Depending on the students and the assignment, the librarian adds to the assignment sheet (either in it or separate) the relevant resource information. She may then review the assignment 10-15 minutes in class, teach a BI special subject hour, or schedule a library class visit. These handouts need not be elegant as long as they are adequate, accurate, and legible. They may be important public relations tools recycled as general handouts, but they must be adequate to the specific assignment first.

Next the liaison librarian must be available to the staff at the reference desk, both to clarify the assignment and to demonstrate the particulars of indexes and reference tools if needed. When students have finished the work, the librarian evaluates, formally or informally, the experience with the faculty member, making appropriate changes so that the commitment to library use continues. Finally, the librarian, often with the faculty member, publicizes successful projects to the rest of the department and to the library, to relevant administrators, to professional colleagues, so that the assignment gains political value. Such library research programs will have a long life only if the college supports a library budget that can keep materials current and in adequate supply. If the library is a weak ancillary to classroom instruction, college funds will go to glamor projects or whatever can be "pointed to with pride." Integrating library skills into coursework is a matter of survival.

Examples

Out of the many assignments developed at HVCC a few may serve as models. In Electrical Construction and Maintenance students do not have to take English. However, they are asked to research their career and job opportunities using the *Dictionary of Occupational Titles, Occupational Outlook Handbook,* professional

and trade journals, the state industrial directories, even *Thomas'*
Register and the construction estimating guides. If they plan to
leave the area they are asked to compare wages and the cost of
living here and there. They may work as teams but must prepare
individual written reports.

In Children's Literature students are asked the hypothetical question:

> On your new job, the principal says that since you are just out
> of school you must be up on all the latest in preschool educa-
> tion and would you please spend the money set aside for books
> and media.

Students then, following a bibliographic instruction class and introduction to materials, consider how to decide what they want, how
to deal with the book trade, how to find reviews and suggestions,
and how to locate free materials. The required result is a list of
"purchases" and a justification which includes an analysis of the
needs of the school (in this case the site of their practicum).

For Criminal Law a full packet was developed to lead students
through the complexities of legal terminology, statutes, case law,
jurisprudence and legal analysis. The presentation included a lecture with slide-tape. Each team of students was given a case to
analyze and present to the class, either for the defendant or the
prosecution, the class acting as jury. This assignment has now
evolved to include three hours of a data base research lab in the
Lexis practice files.

In Sociology, *Resources for the Study of Culture* leads students
through the maze of Library of Congress subject headings. This is a
particularly difficult assignment for freshmen because there is no
one place they can find a list in the card catalog of the cultures
represented by works in the collection. The guide introduces students also to the practice of quickly surveying the possible resources (print, nonprint, books, journals, the reference librarian)
before settling on a topic. There are only three requirements for the
content of the report: students must use scholarly resources and apply concepts learned in class, they must write 5-10 pages, and they

must consider the bias of what they read: how will this look to a member of the culture being analyzed?

In Biology for Non-Science Majors students select an energy source such as petroleum, conservation or biomass. They prepare a written report on its advantages and disadvantages and then participate in a debate among sources. The report covers aspects such as availability, cost, environmental impact, energy technology, and potential. Students may start with the *Readers' Guide*, but many soon become comfortable with *Commodities Yearbook* or *ASHRAE Journal*.

In Money and Banking students read their personal copy of the *Wall Street Journal* throughout the semester, cutting out articles of potential interest. They then settle on a topic based on these articles, summarize and mesh the articles, supplement this with research in the reference and periodicals collection (which may be very sketchy) and submit a 3-5 page report. In other courses students may prepare personnel administration case studies combining personal experience with library research, or prepare for a debate in human services, or annotate book reviews on a work of nonfiction they themselves have reviewed, or research answers to a crossword puzzle in ancient history, apply statistical analysis to psychology articles, prepare a description of a Standard Metropolitan Statistical Area based on reference books such as *County and City Data Book*, industrial directories, atlases, telephone books, etc. or they may design their own small business in all its legal, financial, promotional and spatial complexity. Students in Data Processing and in Retailing may work on case studies while students in Construction Technology may research construction standards or the use of open land.

CONCLUSIONS

Can we therefore draw any conclusions about how to run such a program? In retrospect and in crystal ball gazing it seems fairly simple. The librarian bears the responsibility for general education at the (community) college, having access to all the information and resources necessary to enliven a class, extend horizons, and facilitate independent learning. The library layout must encourage discovery, but for libraries to be centers for independent learning one must be at least a little passionate about getting students involved through their coursework. Collection building must support issues, not just the curriculum, so that the resources support the whole person, so that serendipity and exploration are encouraged. Finally, spread the load and share the glory. Involve as many of the professional staff as possible in carefully prepared outreach. Share ideas, establish both the librarians and faculty members as resource people neophytes can turn to. Above all, communicate informed contagious enthusiasm. If there is an information virus, be one of the people who is a carrier.[5]

REFERENCES

1. Available from SUNYLA Bibliographic Competencies Task Force. ℅Mary Beth Bell, Assoc. Library Director, Community College of the Finger Lakes, Canandaigua, NY 14424, or the author.

2. Hudson Valley Community College. *General Catalog, 1986-87.* Troy, NY, 1986, p. 9.

3. Middle States Association of Colleges and Schools. *Characteristics of Excellence in Higher Education.* Philadelphia, 1982, p. ii.

4. Ibid., p. 23-24.

5. Henson, Keith. "Information as a Communicable Disease," *Coevolution Quarterly*, Summer 1984, no. 42, p. 98.

BIBLIOGRAPHY

American Association of Community and Junior Colleges. *Strengthening Humanities in Community Colleges.* Washington, 1980.

Center for the Study of Community Colleges and ERIC Clearinghouse for Junior Colleges. *The Humanities and Sciences in Two-Year Colleges.* Los Angeles, 1980.

Commission on the Humanities. *The Humanities in American Life.* Berkeley, Univ. of California Press, 1980.

Gagné, Robert M. *Principles of Instructional Design.* New York, Holt, Rinehart and Winston, any edition.

Havelock, Ronald G. *The Change Agent's Guide to Innovation in Education.* Englewood Cliffs, N.J., Educational Technology Publications, 1973.

Henson, Keith. "Information as a Communicable Disease," *Coevolution Quarterly*, Summer 1984, no. 42, p. 98.

Hudson Valley Community College. *Self-study Report Written for . . . Middle States Association of Colleges and Schools.* Troy, N.Y., 1984.

_____. Learning Resources Center. [Library Assignment Packets 1978-].

Kirsch, E.D. *Cultural Literacy*. Boston, Houghton Mifflin, 1987.

Middle States Association of Colleges and Schools. *Characteristics of Excellence in Higher Education: Standards for Accreditation*. Philadelphia, 1982.

Root, Christine and Blandy, Susan. "A Reappraisal of Bibliographic Instruction," *The Bookmark*, Fall 1986, pp. 30-33.

SUNYLA Bibliographic Competencies Task Force. *Recommended Library Skills and Competencies for Graduates of Community Colleges in New York State*. Canandaigua, N.Y., 1987.

Turesky, Stanley F., ed. *Advancing the Liberal Arts*. San Francisco, Jossey-Bass, *New Directions for Community Colleges*, no. 42, June 1983.

PART IV:
LIBRARY SKILLS IN COLLEGES AND UNIVERSITIES

University Approval
of Library Research Skills
as Part of the General Education
Curriculum Requirements

Judy Reynolds

SUMMARY. To gain university support for new proposals, librarians must become involved in campus policy and governance bodies. If we do not know where our own universities are headed, we will always be followers and never able to provide leadership. A proactive stance requires a great investment in boundary spanning activities with policy making bodies. At San Jose State University librarians engaged in an education campaign to persuade faculty and administration of the need to include bibliographic instruction in general education requirements. Librarians should strongly encourage open communication with faculty regarding student research skills. Faculty often perceive student research skills quite differently than do librarians.

Judy Reynolds is Library Education and Assistance Program Head, San Jose State University Library, Washington Square, San Jose, CA 95192-0028.

The library at San Jose State now has a two-tiered bibliographic instruction program that is a required part of the University's general education curriculum requirements. Becoming an integral part of the curriculum required a large commitment to involvement in campus governance, realistic planning, marketing and open communications. We were fortunate. In our case the investment paid off and ultimately resulted in a program that benefits our entire student body.

Our story is not unique, although the events have occurred earlier at San Jose State University than on the campuses of many other universities. Communication between the library and other parts of the campus occasionally broke down. New departments and programs were added or dropped, emphasis changed, interdisciplinary programs initiated or dissolved, and the library was the last to know.

Protest after the fact did not improve the situation. The librarians devised a more proactive strategy, forming a network that served as an underground early warning system. We made a special point to have librarians as members of the Academic Senate, the faculty policy body, and its policy and program committees. This enabled us to find out about changes while they were still in the planning stages and usually enabled us to have sufficient lead time to respond.

San Jose State is part of the California State University System campuses. It is one of the larger campuses with about 25,000 students enrolled, eighty percent of whom are undergraduates. Its principle mission is to provide undergraduate and graduate (through the master's degree), education in the liberal arts and sciences, applied fields and the professions.

BECOMING INVOLVED

In 1978 we decided to act when our representative to the Academic Senate reported that the Senate was considering adopting a new general education curriculum, growing out of a new statement of the University's mission. At this time the library had been offering a one unit course in library research through our Library School but it only provided us the opportunity to instruct a tiny portion of our student body. With students facing increasing numbers of required courses for both general education and upper division major requirements, the enrollment in the course was likely to decline even further. The course was not providing sufficient introduction to the library in a time of shrinking budgets. Students increasingly needed to acquire the skills necessary in order to use a more self-service library, ever increasing in size and complexity.

After apprising the Library Director about the opportunity to become involved in the new general education program and being promised support and resources, a brief list of educational goals and objectives was developed. Excerpts from a study by Whitlatch and Keiffer indicating deficiencies in our students' ability to use the library were included in this plan (Whitlatch and Kieffer). The main findings were that when patrons reported not finding books in the catalog, in forty-two percent of the cases the books were correctly listed in the catalog. Only one third of these people asked for help. About one third of the books patrons could not find on the shelf were actually there. And, here again, only one quarter of the people who failed to find materials asked for help. The study provided evidence that problems in library use did not decrease for students in upper division and graduate programs.

GAINING APPROVAL

The Academic Senate's support was the key to our gaining acceptance of our proposal. Our faculty rely on this body of their peers to referee policy and curriculum matters. Obtaining its endorsement was tantamount to active, campus-wide faculty approval of our mission. The importance of changing faculty attitudes is summarized by Breivik. She states that the biggest hindrance to exploring campus libraries as the point of access to information

> is largely an attitude that perceives the librarians as the heart of the institution, which like physical hearts are ignored until a problem arises (for example, negative accreditation reports). This attitude also perceives librarians as passive second-class citizens of academe. (Breivik, 48)

At San Jose State, at that time, librarians had some of the privileges of faculty status including membership on faculty senate committees. We used our status to change our image with the faculty to a more dynamic one. Guskin, Stoffle and Boisse recognized the importance of cultivating this more active relationship.

> The key element in developing a successful instruction program is the relationship between the faculty and the librarians. Without cooperation and communication, librarians cannot prepare relevant instruction programs and faculty will not accept librarians in the classroom. Therefore, librarians must spend a substantial amount of time cultivating faculty members, providing information for them, obtaining information from them, and developing among them the concept of the librarians as a team member in the educational process. (Guskin, 285)

Meisel and Kalick further state that, "librarians who seek to improve communications can be viewed as change agents. They must literally get out of the library to effect changes. In that role they can alter the perceptions of their users and the image of the library" (Meisel, 29).

Our proposal was introduced to the Academic Senate with this justification:

> The primary mission of the University is undergraduate education and its first priority is to insure a reasonably uniform background in General Education for all students! In keeping with the University's goal, the Library Education and Assistance Program's (LEAP) first priority is the improvement of the ability of undergraduate students to make effective use of the library collections, services and staff in order to increase their ability to use the library independently. To achieve this end, LEAP will systematically integrate a unit in the basic composition course which will familiarize the students with basic strategies for locating information on general topics in books and periodicals. In addition, it will offer such other instructional services as may be deemed necessary at this basic level.

The University President gave her full support to the proposal having been advised of it in advance by our Senate Representative who was also on the Academic Senate's Executive Committee. The President's strong support was very persuasive to the faculty and contributed immensely to the ease of implementing the program. We had also met with the Academic Vice President, responsible for curricular and faculty matters, and the Chair of the English Department. These preliminary meetings provided the project with strong support and the involvement of key people from its inception.

FRESHMAN LEVEL INSTRUCTIONS

Our initial proposal noted that a standard reference, *Missions of the College Curriculum* stated that "statistical skills have become more important both in many occupations and for comprehension by the citizen of current developments and that skill in using library sources is becoming more and more essential. Both these skills are frequently ignored" (Carnegie, 11). Breivik pointed out that short-sighted nature of instruction too closely focused on individual courses outside of a cultural context.

> Traditional approaches such as using textbooks, providing reading lists, and putting selected materials on reserve do not, however, provide students with the information-handling skills required for continued learning after graduation. Neither do these approaches ensure that students will know if they are applying their problem-solving abilities to an appropriate information base. (Breivik, 49)

As one of the University's goals was to develop in its students an inquiring mind and to impart to them the ability to continue in the future as active, informed citizens, a library unit was proposed for the second semester of freshman English 1B, the first writing class which might require a documented research paper.

Mode of Instruction

We could not offer an entire course to every student because we could not afford the personnel costs and students would not likely be able to fit it into their schedules. Nor did we expect students, many of whom do not see research as a major component of their adult life, to desire an entire course in library research. Instead we opted to integrate our instruction as "one hour stands" in required general education courses.

From the various options for teaching, tour, workbook, self-paced AV presentation, etc., we selected to teach using the lecture method. Course integrated lectures enabled us to hone in on specific information needs facing our students. Dervin states that people seek information when it fills a recognized gap in their knowledge. Having to write documented papers subsequent to our lectures reinforced the utility of these customized lectures in satisfying information gaps. We felt that a genuine workbook would have been seen as irrelevant busy work.

One of the assets of this method is that it stresses interpersonal communication. A good part of our motivation in offering instruction was to change student attitudes towards the library and market our services. We wanted to initiate a personal contact between the students and librarians, replace stereotypes of librarians and increase users' expectations of success in the library.

A study by Mellon has found that "library anxiety was considerably reduced by interaction with librarians in a fifty-minute session." Her results verify our concern about our approachability problem. "Librarians were unaware of the importance students placed on getting to know the librarians and realizing those people (librarians) want to help me" (Mellon, 164). Further evidence to corroborate Mellon's work is found in a comparative study of biographic techniques by Markman and Leigton. Their evidence indicates the importance of interpersonal factors. A lecture from a librarian alleviated students' anxiety about using the library. A library workbook, on the other hand, left many students feeling "frustrated," "frightened" and "hostile."

At San Jose State, Whitlatch studied student interest in bibliographic instruction. Students were generally (71.1%) more interested in availability of instruction than their instructors (50.4%). Student preference was for one-to-one instruction at the reference desk (82.6%). This option was, for us, neither an economically feasible way to offer help to every student nor was it seen as effective in developing the ability to use the library independently. Desire for research lectures peak in the sophomore year (58.7%). The majority of our upperclass and graduate students also expressed a preference for research lectures.

Specific Objections

Originally, the objectives of this unit were for the students to learn to: (1) Use the library effectively; (2) Recognize the basic elements for bibliographic form and be able to use basic style manuals in their fields and; (3) Plan and implement a basic literature search and evaluate the usefulness of bibliographic citations. This eventually was modified to learning how to conduct a basic literature search, i.e., how to find books and periodical articles pertinent to one's research assignment. The objective was modified because the original objective was too broad and vague. Teaching bibliographic format was deemed to be the responsibility of the English department. The library has concentrated on teaching students to recognize which format book, journal, etc. a reference indicates.

The Academic Senate was quite supportive of our proposal and was pleased that the librarians wanted to become so actively involved in classroom instruction. While the upper division section of the proposal continued in the Senate's Board of General Studies for two more years, we proceeded with freshman English.

In order to work out the details, the next meeting was with the English Curriculum Committee. After the proposal was introduced, they asked who else had such a program. Such required, course-integrated instruction was fairly scarce at the time and allusions to ACRL BIS, the concept of a library college, Louis Shores, Patricia Knapp, Evan Farber and Tom Kirk and their libraries fell on deaf ears. Obviously library literature did not motivate teaching faculty. Although he conceded that the idea was good, the chair's first question was "Why English? Wouldn't it be better to offer the unit in History where documented research papers are the norm?" He went on to point out that since the sixties, many instructors in English had drifted away from documented papers and students wrote more personal narratives. Perhaps we should have briefed the committee chair in advance to avoid the risk of our proposal dying at this point! As I held my breath, the department committee came to our rescue before I could reply. A rallying cry went up for a return to traditional, pre-sixties writing requirements and it was agreed that at least one documented research paper ought to be part of the course. The library then pointed out that English was chosen because of its key role in teaching writing. While History may require research, they are not responsible for teaching students to convert it into lucid prose. This recognition of the key role of the English faculty and, further, our respect for it, cinched the argument. The committee chair, incidently, became a staunch supporter of our project.

Feedback

In fall of 1979 we began teaching in freshman English. All the students were asked to fill out evaluations which asked several questions including: What information was new to you? What part of the lecture was most informative? The evaluations were summarized and the library was surprised to learn that for most students this very basic introductory lecture was just what they needed. For two semesters summaries of the evaluations were sent to the faculty. In one case where an instructor felt the lecture too elementary, the evaluations for his class were tallied for him to review and he revised his expectations. This communication link back to the teaching faculty is one which librarians would be well advised to pursue. While librarians may personally confront students with haphazard and insufficient library skills daily, teaching faculty often assume that their students are much better equipped than is the case. They then become dissatisfied when a librarian lectures on the basic essentials.

One of the greatest benefits of this program for librarians and faculty is that it has increased our effectiveness in working as a team in the classroom. The faculty attending the lecture with their students received a separate evaluation sheet which asked how we could better integrate our lecture into their coursework. This was a trick question. It has persuaded many of the instructors to be quite diligent about explaining their students' assignment to us ahead of time. They are working with us to devise a research assignment that will increase student awareness of information systems and the need for critical evaluations of sources.

The freshman English lecture settled into a comfortable pattern of acceptance over the next two years and the image of the librarians gradually shifted. They became more involved with curriculum and more visible partners in the classroom. This may have been due, in part, to our decision to hold the lecture in the classroom rather than have students make a field trip to that foreign turf—the library. The non-verbal message of seeing librarians as part of the class may have had some persuasive power. Also, as Marshall McLuhen said, "The medium is the message." We tried to communicate that we wanted the students to know about the library. We wanted to tell them about it personally rather than via a workbook.

UPPER DIVISION INSTRUCTION

The Academic Senate's Board of General Studies (BOGS) was responsible for overseeing approval of general education courses. To some extent it was easier to become involved with the next phase of the general education program. With the continued support of the University administration and enhanced viability as a result of the freshman program, we also requested a unit in the junior level writing workshop, an upper division general education requirement. Our objectives for that course are for the students in each major to: (1) Become familiar with the basic reference tools and indexes in the discipline; and (2) Acquire a basic concept of how information is organized and accessed in the discipline. Each librarian, responsible for a subject area with a junior level course, contacted the appropriate curriculum committee to discuss the library unit. Many of these librarians already had close contact with the teaching departments. This initiative provided an important opportunity to become a more active partner and cement those ties even more solidly.

At this level, the library's involvement met with no opposition. The three unit junior writing class was an additional general education requirement, introduced at a time when most departments were battling to keep all the upper division courses in their departments. The explosion of information made it difficult to condense the required courses into two years of classes. In addition, funding for education was very tight and fewer courses could lead to cuts in a department's faculty.

The result was that many departments opted to teach the writing course themselves. This was an opportunity for the librarians, as it meant we could tailor our lectures to a fairly precise audience. What's more, this audience would have had some exposure to university library research and would be interested in their topic. The teaching faculty, in almost all cases was thrilled to have us. Why? Because they came from disciplines such as biology, business and art and, initially, they did not feel comfortable about having to teach a junior level course in writing.

After two years of shouting matches at BOGS meetings and the Academic Senate, the junior class finally got underway in fall of 1981. The librarians had been prepared for a year and were eager to talk to the classes. As many of these lectures involve discussion of sophisticated indexes and other reference tools, they were held in the library. Some now involve demonstration of automated information systems, not available in the classroom.

In some areas the number of sections of a course is too large a workload for one librarian. Because of this and because we take our teaching responsibility very seriously, we trained additional librarians to give each lecture. This gives us flexibility and emergency coverage. All the lectures for a particular department are scheduled by the librarian responsible for the subject area, once again strengthening our ties with the teaching faculty.

Evaluation of the content of these lectures is a constant focus of the subject librarians. Now, with the advent of word processing, many of the librarians are experimenting with new teaching methods and involving the faculty in these projects. We have even had some success in reducing the number of "treasure hunt" assignments when the librarians are consulted about the assignment ahead of time. The chair of BOGS summed up the faculty view of the junior level library unit saying "It's the best thing about the whole course."

FUTURE PLANS

Building on our successful instructional activities we have several new projects and plans for bibliographic instruction. We are experimenting with a pilot program of individualized tutoring for foreign students on library exercises after their freshman level library lecture. We are working with the Educational Opportunity Program to introduce disadvantaged students to the library during a summer campus orientation program designed to bridge the transitions between high school or junior college and the University. We would like our instruction to be formally required in graduate research methods courses where we are now only involved by invitation. Individual librarian instructors are experimenting with teaching new technologies such as CD ROM and others are exploring alternative teaching techniques designed to elicit more student involvement and develop students' critical thinking skills.

CONCLUSION

If you or your library wish to increase your involvement on campus, here are a few points to keep in mind.

1. Become involved in campus policy and governance bodies. You may learn of opportunities while they are still in the planning stages when you can have the greatest impact.
2. Be realistic. Look at the available resources for the program and develop a plan which allows you to provide the type and quality of program that will benefit as many students as possible.
3. Discuss your well-outlined proposals in advance with the major influential individuals and convince them to become stakeholders in your proposal, insuring their support.
4. Acknowledge your need and respect for the teaching faculty's support in their role as powerful student opinion leaders.
5. Keep the faculty informed about how well your program is working, especially from the students' point of view. They often don't realize how much help students actually need, es-

pecially in our multi-cultural environment. It is incumbent upon you to keep this system of communication lines open.
6. Be patient. In addition to looking ahead and planning for the future, look back a few years and you might be surprised how far you've come.

REFERENCES

Breivik, Patricia Senn (1986). Library-based learning in an information society. *New-Directions-for-Higher-Education* 14(4):47-55.

Carnegie Foundation for the Advancement of Teaching. *Missions of college curriculum: a contemporary review with suggestions*. San Francisco, Jossey-Bass, 1977.

Dervin, Brenda (1977). Useful theory for librarianship: communication, not information. *Drexel library quarterly* 13(3):16-32.

Guskin, Alan, Stoffle, Carla J., and Boisse, Joseph (1979). The Academic library as a teaching library: a role for the 1980's. *Library Trends* 28(2):281-296.

Markman, Marsha C. and Leighton, Gordon B. (1987). Exploring freshman composition student attitudes about library instruction sessions and workbooks: two studies. *Research Strategies* 5(3):126-134.

Meisel, Gloria B. and Kalick, Rosanne (1984). Marketing bibliographic instruction through improved communication. *Community and Junior College libraries* 2(3):21-30.

Mellon, Constance (1986). Library anxiety: a grounded theory and its development. *College and Research libraries* 47(2):160-165.

Whitlatch, Jo Bell and Keiffer, Karen (1978). Service at San Jose State University; Survey of Document Availability. *The Journal of Academic librarianship* 4(4):196-199.

Whitlatch, Jo Bell (1981). San Jose State University Library Services: results of the Spring 1980 faculty and student user surveys. Educational Resources Information Center (ERIC), #ED206279.

The View from Square One: Librarian and Teaching Faculty Collaboration on a New Interdisciplinary Course in World Civilizations

Paula Elliot

SUMMARY. Amid growing trends toward curriculum reform on many campuses, librarians may find an opportunity to contribute significantly to the improvement of undergraduate education. In the Bibliographic Instruction and Writing Across the Curriculum movements, recent developments suggest that librarians may work more closely with their classroom colleagues to create more effective learning situations. While curriculum reform has a most apparent impact on user education, it also touches upon collection development (and bibliographic control), reference and circulation activity, professional development and the library's public image. At Washington State University, the library is prominently represented on a campus-wide committee to develop a new core course under the auspices of the National Endowment for the Humanities. The librarians involved have expanded their professional practice in unexpected ways, causing an increased respect for the library among teaching faculty, and an added dimension to their careers as academics. Their experience is offered as a model for those whose institutions are similarly undergoing reforms in general education.

In 1986, Washington State University received a grant from the National Endowment for the Humanities to develop a freshman course in World Civilizations, with an anticipated implementation in Fall 1987. Interdisciplinary in its approach, the course would address students' apparent inexperience with historical, cultural and

Paula Elliot is Reference/Instructional Librarian and Music and Theatre Specialist, Holland Library, Washington State University, Pullman, WA 99164-5610.

conceptual issues. It was further hoped that such a course would stimulate students' interest in other humanities course offerings. The award coincided with the establishment of WSU's Commission on General Education and the All-University Writing Committee. With such widespread attention to curriculum reform, the NEH project sparked immediate interest across campus.

Recognizing that "better undergraduate education means better integration of libraries in the learning process,"[1] librarians at WSU perceived in these University efforts an opportunity to expand their programs in User Education. This article documents the process of one library's involvement in the curriculum reform movement on its campus, in bibliographic instruction, collection development, media production, faculty enrichment, and public relations.

GROUNDWORK FOR THE NEH PROJECT

The NEH grant was written by a literary scholar and a historian, in a collaboration which itself evidenced concern for a sharing of disciplines in the proposed course. The authors emphasized "the need for such a core course to transcend the limits of any single cultural tradition or approach to learning. Student intellectual growth rather than departmental or college aggrandizement [would be] the aim."[2] Shortly after the award, the two formed an invitational committee representing a variety of interests, including two librarians: Director of Libraries Maureen Pastine, who serves on the Commission for General Education and the All-University Writing Committee, and reference librarian Alice Spitzer, who co-coordinates Library User Education. Spitzer is also known for her long and effective involvement in the freshman writing program, and for her frequent professional activity on international development projects.[3] To develop an interdisciplinary faculty, this Steering Committee selected faculty to plan, and ultimately teach, the course. In the Fall of 1986, invitations to apply for consideration were sent to every faculty member on campus, including librarians. The response throughout the disciplines evidenced a genuine interest in the enterprise. From among 90 applications, 30 faculty were selected to participate. The finalists, from amid a dizzying array of credentials, represented ten academic departments[4] and a much wider range of interests. In addition to scholarly success, their outstanding teaching ability weighed heavily in their selection. Twenty would receive summer stipends from the NEH; the remaining group (including two librarians who are on twelve-month appointments) would serve in a volunteer consulting capacity.

After the selection of the faculty group, the Steering Committee disbanded; the Director of Libraries' role in the project became an advisory one. The two librarians selected for the project were Alice Spitzer, the reference/instruction librarian mentioned earlier, and Paula Elliot, a reference/instruction librarian relatively new to WSU, who possessed a particularly strong background in the arts and humanities. Their combined abilities produced a highly experienced team. While an interest in the improved teaching of humanities at WSU had prompted their participation, they felt an equally strong professional concern for the inclusion of a library-instruction component in the course. Should World Civ 110-111 become a freshman requirement, as was hoped by its authors, introductory library use would touch every incoming freshman. The Director of Libraries supported their presence on the project to ensure such a measure. But the librarian's involvement took them beyond this expectation into several other creative and influential activities.

In the Spring of 1987, the two sought guidance in a variety of ways. A literature survey, published queries, and a nationwide letter inquiry[5] yielded no precedent for librarians' ground-floor involvement in the creation of such an interdisciplinary course as part of a core-curriculum design.[6] Their approach was informed, however by existing principles which foster independence of inquiry. Summarily,

> a *BI* program that can teach all . . . learners to approach any inquiry, scholarly or not, with appreciation of the complexities and ambiguities involved, will improve the preparation of those destined for scholarship; but more important, it will make a contribution that is uniquely our own to an educated citizenry.[7]

A commitment to lifelong learning guided the instructional decisions of the librarians on the project, which afforded them the opportunity to set such principles in motion.

THE COLLEGIALITY CONNECTION

It must be remembered that in any creative enterprise, the amount of time and energy invested to produce a result is staggeringly large in proportion to the product presented. The design of the new course "World Civilizations 110-111" involved countless hours of discussions among the selected faculty. Beginning in January, 1987, weekly meetings were held to discuss ideology, theory, content and presentation. In the course of these meetings, as might be imagined, this group became a well-acquainted and cohesive unit.

The diversity of approaches to a common problem was an unexpected revelation to all involved. While empathetic to the enterprise of interdisciplinary humanities education, each participant represented a particular, often narrow, academic bias. A large part of the exercise for everyone was to determine a common vocabulary, and initiate one another to the subtleties of a specific academic approach. To engage in this kind of dialogue increased each participant's sensitivity to the isolation fostered by academe's departmental structure.

For the two participating librarians, the leap toward interdisciplinary understanding was not so difficult. Their "department," of any on campus, was the one where all disciplines meet. At its best, their practice of reference had given them (as for all reference librarians) the opportunity to discuss with researchers, sometimes in detail, scholarly concerns which range across the spectrum of knowledge. As public service librarians, they knew many of the faculty on the project. Their evident comfort with the "interdisciplinary problem" earned them early respect from teaching faculty. And their contributions at this juncture caused high visibility for the library among the numerous departments represented.

THE MATERIALS COMMITTEE

The task of creating a new course entailed a division of responsibility among participants. A Curriculum Committee was delegated to draft the syllabus for the course; a Visiting Speakers Committee was formed to select and invite consultants; and a Materials Committee was named to identify audiovisual media and printed information to support teaching. The likely chair of the Materials Committee was librarian Alice Spitzer, who chose librarian Paula Elliot and Paul Brians, of the English faculty, as her collaborators.

The first task of the Committee, in the spring of 1987, was to identify and list films which would appropriately correspond to material being taught. The committee perused catalogs provided by WSU Libraries' Instructional Media Center (IMS), previewed films, and produced a selective list of titles available through IMS. The list was arranged to correspond to the newly-produced syllabus. Additionally, they recommended some films for purchase by the project. These films would be housed in IMS, available to the campus community and beyond, evidencing another advantage of the library's involvement in the project.

In developing the first-semester syllabus, the Curriculum Committee determined that one of the recommended films would be shown each week as part of the course. Student viewings would be out-of-class, and could occur at one of several times and locations. In this effort the libraries' IMS (Instructional Media Services) unit played a key role in making necessary arrangements.

As the syllabus became more refined, the materials committee was able to proceed with more concept-specific projects. The three members of the Materials Committee shared a strong conviction that the arts must be consistently incorporated into this introduction to world cultures. Their expanding activities took them beyond the identification and listing of materials, and into procurement and, ultimately, creation of them.

Since the library does not possess a slide collection, they pursued the ramifications of starting one, and investigated sources for the purchase of slides. Using the library's art resources, they identified illustrations for lectures. They have developed a slide collection in support of the course, and have created an indexing system to facilitate access as the collection grows. Currently each department involved in teaching the course holds one copy to the slide set. Other provisions for control of the collection are being considered. The process of identifying sources naturally led to a practical assessment of the library's ability to meet the material needs of the course; the library's involvement on the project could influence the way in which certain acquisitions are approached.

Private collections were also heavily drawn upon where necessary. One notable instance was in the creation of the "World Civ

111 Soundtrack," a taped anthology of music selected to convey the sense of a particular lecture's content. The Materials Committee utilized their combined audio collections, the refined recording abilities of one member, and the discographic skills of another to produce a series of cassettes specifically tailored to the teaching concerns of the second-semester syllabus. While the selections were, of course, highly subjective, they reflected the committee's combined knowledge of both world and Western musics. The final tapes evidence a sensitivity for course content and an awareness of student needs. Supplementary textual material provides teachers with background notes on the music, and complete discographic citations. This is the kind of project which would have been difficult to accomplish at WSU without access to private collections. The NEH Project, through the Materials Committee, has directly influenced the improvement of WSU's audio collection.

The committee anticipates further film selection, illustration identification, and the creation of an audio tape for the first semester, which, enhanced by new acquisitions in ancient music for the libraries' audio collection, will enable music to be addressed fairly early in the curriculum.

VISITING CONSULTANTS

In the Spring of 1987, and again in 1988, individuals with expertise in establishing interdisciplinary undergraduate courses were brought to campus for a brief visit. In addition to advisory meetings, each visiting consultant gave a formal address, open to the community. In the course of one or two days they met with the NEH committee as a whole, the curriculum committee, and sometimes the Commission on General Education. In each instance a meeting was scheduled with the director of libraries and the two library representatives to the NEH project. In these small sessions, the librarians attempted to gain some insight into library inclusion on similar projects. While each consultant congratulated WSU on this aspect of the proposed course, each also viewed it as novel and a little unexpected. This reinforced for Spitzer and Elliot what instructional librarians instinctively know: that library user education concepts remain foreign to many teachers of undergraduates, however accomplished and principled. These discussions provided the opportunity to talk informally about theories of course-related library user education, with some of the leaders in interdisciplinary teaching. If WSU librarians were unable to gain any insight, the situation afforded an opportunity for them to suggest to the visitors the inclusion of a library component in their own courses.

THE PLANNING COMMITTEE

The NEH grant provided for two summer workshops to train participants in less-familiar aspects of world cultures. It was assumed that most faculty's educations had provided an adequate background in Western traditions, as was the custom in previous generations. Therefore the summer workshops would address basic knowledge in India, China, Japan, Africa, and the Middle East.

The two librarians, experienced at conference coordination, volunteered to make arrangements for the Spring 1987 workshop. They created a timetable, drew up a list of supplies and a checklist of preparations, arranged for refreshments, set up meeting rooms, reserved films, hung maps, posted posters of exotic places, provided for the taping of lectures, and hosted a reception.

The success of the workshop led to the formation of a new sub-committee on which both librarians sit. The Planning Committee combines the activities of the initial visiting lecturers committee with necessary preparations for weekly faculty meetings and future summer workshops. It is, besides, a steering committee for the administration of the project.

The two librarians on the projects also serve on other University committees which have a relationship to the project. Sometimes the relationship is coincidental; sometimes it is directly because of their involvement in the World Civ effort. Because of their ability to interact with many different campus groups, ties are strengthened in a variety of ways, to the benefit of the project, the library, and beyond.

BIBLIOGRAPHIC INSTRUCTION

The introduction of a library-use component into the pilot classes of World Civilizations would effect its inclusion once the course underwent full implementation in the freshman curriculum. It was

therefore necessary to consider carefully the nature of this component, its value to the course, and its value to the students. It could
conceivably revolutionize bibliographic instruction at Washington
State University.

Introductory sessions at WSU had traditionally centered around a
library tour which highlighted certain types of sources. Encouraged
to experiment, the librarians felt that a different approach might be
more effective. Taking the opportunity to address freshman user
education in an innovative way, the librarians attempted to determine the most important library-use concerns of incoming students.

Drawing on their years of one-on-one interactions with students,
and encouraged by recent writings in user education,[8] and influenced by the recent national studies which cite students' lack of
evaluative ability,[9] they determined that one of a student's greatest
obstacles in library use arises in simply asking a question. As a
primer for fundamental investigatory skills, a session on question
analysis formed the basis of the library component for the first semester.[10]

World Civilizations 110-111, as implemented in 1987-88, was
comprised of two class sections of fifty freshmen each. Students to
take the pilot course were recruited by letter during the preceding
summer, and, for testing purposes, respondents were then selected
to represent a cross-section of the incoming class. In the syllabus,
the forty-five class sections were packed with lecture information;
the curriculum committee, confronted with the task of preparing the
new course, felt it had reduced the study of world cultures to its
barest bones. Although the committee agreed that library use must
be included (and, in fact, a short research project was required in
the course), there was no provision in the syllabus for an in-class
library presentation.

Given the special circumstances of the pilot project, special,
small, out-of-class sessions were held; students were required to
attend one as homework. In the session, they completed an exercise, inspired by Oberman-Soroka's "Question Analysis and the
Learning Cycle" (see note 10), which asked them to divide a set of
cards into two groups. On the cards, as in Oberman-Soroka's exercise, were conceptual and factual questions. These, however, were
of a historical nature, and drawn from the text for the course.[11] A

discussion on the attributes of such questions ensued, and, following Oberman-Soroka, a chart was made on the board to illustrate to students the breakdown of complex conceptual questions into simple factual components (e.g., who, what, when, where, other). In a session of this sort, through direct classroom feedback, the librarian was able to observe the students' grasp of the material. The session also included a brief introduction to types of related resources.

The mechanics of locating a book in the WSU system was also deemed important for freshmen. Implicitly, subject headings and call numbers would be addressed. In response to campus-wide reforms in writing, the evaluative component of the exercise asked that students examine a book that they found and write a few paragraphs on its apparent usefulness.

On a worksheet provided, the students' first task, in a departure from Oberman-Soroka's procedure, consisted of formulating their *own* conceptual questions, based on a topic of interest in McNeill. (All had been asked to bring the text to class; topics were selected from the index.) This formed the basis of the homework for the library component. Students were than asked on their worksheet to design a conceptual question using the factual components they had listed. These components would help categorize their chosen interests into contexts of time, place, surrounding circumstances, etc. Using this breakdown, they could then attempt to locate a book using the library's online catalog. The categorical components which they had listed provided subject headings.

A worksheet guided each student through the use of the library's online catalog, and space was provided for the student to identify and jot down bibliographic elements and call number. Space was also provided for the written commentary on the book's usefulness previously mentioned.[12]

Faculty teaching the pilot sections agreed to incorporate points for the library project into the final grade. After reviewing the completed worksheets, librarians felt that the students exhibited a good grasp of the material presented, but their ability to transfer such principles into other research activities cannot yet be determined. Students' reactions to the assignments suggested that they were glad to have been introduced to the material and thought it might be useful in the future.

The second semester's library project provided independent experience in the selection and evaluation of sources. To continue an introduction to different kinds of sources, and to expand upon the evaluation of information, a bibliographic essay was assigned. This was expected to reinforce students' skill at locating books, and introduce them to the use of indexes and encyclopedias, while encouraging a critical look at the varieties of available information. Worksheets assisted in the location of sources, preparatory to the writing of the essay. This approach discouraged last-minute encyclopedia cribbing. In the process of assessing a source's quality, students would learn something from its factual content. No librarian's presentation was planned, but students obtained appropriate assistance from reference librarians. Successful completion of the essay was assessed for the final course grade. It is hoped that high grades will encourage the application of these investigatory principles to assignments for other courses.

Instructors for the pilot sections of the course have been very supportive of the course-related instruction presented by librarians. There is, however, among the entire NEH faculty, a vital concern for the overwhelming amount of "material to be covered." Some faculty doubt the appropriateness of "teaching skills" in such a course. (This attitude exemplifies the discipline-based isolation which has caused communication difficulties throughout the enterprise.) The librarians are confident that conscious integration of skills with content, as in the pilot exercises, will dispel these reservations.[13]

THE WRITING CONNECTION

Influenced by new University concerns for writing, the NEH project provides that World Civilizations enrollees be placed in special, related sections of English 101. During the pilot, half of World Civ students are scheduled for English 101 in the first semester, half in the second. Since English 101 typically addresses some aspects of the research process, and not all students are exposed to these at one time, it was important to introduce different, yet related, bibliographic skills in World Civ. (This risk of overlap incidentally contributed to the instructional librarians' decision to introduce question analysis rather than the use of tools.)

It is evident that very close communication must occur between English 101 Teaching Assistants and instructional librarians involved in this course. WSU's existing program in User Education has fostered strong links between the library and the writing program, and the communication is strongly supported by administrators in the Library and the English Department.[14]

THE "EVENTS" ASSIGNMENT

In addition to film viewings, examinations, map quizzes, the library component and the research report, students in World Civ 110-111 are expected to attend several related cultural events on campus and report on their experiences. This "Events Assignment," while not necessarily teaching library skills, was developed by the two librarians on the NEH project. In part, it is their attempt to build audiences for the high-quality, under-attended exhibitions, performances and lectures at their institution. It also is their attempt to integrate such experiences into undergraduate education, in preparation for a rich cultural life. For enrollees in World Civilizations, selected events provide a natural extension of the course, as the relationship of such events to course content is emphasized in the grant proposal.[15] For students in the special English 101 sections (and in other courses as well), such a relationship is reinforced by this writing assignment, which has also been used in several traditional sections of English 101. It takes many forms, and sometimes includes library investigation.

CONCLUSION: WHAT THE TITLE IMPLIES

The title phrase "working with faculty" suggests a highly energetic level of collegial interaction which goes beyond the customary services of our practice. ". . . to build library use into a new interdisciplinary course" implies a high level of commitment to every aspect of the project. Current leaders in our profession suggest that "librarians must be part of long-range planning committees and task forces for proposed new courses and/or general changes in the curriculum and direction of the university."[16] Academic librarians, from their interdisciplinary vantage point, are ideally qualified to assume leadership roles in core curriculum development on their campuses. From their investment of energy and expertise, comes the welcome stimulation of open dialogue, and the rewarding opportunity to assert a dynamic influence on the direction of undergraduate education.

REFERENCES

1. Patricia Senn Breivik, "Making the Most of Libraries in the Search for Academic Excellence," *Change* 19(4):46.

2. Richard Law and T.L. Kennedy. *The Humanities Core Curriculum Project*. Grant proposal to the National Endowment for the Humanities, [n.d.].

3. In addition, the committee included faculty representing economics (also University Ombudsman), history (chair and coordinator of the Asia Program), and English (coordinator of departmental humanities offerings and director of composition).

4. English, History, Sociology, Anthropology, Economics, Mathematics, Women's Studies, Fine Arts, Architecture, the Libraries, Environmental Science, Honors Program, Foreign Languages, Asia Program, Philosophy, Comparative American Cultures, Biochemistry.

5. The list of institutions queried was gleaned from the table of contents in Kevin Reilly's collection of contributed papers, copyrighted by the World History Association, *World History*, (New York: Marcus Wiener Publishing, Inc., 1985). A more recent list of interdisciplinary programs appears in *Interdisciplinary Undergraduate Programs: A Directory*, (Oxford, OH: Association for Integrative Studies, 1986).

6. Informal sources have provided information on such programs at Earlham College and DePaul University.

7. Frances L. Hopkins, "Bibliographic Instruction as a Liberal Art." *Back to the Books: Bibliographic Instruction and the Theory of Information Sources*. Papers presented at the 101st Annual Conference of the ALA, ACRL Bibliographic Instructions Section. Ross Atkinson, ed., (Chicago: ALA, 1983):20.

8. e.g., Pamela Kobelski and Mary Reichel, "Conceptual Frameworks for Bibliographic Instruction." *Journal of Academic Librarianship* 7:73-33; Anne Beaubein, Sharon Hogan and Mary George, *Learning the Library*, (New York: Bowker, 1982); Cerise Oberman and Katina Strauch, eds. *Theories of Bibliographic Education*, (New York: Bowker, 1982), for thoughtful essays on the nature of user education in support of learning.

9. National Commission on Excellence in Education, *A Nation at Risk*, (Washington, DC: United States Department of Education, 1983). *Alliance for Excellence*, a response to this document from the library profession (U.S. Depart-

ment of Education, 1984), examines the role of libraries in addressing this concern.

10. Publications informing this approach are Sharon Hogan's "Research Problem Analysis" in *Learning the Library*, and Cerise Oberman-Soroka's "Question Analysis and the Learning Cycle," *Research Strategies* 1 (Winter 1983):22-30.

11. William H. Mc Neill, *A History of the Human Community: Prehistory to the Present*, (Englewood Cliffs, NJ: Prentice-Hall, Inc., 1987).

12. The questions and worksheets used in the library exercises may be found in the Appendix.

13. Keith Stanger posits that teaching faculty are the best-qualified to demonstrate and inspire investigation within their disciplines in "On the Limits of Bibliographic Instruction: An Opinion Piece." *Research Strategies* 1:31-34. Interdisciplinary instruction forces a closer collaboration between librarians and teachers in this regard.

14. The reader is referred to Alice Spitzer's article, this volume.

15. Law and Kennedy: 3.

16. "Academic Colleagues in Concert." *C&RL News* 49:71.

APPENDIX

Questions on Cards for Analysis Exercise

Simple, Factual

When was the golden age of Athens?

Name the twelve tribes of Israel.

What are three schools of Chinese thought?

Where is Mecca?

Who was Empress Theodora?

What agricultural tools were used in the New Stone Age?

Define "ecumene."

Conceptual, Complex

Compare Aristotle's philosophy with Plato's, and discuss the departure of the student's from the teacher's.

How did the arrival of Buddhism in Japan change centers of power in   Japanese culture?

What was the role of Joan of Arc in the Hundred Years' War?

What were the implications of Asoka's reign?

What was the primary effect of Alexander's conquests, particularly in   India?

How do Sumerian temple communities compare to Mayan temple   centers?

Explain the earliest ramifications of the discovery of movable type in   Europe.

Name_____Section_____

World Civilizations 110
Library Use Project • Part I

Introduction

What you look for in the library, and how you look for it, depends on the kind of question you have to begin with. The purpose of your library class session and related worksheets is to acquaint you with techniques of **question analysis**, the art of identifying key ideas in order to pursue information with clarity and direction.

To begin with, there are two types for questions. One kind looks for **facts**; the other asks for **concepts**. It could be said that "fact" questions are short-answer questions, and "concept" questions are more in-depth.

– Discussion –

It is possible to break down a conceptual question into several smaller factual components and keywords. Doing this enables you to take a look at the more manageable elements of a complex question. As a group, we'll ask a conceptual question, and work through a sample of the chart that you'll find on your worksheet. **Please note that this technique is useful for exam essay questions and other apparently complex problems.**

– Discussion –

Beginning Investigation: Constructing a Research Question

During class we reduced a complex question to simple components. In the next exercise, you will construct your own research question from similar components, based on background information in your textbook. Choose a topic of interest from the index of McNeill. Fill in the space below.

Topic_____Page____Librarian's initials_____

(over)

HOMEWORK

Complete the chart below, separating out the basic information components you can identify from your background reading. Remember, there can be a number of terms in each column.

Who (names)   When (dates)   Where (places)   What (related info)

Synthesize these terms into a conceptual question about your topic.

_____

_____

_____

_____

_____

_____

_____

Turn in the worksheet to your World Civ instructor **by September 21** for a

check._____

Name_____Section_____

World Civilizations 110
Library Use Project
Part II

AT THE LIBRARY: USING "COUGALOG"

This is the part where you explore the library to find books on your topic. You'll be using "Cougalog," WSU Libraries' online (computerized) catalog.

THINGS TO REMEMBER

1) Cougalog is set up to help you find **books only.**   (Magazine titles are also in Cougalog, but this part of the system isn't complete yet.)

 2) The books in Cougalog are more recent than the ones in the card catalog. (For research in the humanities, the card catalog is also particularly helpful. But this project is to acquaint you with Cougalog, and is designed to make sure you use it.)

3) Cougalog terminals are located in the reference room of any WSU library.

4) There are instruction sheets beside every Cougalog terminal.

5) There are help screens in the system. Try them.

STEP RIGHT UP TO THE TERMINAL

TYPE F SUK. This stands for "Find Subject Keyword." **Subject keyword** means **topic.** Right after F SUK, type in your topic. Hit Return.

If the computer tells you there are lots of "hits" on the subject, read the instruction sheet to find out what to do next.

If the computer tells you there are "zero hits," press "Clear," type F SUK again, and try a **related term** from your chart. If it tells you there are too many, try adding a related term to your original one. Keep experimenting till you get some results.

What term worked?_____

By now, you've seen a title on the screen for a book you'd like to find. Type "L" (for "locate"), space, and the number in front of the title. Jot down the number in front of the title._____ Press return.

In the spaces below, write down the details that you see on the screen.

AUTHOR_____TITLE_____
—

CALL NUMBER_____
LIBRARY_____

(over)

Now, type "S" (it means "select"), space, and the number of the item again.
Note what you see on the screen this time.

TITLE_____
–

AUTHOR_____
–

IMPRINT
      Publisher_____

      Place of publication_____

      Date of publication_____

PAGINATION
      How many pages in the book?_____

      Does it contain a bibliography?_____

      Does it have illustrations?_____

*These details tell you a lot more about the book. They are the components of a **bibliographic citation**, formal information used to describe published items.*

FINDING YOUR BOOK

About call numbers.

A **call number** is a letter-number "code" assigned to each book in the library. It assures that the book can be found in the same order on the shelf at all times. Call numbers serve to organize information into categories. You'll discover that books on the same topic have related call numbers.

In Holland Library, call numbers that begin with LETTERS are on the SECOND FLOOR. Call numbers beginning with NUMBERS are on the THIRD FLOOR.

Using the call number for your book, locate in on the shelf. **Photocopy the title page of your book. Attach the photocopy to your worksheet.**

Note that the title page contains some of the bibliographic information you jotted down above when using the "s" command on Cougalog.

Name_____Section_____

World Civilizations 110
Library Use Project
Part III

USING THE BOOK YOU FOUND

Some books are more useful than others. This section is to give you some techniques for evaluating information. Examine the book you chose. Answer the following:

Does it have a preface?_____ A table of contents?_____ An index?_____
Bibliography?_____ Footnotes?_____ Endnotes? _____ A list of references?_____

These sections give you many clues about the book's contents. They can help you determine its usefulness. **Notice other components** which are helpful in determining a book's value:

Is this book from a University press? _____ *University presses publish scholarly material which shows a lot of research.*

Are there other books by the same author listed in the front of the book?_____ *If the author is a known expert, she or he may have written a lot on the topic.*

Can you tell the author's profession? _____ Institutional affiliation?_____ *If the author is connected to a college or a university, this suggests some credibility.*

Does the author acknowledge the advice of special people?_____ Financial support? _____ *This tells you who was behind the author in the creation of the book.*

Is there an introduction by somebody other than the author? _____ *Sometimes another authority introduces the writer and the book in a special statement.*

Has the book gone through a number of printings or editions?_____ *This can show that the book is an acknowledged classic, has sold well and influenced subsequent research.*

HOMEWORK: PUTTING IT ALL TOGETHER

Using the back of this page, or a separate sheet, **attached,** write what you **think** this book could tell you. Consider when it was written, who published it, whether the preface or introduction tells you anything about the author's credentials, its intended purpose, how it appears to be organized, and why footnotes and bibliographies might be helpful. **How could this book help you answer your own research question on page 2?**

This part is due to your World Civ Instructor by October 12.

Library Use Project
World Civilizations 111
Spring 1987

Name _____

Your library project this semester will be in two parts: 1) This packet of five worksheets, and 2) a bibliographic essay. The project is designed to acquaint you with the many kinds of information available at the library. It gives you an opportunity to discover for yourself the relative value of one resource over another.

In last semester's library project, you began to explore this kind of activity, while acquiring some useful skills for beginning research:

• How to define what you want to find out
• How to locate a book in Holland library
• How to determine a book's usefulness

This semester's project will expand upon what you know, and will introduce new concepts. It is designed to allow you to discover and evaluate for yourself:

• The kinds of resources available
• The kinds of information each provides
• The strengths and limitations of each source

The worksheets attached will introduce you to a variety of information sources. You'll have a chance to look at:

• Dictionaries and encyclopedias • Books again
• Indexes to journal articles • Articles in journals
• Atlases • Newspapers • Bonus materials

Using the index to McNeill for 1500–present, determine a topic that interests you.

The topic you intend to pursue is:_____

_____

Exploring each source you'll do two equally important things:

• Learn about your topic   • Learn about the source itself

This kind of critical approach is an important aspect of research; it's the groundwork for investigation on **any subject at all**.

WHY GO THROUGH THIS?

These pages will help you to prepare a bibliographic essay, which will describe the information you found. In the essay, as on the worksheets, you will note the characteristics of each source, the kind of information it's good for, and the way it gives you that information. You must also note how it relates to your topic.

GETTING STARTED

Get a little background on your topic. Use McNeill, or another textbook, a historical novel, a movie, a professor, a friend. To begin your investigation, under each category make a list of **keywords**—simple concepts—to organize what you already know.

Who   **What**   **When**   **Where**   **How**

A •FINDING BASIC INFORMATION

Look up your topic in two encyclopedias, from your list or your explorations. Compare the way in which each treats your topic.

Fill in below: **#1**   **#2**

	#1	#2
Encyc. Title		
Length of entry		
How detailed?		
Bibliography?		
How factual?		
How analytical?		

Scan the articles. If you find good **keywords,** add to your list. Read your comments in the space above. Circle the number, above, of the encyclopedia which seems more useful for your topic. **On the reverse of this page, write several sentences explaining why. Or why not. Discuss both encyclopedias.**

B •FINDING PERIODICAL ARTICLES Part I: Using Indexes

Identify two articles on your topic using indexes on the list. Try to use a different index for each article. Fill in the details on each article below. For help with the abbreviations, consult the front pages of the index.

1 Index used_____
Article title_____
Author_____Journal abbreviation_____
Volume_____Pages_____Date_____
Full name of the journal_____
KEEP GOING; WE'LL COME BACK TO THIS BOX!

2 Index used_____
Article title_____
Author_____Journal abbreviation_____
Volume_____Pages_____Date_____
Full name of the journal_____

KEEP GOING; WE'LL COME BACK TO THIS BOX!

Observations
From your use of the **indexes** cited above, does one seem better suited to your needs?_____Which one?   **1**   **2**
Why? Or why not? Refer to the information you jotted in the blanks. Write about your observations here and on the back.

C •FINDING PERIODICAL ARTICLES Part II: Locating Journals

PLEASE READ THIS!

A **citation** to an article (whether you get it from an index, or a footnote, or a bibliography, or your teacher) has elements which help you to find it. You jotted them down on the previous page:
>•**Author of the article**
>>•**Title of the article**
>>>•**Name of the journal the article is in**
>>>>•**The specific issue of the journal**
>>>>>•**The pages inside the specific issue**

This is absolutely all the citation tells you.
What you need to know next is:
Does the library have this journal?

HOW TO FIND OUT:
Consult the **green microfiche,** our "List of Journals and Serials." It's kept on racks on the counter near the reference desk. The green fiche lists everything we subscribe to. It will tell you if we get a periodical, and give its **call number.**

Look for the **TITLE OF THE JOURNAL** you want to find.
Beside the title, you will see its call number and its location.
This completes the information you need in order to find an article.

ON WITH THE PROJECT!

•On the preceding page, in the box provided, write the call number for each of the journals which you identified.
•With the call numbers, find your periodicals upstairs, bound like books, or across the hall on microfilm.
•Locate the two articles for which you wrote citations.
•Scan them to get a sense of their content. Add to your list of keywords.
•Photocopy the first page of each article and attach the copies to this packet.

OBSERVATIONS
•Which of these two articles would you be more likely to use in a report on your topic? Why?
•Were there any frustrations in this procedure? What? How were they resolved?

Write on the reverse of this page. Your comments should discuss the appropriateness (or inappropriateness) of the articles to your topic. If you had to deal with problems, please note what they were <u>and</u> what you did.

D •FINDING BOOKS

This is where your list of keywords will be most useful.
Cougalog, the WSU Libraries' database catalog, is designed to
respond to keywords. **If one keyword seems not to work, try
another from your list.**

To search by **subject,** press the **F2** key. On the screen, see "F
SUK" for "Find Subject Keyword." Type in your topic, and press
RETURN. Try other terms from your list, too. Use the help
screens for instructions.

Find two books on your topic. Fill in the blanks.

1 Author_____
Title_____
Place_____Publisher_____Date____
Call number_____Library_____
Is it checked out or otherwise unavailable?_____

2 Author_____
Title_____
Place_____Publisher_____Date____
Call number_____Library_____
Is it checked out or otherwise unavailable?_____

Locate the books using their call numbers, and spend some time
with them. Note for each: the date of publication, whether there's
a bibliography, a discography, illustrations, musical examples,
facsimiles, other attractive features...or not.

Of the two books, which seems to provide better information on
your topic? Circle one: **1**   **2**

**Write your observations about the two books on the back
of this page, and explain your choice.**

F •BONUS MATERIALS

Consider other items which might help you get a fuller understanding of your topic. Try consulting **Cougalog** or the **Card Catalog,** the **Reference Catalog** or a **Reference Librarian,** to find something from one of the following categories.
Use your keywords and think of broad subject areas which relate to your topic. Use your imagination and the Cougalog to locate materials in this group. And **ask a librarian** for suggestions.

•Atlases
    •Almanacs
        •Art prints
            •Guide books
                •Statistical sources
                    •Films (IMS—library basement)
                        •Newspaper indexes & articles
                            •Anything else you choose

For this source, note the following:

Author (or person responsible)_____

Title_____
Place of
publication_____Publisher_____Date_____

What kind of item is this?_____

How did you find it?_____

Is it useful to you in learning about your topic?____Or not?_____
                    Why? Write below.

Bringing an Interdisciplinary World View to English 101 — The Library's Involvement

Alice M. Spitzer

SUMMARY. Washington State University received a National Endowment for the Humanities grant to offer a pilot two-semester World Civilization course as part of the general education core curriculum. Two reference librarians were selected as members of the interdisciplinary faculty group to design the course, to relate it to the required Freshman Composition (English 101) course and to ensure the integration of basic library use skills. The two librarians were asked to develop library/classroom integrated assignments to meet course objectives and to serve as models for those teaching the course. The focus of the assignment is on selection and evaluation of information sources that approach a topic from a particular viewpoint (i.e., liberal, conservative, or middle-of-the-road), provide a popular or a scholarly treatment of the topic, and reflect a targeted audience approach (e.g., layperson or professional).

Washington State University presently has only one course that is a general requirement of all students—one semester of freshman composition (English 101). It was this class, therefore, that the WSU Libraries targeted as a potential vehicle for teaching basic library skills to as many students as possible. For the past ten years a library project has been an option for all instructors of English composition. Over the years, the project has evolved from a short unsupervised research paper to more structured library assignments. The librarian responsible for coordinating user education in the Humanities and Social Sciences has assumed a greater role in the de-

Alice M. Spitzer is Public Services Librarian at Washington State University Libraries.

sign and implementation of the projects, and this closer cooperation between the Library and the English Department has ensured a more successful library experience for the students.

Currently, through a large grant received from the National Endowment for the Humanities, the University is in the pilot phase of developing and teaching a two-semester World Civilization course (see Paula Elliot's article in this same volume) which, along with freshman composition, will form part of a new core curriculum. This core curriculum is one component of a major general education reform on campus. The inclusion of library involvement in this educational reform effort has been widely accepted. Director of Libraries, Maureen Pastine, sits on all the major committees (Commission for General Education, Writing Across the Curriculum, World Civilization Advisory Committee), and two reference librarians, Paula Elliot and Alice Spitzer, were selected as members of the interdisciplinary faculty group which is designing the World Civilizations course.

One of the objectives stated in WSU's proposal to the National Endowment for the Humanities is the integration of English 101 (composition) with the core curriculum. In other words, the content of the composition class would be tied more closely to that of the World Civilizations course. Through emphasis on world rather than western civilization and on interdisciplinary content, it is intended that the course will transcend the limits of any single cultural tradition or approach to learning. This emphasis carries over to the English composition class, for which a whole new syllabus is being developed. Professor Susan McLeod, Director of Composition, selected a group of four teaching assistants (instructors) who would design and implement the new syllabus. Alice Spitzer, Coordinator of User Education for the Humanities and Social Sciences Library, was asked to join this group as an advisor. The charge to the Pilot English 101 Committee was:

1. To develop the curriculum for the pilot English 101 class, a curriculum coordinated with, but independent of, the World Civilizations course.
2. To develop a model syllabus for use of all TAs (teaching assistants) after the pilot years.

3. To develop model writing assignments, including library assignments, based on the course objectives.

After several weeks of discussion, the Pilot English 101 Committee arrived at the following objectives for the new English 101 class:

1. To introduce students to academic thinking and writing tasks, and to develop the verbal and analytic skills common to academic writing (defining terms; drawing inferences; classifying; generalizing; hypothesizing; paraphrasing; summarizing; separating fact from opinion; gathering, synthesizing, and evaluating information; structuring an argument).
2. To teach students basic library skills, especially information retrieval.
3. To help students understand writing as a mode of learning, writing as a tool for thinking.
4. To introduce students to texts and ideas which have been important in various cultures and civilizations, to help them understand more fully the ideas introduced in their World Civilizations class.

For the librarian on the committee it was important to keep two things in mind when working with these objectives. English 101 is not meant to be a research course; there are other, non-required courses in the department that meet that need. Therefore, the traditional full-blown research paper would not be the most appropriate vehicle for teaching basic library skills. Secondly, the library assignments should not be something developed and taught in isolation of the other three objectives. Integration of the objectives would make it easier for both instructors and students to incorporate the library assignment into the normal flow of the course.

The task of developing suitable library assignments was made easier in several ways. The Director of Composition is a staunch library supporter who has emphasized with all her instructors (close to 60) the importance of incorporating library skills into the freshman composition class. The instructors themselves are, in general, an interested, hard-working, creative group ready to accept and try out new ideas in their classes. Because of the diversity of interests among the instructors who would eventually be teaching the new syllabus, it was decided that there would not be just one generic library assignment. Rather, the librarian would work with instructors individually to develop a variety of assignments that met the course objectives and which could serve as models for others teaching the class. Although only four teaching assistants would be involved in actual pilot classes, a number of other teaching assistants were interested in trying to get their students away from black and white views of the world and wanted to create library projects that were more content based and intellectually challenging than their previous, more personal writing had been. Greater consultation between the teaching assistants and the librarian has tremendously increased the workload of the librarian; but the result has been a larger, more enthusiastic pool of instructors than would have been possible using only the designated pilot group and a greater library awareness among these graduate students.

As mentioned before, the curriculum of the pilot English 101 class is coordinated with but independent of the World Civilizations course. This independence is not only desirable but necessary because students may take Composition concurrently with either semester of World Civilizations, a course which, at present, has a chronological framework. The pilot composition syllabus was organized around ideas that span a variety of time periods and cultures: religion, political theory, the arts, science and philosophy. Depending on the particular interests of an instructor, a library assignment could be developed to fit into any of these areas. At the same time, it could dovetail with particular writing skills the instructor is working on. The flexibility not only helps the instructors, but also the librarians. Because the library assignments can be incorporated any time during the course, we are able to spread the workload out over the whole semester, rather than be locked into having all classes come to the library at a certain time. The variety of assignments also challenges the reference librarians, who were getting pretty bored with abortion, gun control, and the 55 m.p.h. speed limit!

Virtually all of the assignments include using journal indexes to find articles, using our microfiche list of journals to identify our call number for the journal, and then locating the bound journal in the stacks or on microfilm. In addition, many of them use COUGA-LOG, the Library's online catalog, to find books, and some assignments require use of newspaper indexes and our microfilm newspaper backfiles. These are transferable skills that can be used in any subject area and any library. When the classes come to the library, the instruction is tailored to meet the students' needs for that particular assignment. There is no intention of telling them everything they might ever need to know about the library. As a rule of thumb, we try not to talk for more than 20 minutes so that the majority of their class period can be devoted to hands-on use of the indexes or catalog with the librarian available to help students individually. We have found that this immediate reinforcement of what they have been taught stays with them longer. Because the library work they are doing relates directly to their assignment, they pay closer attention to the instruction being given and begin working more diligently. Except for very extraordinary cases, we require that the instructor be present during the whole class time in the library. Not only does this reinforce students' sense of the importance of the library instruction, it also means there is someone else available to help answer students' questions.

The instruction that is given to students varies with the assignment, but there are certain things we always try to incorporate. Both instructors and librarians emphasize that any topic can be approached from different viewpoints (e.g., liberal, conservative, middle-of-the-road), have different levels of treatment (from popular to scholarly), and reflect different audiences (e.g., laypersons, professionals in the field). The timing of an article is also important. For instance, a newspaper article reporting an event at the time it happened will need to be evaluated differently than a scholarly journal article on the same event which is written many years later.

Indexes and bibliographies are discussed in terms of the type of information that they will lead to. For instance, *Readers' Guide to Periodical Literature*, which most students are familiar with, will lead them to the kind of magazines they can find on the newsstand. Much of the information in these magazines is aimed at a general audience and is written in nontechnical language. Contrasted with *Readers' Guide* are indexes which generally list articles in more scholarly journals. These are written for specialists in more technical language, they're longer and more in-depth. Some assignments require students to use two different types of indexes to locate a popular and a scholarly article on the same topic. They then compare the articles for length, vocabulary, point of view, audience, and other factors.

Over the years we have developed a series of worksheets which are used for class projects. The worksheets vary depending on what is required of the specific assignment at hand. Some examples are: (1) locating books and journal articles, (2) locating books, journal articles and newspaper articles, (3) locating magazine and newspaper articles, and (4) locating biographical information. The worksheets are handed out to students when they come as a class and are referred to throughout the session. They give step-by-step instructions for locating a particular kind of source with space to fill in citations they find on their topic. Instructors may or may not require students to hand in the worksheets, although we encourage them to do so.

So, what kind of assignments are considered appropriate to the new syllabus? A "tips" sheet was developed to give instructors some basic guidelines.

TIPS ON DESIGNING A LIBRARY ASSIGNMENT

English 101 (World Civilization Section)

1. The objective is to teach students basic library skills, especially basic research strategies and information retrieval:
   a. Narrowing a topic,
   b. Identifying relevant books using the online and card catalogs,
   c. Identifying relevant journal and newspaper articles using a variety of indexes,
   d. Using call numbers to locate books and bound journals in the stacks, and
   e. Locating and using library resources on microfilm.
2. The content of the assignment should relate to some aspect of world civilization. It should broaden the students' horizons, exposing them to a range of viewpoints, different parts of the world, and/or various aspects of civilization.
3. If you, the instructor, have expertise or interest in a particular

subject (e.g., music), consider building an assignment around it. Students will gain from your knowledge and enthusiasm.

4. Consider building an assignment around an appropriate event happening on campus (e.g., a debate on the Central American Peace Plan).
5. Consider an invited speaker or a film as a catalyst.
6. Incorporate a series of assignments leading up to a research paper, for example:
   a. Freewriting on a topic,
   b. A summary of a short article,
   c. A review of a longer article,
   d. An interview with someone on the topic,
   e. A paper that compares and contrasts two articles on the topic, or
   f. An annotated bibliography on the topic.
7. If the entire class is writing on the same subject (e.g., art), build some element of choice into their final project (e.g., compare/contrast two artists' work but let students choose which artists they will write on).
8. Work closely with the library instruction coordinator to ensure that sufficient and appropriate library material is available. Special handouts or worksheets may need to be developed.
9. Be sure the librarian has a copy of the assignment well in advance of the class' visit to the library so that he/she will know what your expectations are for the instruction session.
10. Use library reserve services when appropriate. Any material that will be heavily used by an entire class over a limited time may be placed on reserve.

The project is still in a very early stage, but already a number of suitable and workable assignments have emerged. Because there is a lot of communication between the instructors, successful assignments tend to get repeated and modified. One example is the "travel paper." Frustrated by his students' ignorance of the rest of the world, one instructor decided to have his students do their library project on world capitals. The librarian did some quick checking and came up with a list of 35 cities on which the library had sufficient information because both the instructor and the librarian felt it was important that students not be too frustrated in their early library use. Each student chose a city from the list and the final product was to be an article for a travel magazine. Students were asked to give an account of the city, illustrating its characteristics, indicating the types of activities a traveler may expect to engage in and the sorts of places he or she may go. Examples of travel articles were gathered and discussed by the class in advance of their library visit. In the library, students were shown how to use the *Readers' Guide*, the *New York Times Index*, and the online catalog. This assignment was adopted by other instructors. One had her students write a report to acquaint U.S. government diplomats with the city where they and their families would be stationed. Another used the format of a travel brochure.

Another assignment that has been modified and used by several instructors is a biographical paper. One had students choose historical figures; another chose 20th century world leaders. A special worksheet was developed which led students to biographical reference sources, the online catalog, the *New York Times Index*, the *Personal Name Index to the New York Times Index*, and various journal indexes. Historical news events, especially those of an international nature or with international impact, have been the basis of several assignments. Students chose, sometimes from a list provided, an event that they were to research and write a report on. Examples of some of the topics are "Moscow Puts First Man in Orbit Around the Earth," "Kennedy Proposes Alliance for Progress," and "Cuba invaded at Bay of Pigs." In writing up the event, students had to report not only on the who, what, where, when and why of the event, but also on contrast of opinions, consequences and characterization. News magazines, newspapers and books were the main sources of information.

One last example of a very successful assignment was that based on a week of speeches, debates and films centered on the theme of Central America held during fall semester of 1987. The final product of the assignment was a 5-7 page research paper on some aspect of Central America (social, economic, political, cultural, etc.), but there was a progression of shorter assignments leading to it. First students were required to attend either a debate on the Central

American Peace Plan or a lecture by the mother of Benjamin Linder, an American killed in Central America. Students were then given a librarian-prepared list, "Foreign News Magazines and Newspapers in English" and asked to come to the library on their own to locate a short (1-2 page) article on Central America written from a foreign viewpoint. A short summary of the article was to be written and turned in. Next, a formal instruction session in the library taught students how to locate books and journal articles on Central America using the online catalog and a variety of journal indexes. The assignment was to locate two articles, each 5-15 pages in length, and write a 2-page evaluative review of each. By this time the class had gained some familiarity with the topic and were ready to tackle their final research paper, described above. Although some students tired of the topic, most felt their writing improved over the succession of assignments as their knowledge of the subject increased. The flexibility in choice of topic for their final paper helped reduce the potential for frustration because students could pursue their individual interests.

Librarians at Washington State University consider the new core curriculum to be a golden opportunity to integrate library skills and research strategies into courses which will reach all entering freshmen. Although still very much in a pilot phase, the syllabi for both the World Civilizations classes and the restructured English 101 include library assignments which complement rather than duplicate each other. The library projects in the World Civilizations course emphasize different concepts (e.g., question analysis) than those in English 101 (e.g., varying ways a topic can be approached through different indexes). Teaching faculty's high regard for the librarians' wide-ranging contributions in the development of both classes has helped ensure acceptance of library instruction as an integral part of the courses.

Improving and Integrating Bibliographic Instruction

Sarah Pedersen
Sara Rideout
Randy Hensley

SUMMARY. Instructional librarians at the University of Washington Undergraduate Library and The Evergreen State College Library have received seed grant funding from the Washington State Center for the Improvement of Quality of Undergraduate Education to sponsor two seminars and a small conference on linking library instruction to undergraduate teaching. The focus of the project is on critical thinking, evaluation of sources, and integration of library instruction into the curriculum. Emphasis will be placed on "critical thinking" and the larger context of the particular discipline. A major purpose is to develop a model program for use in other academic libraries.

Instructional librarians at the University of Washington Undergraduate Library and The Evergreen State College Library will be sponsoring two seminars and a small conference in order to explore ways of connecting library instruction to important trends in undergraduate teaching. The activities will focus on critical thinking, evaluation of sources, and integration of library instruction into the curriculum.

Following is the text of the seed grant proposal to support those discussions which was funded by the Washington [State] Center for the Improvement of Quality of Undergraduate Education:

Sarah Pedersen is Dean, Library Services, and Sara Rideout is Reference Librarian/Member of the Faculty, Daniel J. Evans Library, The Evergreen State College, TA-000, Olympia, WA 98505. Randy Hensley is User Education Librarian, University of Washington Libraries, OUGL DF-10, Seattle, WA 98195.

123

I. Problem Statement

Both the University of Washington Undergraduate Library and Evergreen State College Library have active and successful instruction programs aimed at undergraduates. Librarians in both institutions emphasize the need for teaching to take place in context, and acknowledge that library instruction is most effective when it is an extension or expression of what goes on in the classroom. There has, simultaneously, been great emphasis placed on *process*. Librarians want to avoid the mechanical transfer of content — for instance, the use of a "master bibliography" — and to stress the development of critical research skills that will be integrated with students' other intellectual activities. Yet, the idea that good researchers are created by emphasizing process and insisting on context needs closer examination.

What appears to happen is that students think that there is *a* process. Certainly we talk about this so-called process in very idealized and abstract terms so that it is difficult to determine what, precisely, it means or "stands for." There is also a tacit assumption by students that if they discover "the process" they will uncover "the facts" or "the answer." Further, the idea of context — what librarians call the research question — could be approached more critically by students if it is seen in the larger context of the particular discipline or discourse domain. Our assumption is that an examination of these issues will lead to teaching practices that enhance students' abilities to analyze a research question or information need; to understand the range of choices available; and to appreciate the creativity and judgement implied by effective research.

We are interested, now, in exploring the questions and problems that arise in library instruction out of the consideration of context and process. We are especially interested in developing ways of talking about and teaching these concepts with others in other disciplines, with the goal of integrating critical library and research skills into the student's overall education.

II. Objectives

Our purpose in applying for this grant is to develop a model program that will have applicability in a variety of institutional settings. We would like to sponsor a series of working seminars and a conference in which we explore the following questions and concerns:

- What is behind this term "process?" How can we talk about it in conceptual terms that avoid the sense by students that to discover the "process" is the route to "the answer?" For instance, would it be more effective for us to talk about and teach criteria thinking, as suggested by Craig Nelson rather than to talk about process.
- What do librarians mean when they speak of context? Here we might want to examine the different discourse domains in which research is done, and to make explicitly part of our teaching the conventions and values in those discourses that dictate rules for gathering evidence, making arguments, organizing information, and using language that is relevant to subject assignment and control. How can we include students' personal contexts in this discussion?
- What is the connection for us between pedagogy and practice? Librarians are professionals *and* teachers; there are differences between the goals and the activities of these two aspects of what we do. Are we out to teach students to be librarians; or is the nature of their instruction different? Our sense is that instruction should be more consciously focused on integration of research skills into the overall intellectual development of students, and that we are not concerned with making mini-librarians.
- How should the pedagogy of library instruction be brought to the service model that we use at the reference desk? Craig Nelson uses a concept called connected teaching in which a researcher — master teacher — teaches by recounting and recreating the research process in science. Would the idea of connected teaching be applicable to librarians in their one-on-one interactions with students in the library?
- How can the library itself best be used as a teaching tool? What teaching practices are most likely to make the library a teaching tool rather than a substitute teacher? That is, in what ways can we effectively use the resources in the library with-

out allowing the physical environment — its limitations and arrangement — to impose upon and dictate how and what we teach. Are there parallels between the library in research, the medium in art and the laboratory in science?

- What are effective ways of teaching students to evaluate information? Evaluation of sources has some unique characteristics in library research which can indicate the completeness and quality of a search; would this more specialized type of evaluation complement the students' work at evaluating and synthesizing their sources?
- Can Uri Treisman's ideas about group work be brought to library instruction? Can group work provide peers with support which will help them overcome the impersonal and authoritarian impression students receive of libraries and the research process? Could group work better accommodate and utilize cultural differences?

During the working sessions, we would like to invite librarians from other institutions (besides TESC and UW) and people from other disciplines who have experience integrating instruction, and who have incorporated critical thinking into the teaching of a particular discipline. We think that it would be especially helpful to consult and work with people who have developed writing-across-the-curriculum or interdisciplinary writing programs. The proposed model library program will evolve out of these working sessions, and will include specific guidelines and materials for teaching students about process; for introducing students to various kinds of evaluation that can be done in libraries; and for integrating library work into classroom activities in a way that draws on the conventions of a particular discipline or discourse.

III. Implementation Plan and Timetable

Workshop and conference activities would occur Fall of 1988. TESC and UW librarians would host two small seminars (15 people including TESC, UW, other libraries, plus one or two consultants) in which we would explore the questions listed above. We would then broaden the audience to a conference near the quarter's end to which we would invite regional academic librarians in order to begin dissemination of ideas.

Winter quarter we would plan for implementation of our ideas into a course plan for Spring of 1989 at TESC. A workbook or discussion paper would document the plan. The Spring course would be a continuation of the current library instructional time commitment but would be integrated with a program rather than stand alone.

Based on the success or discoveries of the Spring program we would seek external funds to allow a full year's integrated research instruction as a demonstration project in the 89/90 academic year.

IV. Personnel

- Sara Rideout, Reference Librarian/Member of the Faculty, The Evergreen State College
- Sarah Pedersen, Acting Dean of Library Services, The Evergreen State College
- Randy Hensley, Instructional Librarian, University of Washington Undergraduate Library

International Students' Acquisition of Library Research Skills: Relationship with Their English Language Proficiency

Dania M. Bilal

SUMMARY. This study examined international students' acquisition of library research skills in relation to their English language proficiency. The experimental study involved 13 students who were studying English at the Florida State University Center for Intensive English Studies (FSU-CIES) during the 1987 Spring semester. Results of the Pearson Product Moment Test showed a moderate correlation (r = .43) between the students' exit TOEFL scores and the posttest library skills scores. Other findings were: (1) The students mastered 80% of the material taught as measured by Shannon Entropy; (2) Lack of command of the English language, lack of self-sufficiency, and absence of the conceptual awareness of library research were major obstacles to comprehension of the material.

INTRODUCTION

The 1980s have witnessed an emphasis on teaching the effective use of the library to international students, particularly those from developing countries. This new interest can be attributed to many factors including an obvious lack of self-sufficiency, unusual and unique learning patterns of students from developing countries as well as the increase in their enrollment on American campuses.

There is no doubt that most writings in the library literature are

---

Dania M. Bilal was Assistant Reference Librarian at The FSU Strozier Library, at the time of the study.

129

speculative in regard to the problems and difficulties international students experience in using the American academic library. To determine whether international students do experience difficulties in using the library, an experimental study testing the impact or effectiveness of library instruction is an important undertaking.

The main purpose of this study was to examine whether international students' acquisition of library skills was related to their English language proficiency. As is true of other case studies, the limitations of this study reside in its small sample and in its results which may not be easily generalized to other situations.

The Florida State University Center for Intensive English Studies (FSU-CIES) was the site for this experiment. The Center provides English programs to aid students for whom English is a second language. It prepares students in the English language skills needed for university level studies in the United States. It places a greater emphasis on the language skills needed for research paper writing at the expense of library coverage. This approach includes tours of the library as well as a rudimentary introduction to the card catalog and other reference sources. The Center considers research papers an integral part of composition courses at the advanced English levels in view of its goal to prepare the students for university level work. It now conducts two short sessions per semester. More recently it introduced with the cooperation of this investigator a six-week library skills course for the low advanced English level students.

The first study of international students' library skills began in 1969 with Mary Lewis.[1] In her survey of sixty Asian college students at the University of Hawaii, she found that the students experienced fifteen difficulties in using the university library including the card catalog, and finding materials on library shelves. Lewis' study revealed for the first time the special problems that group of international students encountered and suggested solutions through specifically designed library instruction programs.

To learn about the adequacy of library skills possessed by international students as compared to the native-born, Frank Goudy and Eugene Moushey[2] surveyed the directors of 44 university libraries of which their parent institutions had at least 10% of their student body from other nations. They found that the students as a group had more problems in using the library than did the native born.

Many American institutions of higher education respond to the need of foreign students but often the libraries in those colleges and universities do not. In a survey of international offices of 54 institutions, Laura Kline and Catherine Rod[3] found that 98% of the offices offered general orientation programs. At the same time only 56% of the fifty-four libraries surveyed provided special instruction programs such as formal courses.

A more recent study was conducted by this investigator to examine the perceptions of international students from developing countries with regard to the importance of and the success in using the library. Reference librarians' perceptions of the students' success in using the library and the importance of library knowledge to the students were also examined. A comparison of both groups' perceptions revealed similarities and conflicts in certain areas of library knowledge. Most reference librarians commented on the difficulties in dealing with foreign students, in general. They cited cultural and educational background and lack of command of the English language as major problems.[4]

RESEARCH QUESTIONS

1. To what degree did international students' English language proficiency influence their acquisition of library skills?
2. How much learning did the students acquire at the end of the six-week period as measured by Shannon Entropy?
3. What kind of problems did the students encounter in learning library skills?
4. To what degree did members of the experimental group improve on the posttest?
5. To what degree did members of the experimental group perform better on the posttest than did those of the control group?
6. To what degree did members of both groups perform in similar fashion when previous formal instruction was not a factor?

METHODOLOGY

The experimental method was employed with a course in bibliographic instruction designed by this investigator. The course was structured around the following areas: Tour of the library; library terminology; classification systems; card and online catalogs; Library of Congress subject headings; periodical indexes; dictionaries and encyclopedias; and government publications. Because of time constraints, government publications, dictionaries and encyclopedias were briefly discussed. A total of seven weeks were allotted to the course which met twice a week for two consecutive hours. In each session the lecture method was employed. A two-hour tour of the university's main library, Strozier, was conducted during the first session.

The study was limited to existing high intermediate English language level students who served as the control groups, and to existing low advanced English language level students who served as the experimental group.

The experimental group consisted of seven students, six graduate and one undergraduate. Their countries of origin were China, Iraq, Japan, Taiwan, and Thailand. Their fields of study were Business, Computer Science, Education, Interior Design, Home Economics, and Mathematics. Five hundred and fifty is an acceptable TOEFL (Test of English as a Foreign Language) score for graduate admission to the Florida State University. At the time of the study, the highest score received by a student in the experimental group was 510. Three of the students had been awarded a scholarship by their home government to pursue graduate study in the United States. The group had previously been exposed to the library before the instruction and had made a slight use of the university's main library online catalog (LUIS) and *Readers' Guide to Periodical Literature* as part of their composition class.

The students were highly motivated to learn the effective use of the library. This was reflected through their high attendance record which averaged 98% over the six-week period, the highest among all classes at the Center. The students expressed their belief in library research skills as imperative for academic success and in learning them at CIES since the university's library did not, at that time, offer any formal library instruction programs.

The control group consisted of six graduate students from developing countries for which the highest TOEFL score was 490.

INSTRUMENT

The instrument used to test the students' library skills was prepared by the investigator. It consisted of forty-four items apportioned among six units: I. Library Terminology; II. Classification Schemes; III. Card Catalog; IV. Periodical Indexes: Interpretation of information from the Social Sciences Index; V. Choice of Indexes: Finding the best index to use for some wanted information; and VI. The Library of Congress Subject Headings. The questions were selected from a pool of items generated for each unit. The items in the pool were judged by this investigator and two other reference librarians to be representative of the minimal skills foreign students should possess to be able to function in the academic library. The instrument was pilot-tested and its .80 internal consistency was determined through the application of the alpha coefficient special computation of Kuder Richardson Formula 20. This formula is considered highly useful in estimating the internal consistency of the test items. It is specifically employed when test items are scored dichotomously as it is the case in this test. In scoring the test unanswered questions as well as questions with two answers were counted as wrong answers.

PROCEDURES

During the first week of Spring semester 1987, a pretest was administered to the experimental group. Questions regarding any ambiguous items, directions, or examples were encouraged. The students had difficulties understanding the meaning of terms like "article," "review," "periodical," "evaluation," "critique," "book review," "abstract," "index," "bibliography," "stacks," "classification," and "biography," to name only a few. They needed an average time of forty-five minutes to complete the test.

The highest possible score was 44. The range of scores was from 21 to 38.

After the pretest, still during the first session, the students toured the Strozier Library. The investigator defined unfamiliar library terminology in much more detail than is normally provided to American students. Such elements as fine, interlibrary loan, reserve desk, index tables, reference, circulation were unfamiliar to the students. The tour took twice as long as is normally the case, two hours instead of one hour. To reinforce the instruction provided during the tour, an assignment about library services and facilities was handed to the students. They were also required to ask the reference librarians in the general reference area as well as in the science and documents areas any questions related to the location of certain materials in their departments. The purpose of the latter was to encourage the students to approach the reference staff in order to overcome a natural barrier, the reference desk.

Teaching started the second week of classes. During each session, in-class exercises, writing on the board, class discussion, handouts of each unit, and transparencies were used as teaching aids in support of the lecture method. In addition, the students were required to regularly use the library to complete class assignments.

During the last week of classes, the posttest was administered to the experimental group by this investigator and distributed to the control group by their English instructor. Testing time dropped from 45 minutes to 30 minutes, on the average, for members of the experimental group. Members of the control group needed fifty minutes to complete the test similar to the time required for the pretest by the experimental group. The range of their scores was from 9 to 25.

RESULTS

Table 1 illustrates the degree of Pearson r correlation between international students' English language proficiency and their library skills. As shown in Table 1, there was no significant correlation between the pretest library skills' scores of members of the experimental group and their entry TOEFL scores ($r = .06$). A

TABLE 1. Correlation between Pretest/Posttest Library Skills Scores and Entry/Exit TOEFL Scores

N= 7

Library Skills		Pearson r		TOEFL	
Pretest Mean	Posttest Mean	Entry	Exit	Entry	Exit
29.42	39.0	.06	.43	491.0	491.28

moderate correlation, however, was found between their posttest library skills scores and the exit TOEFL ($r = .43$). It should be mentioned that library skills scores increased 10 points during the posttest while those on the exit TOEFL improved only .28. In examining the students' TOEFL scores, the investigator found that the scores of two out of seven students dropped in exit TOEFL, two increased only three points, two improved only ten points, and one stayed the same. It is clear that these sets of scores were unusual when one considers that three students either declined or showed no improvement even though they had studied the language intensively. In fact, the TOEFL does sometimes yield such results with a standard error of measurement of about $\pm$ 14 points. One should proceed with caution here when inferring that the students' library skills were significantly influenced by their English language proficiency since the posttest library skills scores did improve significantly while those of the exit TOEFL did not.

Table 2 provides a view of the extent of the students' acquisition of library skills after instruction as measured by entropy. Entropy was first implemented by Shannon to study the disorder in a system.[5] Here it measured how much knowledge the students lacked in order to become 100% informed. By using Entropy, it was found that the students lacked 40% of library skills taught during the seven-week period and that they acquired 60% of the material. This should be considered a satisfactory performance when one takes into consideration the short period of time allotted to the course.

PROBLEMS ENCOUNTERED DURING TEACHING

Table 3 presents the problems encountered during teaching. The most severe ones were the students' lack of command of the English language and absence of self-sufficiency. The students experienced difficulties in understanding the concept and the process of library research since they explained that they were not required to use the library in their home countries for research purposes. Additionally, they maintained that they had to heavily rely on professors' notes and textbooks as means of study.

The pre/posttest scores of members of the experimental group are shown in Table 4. The t-test was used to determine whether a sig-

TABLE 2. Extent of Students' Acquisition of Library Skills as Measured by Shannon's Entropy

$$H = -\sum P_i . \log . P_i$$

	$\sum P.\text{Log}$		Total	Value	%
	-----		-----	-----	---
	Pretest	Posttest			
	-----	-----			
	-1.76	-0.70	1.06	.60*	60

H= Entropy
$\sum$ = Sum of each score multiplied by log of score
P = Score of student on pre/posttest; obtained by dividing
  i the score of student by the maximum score
*= Obtained by dividing 1.06 by 1.76

TABLE 3. Problems Encountered During Teaching Library Skills Arranged in Rank Order

1. Lack of command of the English language. This required teaching at a slow pace.

2. Lack of self-sufficiency. No previous experience in doing library research.

3. Need of repeated explanation of technical material especially regarding classification schemes; Library of Congress subject headings; and library terminology.

4. Lack of conceptual awareness of library research.

TABLE 4. Pretest/Posttest Scores: The Experimental Group

Pretest	Posttest	Gain	T-test
	N= 7		
Mean	Mean		
29.42	39	9.58	2.42*

*Significant P<.05, df= 6.

nificant difference existed between the scores on the two tests. A significant difference (t = 2.42) in the scores was found with a 9.58 point gain on the posttest. The scores ranged from 34 to 44 while they ranged from 21 to 38 on the pretest. The students demonstrated a relatively high score in Unit Four, Interpretation of Information from the Social Sciences Index. This success could be attributed in most part to the fact that they had been previously exposed to such a skill before instruction. The only area in which the students were still deficient after instruction was in Unit Five: Choice of Indexes, in which they were asked to select the best index for finding some information. It is believed that item difficulty in this Unit and the short period of time devoted to the course may have hindered the students' performance.

Table 5 shows a significant difference (t = 2.34) between the scores of members of the experimental group and those of the control group on the posttest. One could infer that the library skills course did make a significant difference in this regard.

An interesting revelation regarding the performance of members of the experimental group on the pretest and those of the control group on the posttest is provided in Table 6. This test was conducted to determine whether both the experimental and the control groups possessed similar library skills before instruction. It should be noted that the control group was only exposed to a posttest whereas the experimental group was exposed to both tests. As one can see, the mean scores of members of the experimental group on the pretest was higher ($\overline{X}$ = 29.42) than that of the control group on the posttest ($\overline{X}$ = 18.50). The difference between the two sets of scores was significant (t = 2.90).

It is still unclear, however, why the experimental group performed better on the pretest than did the control group on the posttest since both groups had received a brief introduction to the library in the same manner and both had a similar background. It is believed that the 20 point difference in their average TOEFL score may have caused the difference in their performance. Since members of the control group refused to disclose their TOEFL scores to the investigator, it was not possible to correlate their library skills scores with those of their TOEFL. Similarly, the use of the analysis

TABLE 5. Posttest Scores of the Experimental vs. the Control Group

	Posttest	T-test
	Mean	
Experimental	39	
Control	18.50	2.34*

*Significant P<.05, df= 11.

TABLE 6. Pre/Posttest Scores: Experimental vs. Control Group

	Pretest	Posttest	T-test
	Mean	Mean	
Experimental	29.42		
Control		18.50	2.90*

*Significant P<.05, df= 11.

of variance which equates both groups' scores before instruction was not possible.

FINDINGS

1. No significant correlation was found between the scores received by members of the experimental group on the library skills pretest and on their entry TOEFL score.
2. A moderate correlation was found between their score on library skills posttest and their exit TOEFL score.
3. Members of the experimental group mastered 60% of the library skills taught as measured by Shannon Entropy.
4. Members of the experimental group encountered difficulties understanding the use of the library. This is possibly linked to their ability to comprehend the language. Lack of command of the English language, lack of self-sufficiency, and absence of the conceptual awareness of library research were found to be major problems.
5. A significant difference was found between the pretest/posttest scores of members of the experimental group.
6. A significant difference was found between the posttest scores of members of the experimental group and those of the control group.
7. A significant difference was found between the mean scores of members of the experimental group on the pretest and of those of the control group on the posttest. Although formal instruction was not a factor, the experimental group performed better than did the control group.

CONCLUSION AND RECOMMENDATIONS

The experiment showed the utility, efficiency and students' interest in the course. It also revealed that the students were unfamiliar with the American library system; that they were not required to use the library for research purposes in their home countries; that they lacked the conceptual awareness of library research skills; and that they needed repeated assistance in understanding the use of the library.

In the future enough time may be allotted by CIES for a library research skills course since six weeks was to short a term for the students to master the bibliographic enterprise. The students had high expectations and requested that they be taught how to develop research strategies, methods of writing term papers, and ways of compiling bibliographies. A comprehensive course that will include all these elements will be planned at CIES, if time and budget permit.

Although the results of this study cannot be generalized to other situations, some recommendations can be made to reference librarians who are involved in bibliographic instruction. It is extremely important that those librarians become aware of foreign students' backgrounds, cultural differences, and learning patterns. A positive attitude toward these students, patience, willingness to repeat information more than once or twice, and careful listening are prerequisites to teaching library research skills.

To obtain a clear and unbiased idea about the library skills of incoming international students, it is suggested that they be tested on those skills during the same period they are tested on their English language skills. The latter test is often required by centers such as CIES.

Further research is needed regarding the habits and needs of international students with respect to bibliographic instruction. Future studies may compare the level of library skills possessed by international students who are beginning their studies at an English language center with those international students at more advanced levels. Experimental studies in different institutions that involve larger groups are also recommended so that generalization may be more valid.

The question also remains whether a library skills course should be limited to inclusion within the curriculum of the intensive English program. Many international students enter American universities and colleges and due to a higher TOEFL score, bypass the English language program. These students may also share the need for acquiring library skills.

REFERENCES

1. Mary G. Lewis, "Library Orientation for Asian College students," College and Research Libraries 30(May 1969):267-72.

2. Frank Wm. Goudy and Eugene Moushey, "Library Instruction and Foreign Students: A Survey of Opinions and Practices Among Selected Libraries," The Reference Librarian 10 (Spring/Summer 1984):215-226.

3. Laura Kline and Catherine M. Rod, "Library Orientation Programs for Foreign Students: A survey," RQ 24(Winter 1984):210-216.

4. Dania M. Bilal, "Library Knowledge of International Students from Developing Countries: A Comparison of their Perceptions with those of Reference Librarians," PhD dissertation, Florida State University, Spring 1988.

5. J. Aczel, On Measures of Information and their Characterizations. New York: Academic Press, 1975.

PART V:
LIBRARY USE SKILLS
FOR OFF-CAMPUS PROGRAMS

Andragogy Off-Campus:
The Library's Role

Lori M. Keenan

SUMMARY. First introduced to this country by the American educator Malcolm S. Knowles, the term "andragogy" derives from the Greek "andros" meaning "adult or grown up" and "agogos" meaning "one who leads." Educators have long known that the learning of children differs substantially from the way in which adults learn and that, consequently, each demands a unique teaching approach. If children thrive in a highly-structured, fact-oriented, homogeneous teaching environment, adult learners respond much more readily to the open, experientially-based and mutually respecting approach of the facilitator. The following study will examine some of the most widely held assumptions about andragogy, particularly as they relate to the role the library must play in providing relevant reference services and bibliographic instruction to the adult learner in an off-campus setting. A secondary focus will be the efforts being made by one library system, Washington State University, to meet the challenge presented by the unique informational

Lori M. Keenan is Director, Moscow-Latah County Library System, 110 S. Jefferson, Moscow, ID 83843.

needs and demands of its off-campus learners. Present programs and future trends in off-campus library services to adult students at WSU will be examined.

In a recent article on bibliographic instruction, the authors brought to our attention a rather serious oversight committed by our profession. They charge that those of us involved with user education are so intent upon presenting the correct content of our sessions, that we often overlook the most important element of all, those whom we want to educate — our students.

> We tend to consider them, if we consider them at all as an absorbent mass, rather like a sponge, who will operate well in our library only if we can determine the correct things for them to soak up. Therefore, we concentrate on the content of our instruction sessions; students never seem to become to us individuals with knowledge, thoughts, and feelings about the library that must be understood, and perhaps overcome, before learning can begin. Yet without a deep understanding of those we address, designing effective library instruction programs is impossible.[1]

There is an undeniable truth in this statement and one which we, who are involved with dealing with a widely differing clientele, can only choose to ignore at our own peril. The exhortation to become more familiar with those whom we serve is particularly timely, since we are constantly developing more and more sophisticated approaches to all facets of our profession, including bibliographic instruction or user education and reference service.

This paper is an attempt to become more familiar with a very particular group of academic library users who function in a unique setting. Off-campus library users, while they may not represent the largest slice of our client pie, are rapidly growing in numbers and are presenting libraries with new and often difficult challenges. Some of the assumptions that have sprung up around the concept of teaching adults will be examined in light of how these can be brought to bear upon effective bibliographic instruction practices. Furthermore, the efforts of Washington State University in the area of providing good user education and reference service to its ca. 700 off-campus adult students will be described.

WHAT IS ANDRAGOGY?

Andragogy has been defined by Malcolm Knowles, one of its most ardent proponents, as "the art and science of helping adults learn." The term, which has its roots in the Greek "andros," meaning "man" or "adult" and "agogos," meaning "one who leads," was first introduced to the United States by the American educators Lindeman and Anderson in a 1927 monograph which attempted to show that the life experiences of adults have a definite impact on how they learn. It was not until 40 years later, however, that Knowles was able to elaborate upon this idea and publish his formulations in his landmark 1970 publication *The Modern Practice of Adult Education: Andragogy vs. Pedagogy*.

Knowles believed that adults are existentially different from children and therefore learn in a different manner. His theory is based upon four assumptions aimed at describing the adult learning process: (1) as a person matures the self-concept moves from dependency toward self-direction; (2) maturity brings an accumulating reservoir of experience that becomes an increasing resource for learning; (3) as the person matures, readiness to learn is increasingly oriented towards the person's social roles; and (4) as the person matures the orientation towards learning becomes less subject-centered and increasingly problem-centered.[2]

Although Knowles' theory gained a fair share of credibility among educators involved in adult education, it was not without its detractors. The debate that ensued almost immediately following the appearance of Knowles' book has lasted to the present and does not seem to be abating. Critics of the concept of andragogy have argued that the learning process is fundamental to all learners and that there is no essential difference between the education of children and of adults. Some have perceived andragogy merely as a technique or set of techniques,[3] while others have asked why limit ourselves to children and adults? Why not develop a theory of humanagogy?

> . . . a theory of learning that takes into account the differences between people of various ages as well as their similarities . . . a human theory of learning, not a theory of "child learning", "adult learning", or "elderly learning" . . . that combines pedagogy, andragogy, and geragogy and takes into account every aspect of presently accepted psychological theory.[4]

More recently, critics have warned of the danger of elevating andragogy to the level of an "academic orthodoxy" and have stressed the need for a more pragmatic approach.[5] On the other side of the coin, Brookfield points out the great emotional appeal of the concept to those involved in facilitating adult learning and emphasizes the learner centered aspect of andragogy, along with the potential for "all kinds of humanistically desirable and democratic practices."[6]

As happens frequently with lively and thorough debates, they serve to sharpen and clarify our notions and ideas about things. Over the past twenty years, the image of the adult learner has emerged clearly and has allowed those involved in facilitating the learning process to identify the unique needs and demands of this group. Librarians, who play an essential role in the educational development of all learners, are beginning to become aware of the unique situation of the adult learner.

ADULT LEARNERS:
WHO ARE THEY AND WHAT DO THEY WANT?

In one of the few articles linking andragogy and libraries, the author draws an in-depth profile of the "generic" adult learner.[7] She reports that eighty percent of all adult students are in life role or life circumstance transitions, most of which are triggered by life crises such as divorce, retirement, acknowledgement of alcoholism, the "empty nest" syndrome, etc. While the majority of adult learners are involved in making career changes, many also seek solutions to problems relating to family life, health or an excess of leisure time by returning to the classroom and becoming involved in the educational process. Sheridan stresses that as a result, these learners are often highly motivated and eager to face the challenges presented to them by the academic environment.[8]

This picture of the adult learner is congruent with that drawn up by a number of educators over the years. The typical adult learner tends to be a relatively affluent, well-educated, white, middle-class individual.[9] Yet this group suffers the same insecurities and anxieties that beset most of us when we enter a new and unfamiliar environment.

Many adult learners who are returning to school after a long absence, may feel insecure about their ability to perform academically or to compete against others much younger than themselves. For many, returning to school adds a great deal of additional stress to a life already full with the demands of job, family and society. It is therefore imperative that a unique environment, one which simultaneously nurtures, affirms and challenges, be operative for these students if they are to succeed in the path they have chosen.

Knowles' assumptions about adult learners, i.e., the learner's self-concept, the role of experience, the readiness to learn, and the orientation to learning address the expectations the individual will have of an educational experience and the demands she/he will place upon it. As self-directed individuals with a certain amount of life experience, adult learners are desirous of learning those things they perceive necessary to help them cope effectively with their real-life situations. They will be motivated to learn new knowledge, skills, and attitudes most effectively when these are presented in the context of applications to real-life situations. As a result, we may summarize the demands of adult learners to be those for self-direction, relevance, usefulness, and the opportunity to integrate life-experiences with learning experiences.

THE OFF-CAMPUS SETTING

While we can assess whether adult learners find their educational experience in the traditional setting, among 18-24 year olds, either satisfying and fulfilling or disconcerting and threatening, not enough is known about the off-campus learning experience as a whole to judge its effectiveness or its limitation vis à vis the on-campus one. Certainly, universities are trying very hard to overcome the "second rate" image of their extended academic offerings by involving their top faculty in the planning and teaching of off-campus courses and by providing better support structures for these programs. Within the last few years, libraries too, have taken a much more pro-active role toward off-campus programs. Many libraries have created special positions or departments headed by professionals to meet the informational needs of their institution's off-campus students, faculty, and staff.

Yet it must be acknowledged that off-campus learning too often takes place under less than ideal circumstances and that this situation places an additional burden upon the student in particular. Imagine yourself a graduate student in education, travelling a great distance once a week to take a course in "Advanced Children's Literature" or "Innovations in the Language Arts." While you trust that your instructor will have chosen, besides a comprehensive text, a wealth of relevant materials to be placed on reserve (assuming that the mechanism for such an arrangement exists), the onus in any graduate course, is on you, the student to conduct thorough research of your particular topic. Without having ready and convenient recourse to a number of basic resources in education, the student will be at a distinct disadvantage. Frustration, a sense of helplessness or futility, and even anger, are likely to result from this situation. The value of the educational experience in such a setting will become greatly diminished, damaging not only the institution's credibility, but also the student's own sense of self-worth.

WHAT'S A LIBRARY TO DO?

Working with Knowles' basic assumptions about andragogy, the library can do much to help the adult learner achieve a positive and beneficial learning experience. Let us examine four of these assumptions and attempt to relate them to the kind of service librarians can provide for adult learners who function in an off-campus setting.

1. The Learner's Self-Concept

For Knowles, this lies at the essence of his definition of an adult as someone who has

> a self-concept of being responsible for their own decisions, for their own lives. Once they [adults] have arrived at that self-concept they develop a deep psychological need to be seen by others and treated by others as being capable of self-direction. They resent and resist situations in which they feel others are imposing their wills on them.[10]

Recognizing and becoming sensitized to the adult learner's need for self-direction and independence in her/his course of study, the librarian will endeavor to function much more as a facilitator than an information manager. The emphasis will shift, hopefully, from simply providing information the librarian perceives as being needed, to offering the student the ability to see a number of approaches by which the predetermined goal can be achieved. By empowering students to master their own research strategies, the librarian is reinforcing the individual's need for self-accomplishment and self-direction. The adult learner becomes the consummate end user.

2. The Role of the Learner's Experience

Adults bring to any learning environment both a greater quantity and a different quality of experience than do non-adults. This means that any group of adults will be more heterogeneous in terms of interests, goals, needs, learning styles, and background than traditional college students. It calls, as Knowles points out, for an emphasis to be placed on individualization of teaching and learning strategies.[11] He suggests the utilization of experiential techniques such as group discussion, simulation exercises, problem-solving activities, peer-helping activities, etc., as keys to tap the wealth of experience that resides within adult learners.

For the librarian involved in giving bibliographic instruction to adult learners, there is much to be gleaned from Knowles' insights. Rather than involving the learners in a traditional lecture that stresses transmittal techniques, it might prove fruitful to meet with small groups, encourage group discussion, allow students to question and, hopefully, come to an understanding of how and why bibliographic instruction can be beneficial to them. Setting up situations which foster peer-helping activities can also prove valuable to both student and teacher who might just gain the satisfaction of seeing her/his students develop a deeper grasp of the material by having the opportunity to share the knowledge recently acquired.

Knowles points to another, more subtle reason for utilizing the student's life experience in the learning process. As adults we tend to define ourselves in terms of our experiences. Any situation which ignores or counts as irrelevant those experiences, will be perceived by the individual as rejecting not merely the experience but also the person.[12] In order to create the most favorable learning environment, we need to discover ways of involving the whole person in the learning process, regardless of whether we teach bibliographic instruction, provide reference service or fulfill a need for library support.

3. Readiness to Learn

Throughout life, learning involves the moving from one developmental stage to the next. A teenager is not ready to learn the knowledge and skill required to teach a high school English class. A single mother, who has recently returned to school to complete her undergraduate degree because she needs to provide a living for her family, may not be able to picture herself as a lawyer. On the other hand, the graduate student in the MBA program, who is also working for a high-powered investment company, will have no difficulties envisioning his climb up the corporate ladder.

It becomes the role of the facilitator to perceive correctly where the individual exists on the developmental scale and to assist, not only in allowing the student to master each new stage, but also in challenging the learner to confront the next one. This process is fundamental to good teaching and ought to be incorporated wherever learning is expected to take place, whether this be in the classroom or in the library.

4. Orientation to Learning

As has already been pointed out, adults are motivated to learn new knowledge and skills when these are perceived as necessary to an effective coping with real-life situations. In other words, someone will take the time to master the search protocol of ERIC on CD-ROM if by doing so they perceive they are gaining information which will help them become a better teacher, a better student, or a better person. Librarians involved in teaching library and research skills must learn to utilize this motivating factor. To do so, it becomes essential to learn something about the student in order to allow her/him to see the connection which can exist between such seemingly disparate elements as a bibliographic citation and a life or career skill.

While it may seem unrealistic to expect busy and already overextended librarians to develop the kinds of relationships with their clients described above, it has nevertheless become necessary to adopt a more involved attitude toward particular groups of users. Efforts in the area of reaching nontraditional users such as the handicapped or the foreign student are witness to this. Adult learners, many of whom function in a less than ideal setting, deserve our best efforts to help them achieve the kind of learning experience their more traditional counterparts on campus are receiving. A first step in this endeavor is to recognize that this group of learners is unique and that their needs must be met creatively and enthusiastically.

ONE LIBRARY'S APPROACH

In 1983, Washington State University, in an effort to reevaluate its mission as a land grant institution, responded by expanding its extended academic programs. As a result of generous funding from the Washington State Legislature, the University was able to put into operation WHETS (Washington Higher Education Telecommunication System) and begin the transmission of a variety of courses ranging from computer science and engineering to education and psychology via interactive microwave technology. At the same time, on-site courses at three locations (the Tri-Cities Area,

Vancouver, and Spokane) were being developed. Presently, between 20-25 courses reaching 250 students per term are offered through WSU's Extended Academic Programs.

Although WSU Libraries have provided library service to a small number of students (15-20 per term) for a number of years, it was not until the advent of WHETS and the establishing of WSU Centers at Vancouver and Spokane, that the scope of this service had to be thoroughly assessed. After identifying several successful library extension programs, particulary those of Simon Fraser University, the University of British Columbia, and the University of Victoria in Canada, as well as a number of American models, notably those of the University of Wyoming and Pennsylvania State University, WSU Libraries began to integrate the knowledge gathered into its own plan for action.

Following closely the 1981 ACRL "Guidelines for Extended University Campus Library Services," WSU Libraries, in 1987, created the OCLS (Off-Campus Library Services) Unit headed by a professional librarian, to implement, plan, and guide the direction of a program of library services to an ever-increasing population of off-campus learners.

A vital link between students at various locations around the state and the main campus at Pullman, is the 24-hour toll-free telephone number through which students can have unlimited access to all offices of WSU, including the Libraries. This service is heavily used by students to request materials, services, and assistance with research problems. Although every effort is made to use personal communication with students to create in them a sense of being valued by the University Community, much more needs to be done to convey to off-campus learners how important the success of their educational experience is to those charged with facilitating the learning process.

By gearing bibliographic instruction sessions, given either on-site or over WHETS, to, if not individual-, then at least group- and subject-specific needs of the students, a small step has been taken to meet their need for relevance. Another step in this direction is the making available of subject bibliographies with detailed information of item availability. Students can then choose whether they want to use the material at a library near them or request it from

WSU Libraries. The OCLS Unit will send the requested materials either via a 24-hour courier service to the Branch Campus site or mail it 1st class to a location specified by the student. This service is free to the student and is appreciated for being relatively efficient and expedient.

A traditional limitation to learners in off-campus settings has been the inability to simply browse a good and extensive research collection. COUGALOG, WSU's online catalog, offers a title, author, subject, and call number browse capability and is available to students at all off-campus sites. Access to a comprehensive journal collection at these locations is more difficult to achieve. It is hoped that by this summer, students will be able to browse at least tables of content pages of many of the journals essential to courses taught in the off-campus curriculum. This and the ability to conduct much of their own research by having available a number of databases on CD-ROM will do much to allow students to feel good about their educational experience.

Future plans for bibliographic instruction activities include the offering of intensely subject-specific sessions conducted by subject specialists, either on-site at the off-campus locations or over the WHETS system. It is anticipated that these will enable students to identify information sources most suitable to their own course of studies. Workshops on how to conduct good research under limiting and even adverse conditions are also planned. The challenge here will be to allow students to feel that their efforts are important and add significantly to the value and success of their educational experience as well as to the strength of WSU's programs.

In an extremely perceptive essay on adult learning, David Carr speaks of the need for librarians to become subjectively involved in the learning process and calls us to be nearer to learners and their thinking. He reminds us of the complexity of this process, particularly in the adult learner, calling this "construction of knowing amid the continuities of adult life, one of the most private human acts."[13] As librarians, involved in the metamorphosis of information into knowledge, we play a greater part in the shaping of human lives than we at times care to recognize. By becoming aware of who our clients are, by acknowledging the role we are called to play in the learner's life, we can enter more deeply into the learner's world and thereby give witness to what Carr so eloquently refers to as "the extraordinary instrumentality that is the librarian's touch."[14]

REFERENCES

1. Bobbie L. Collins, Constance A. Mellon, Sally B. Young, "The Needs and Feelings of Beginning Researchers," in *Bibliographic Instruction: The Second Generation*, ed. Constance A. Mellon. (Littleton, Colo.: Libraries Unlimited, Inc., 1987): p. 73.

2. Malcolm Knowles, *The Modern Practice of Adult Education: Andragogy vs. Pedagogy*. (New York: Association Press, 1970): p. 39.

3. Joseph Davenport, Judith A. Davenport, "A Chronology and Analysis of the Andragogy Debate," *Adult Education Quarterly* vol. 35, (Spring 1985): p. 153.

4. Russell S. Knudson, "Humanagogy Anyone?" *Adult Education* vol. 29, (Summer 1979): p. 261.

5. D. D. Pratt, "Andragological Assumptions: Some Counter-Intuitive Logic," *Proceedings of the Adult Education Research Conference*, no. 25. (Raleigh: North Carolina State University, 1984): p. 152.

6. Stephen D. Brookfield, *Understanding and Facilitating Adult Learning*. (San Francisco: Jossey-Bass Publishers, 1986): p. 96.

7. Jean Sheridan, "Andragogy: A New Concept for Academic Librarians," *Research Strategies* vol. 4 (Fall 1986): p. 157.

8. Sheridan, p. 157.

9. Brookfield, p. 5.

10. Malcolm Knowles, *The Adult Learner: A Neglected Species*, (Houston: Gulf Publishing Co., 1984): p. 56.

11. Knowles, *The Adult Learner*, p. 57.

12. Knowles, *The Adult Learner*, p. 58.

13. David Carr, "The Meaning of the Adult Independent Library Learning Project," *Library Trends* vol. 35 (Fall 1986): p. 329.

14. Carr, p. 327.

The BI Librarian's New Constituency: Adult Independent Learners

Jacquelyn Coughlan

SUMMARY. Adult independent learners are becoming an increasingly important and sizeable segment of the college student population. In an effort to identify their unique needs and orientations, this paper reviews some of the literature of theories of bibliographic instruction, examining both the cognitive and behaviorist theories of learning. There follows a brief treatment of the recommended teaching styles appropriate for dealing with adults, and a description of types of approaches to course content. The author concludes with remarks about an instructional experiment, involving students at SUNY Empire State College, the college within the State University of New York that serves adult learners.

The profile of the American college student population is changing rapidly. The notion of the typical 18-22 year old is no longer accurate since "nontraditional" students constitute a large and growing proportion of students in higher education. The increase is largest in the over 35 group. "Many will be enrolled as part-time students, who will account for 46 percent of all students. One out of every three students will be part-time and over the age of 25 (by the year 2010)" (Sheridan, 1986, p. 157).

Among these are the adult independent learners who have often been overlooked by those engaged in library instruction or bibliographic instruction (BI). Most students 35 years or older do not

Jacquelyn Coughlan is a graduate student at SUNY Albany, School of Information Science and Policy. She may be reached at the SUNY College of Technology Library, Marcy Campus, P.O. Box 3051, Utica, NY 13504.

The author wishes to thank Nancy Steele for her invaluable interlibrary loan assistance in writing this paper.

159

recall being instructed in the use of an academic library, and many are intimidated by or unfamiliar with current library technologies.

Decreasing budgets for both academic and public libraries have affected support for this "nontraditional" group. The viewpoint of the public library is that service specific enough for the nontraditional academic student diverts funds and staff away from its open service for all policy. And, while the role of the academic library in relation to these students has not been clearly defined in the past, the academic standards of off-campus courses suffer where there is inadequate library support for them.

This paper reports on a specific project designed to provide BI for this type of student enrolled at SUNY Empire State College. The instructional project and the research conducted in preparation for it, provided an opportunity for the author to reflect on current practices as described in the literature and to undertake an intentional plan for professional development as a teacher of library skills.

The actual instructional effort, organized as a study group, and formulated within a learning contract, was specifically designed in order to experiment with and evaluate strategies appropriate for adult learners. Readings were initiated prior to the beginning of the study group and were also pursued by the instructor throughout the period of instruction. The two specific areas of interest covered in the literature review, and for which the study group experiment is pertinent are: theories of adult learning and bibliographic instruction. This is an attempt to reflect on these concerns by focussing on instructional methods best suited for adults who wish to learn how to use a library effectively. The paper begins with a review of relevant literature and then proceeds to a discussion and evaluation of the study group in that context. In order to understand the differences in approach between behavior and learning theory, particularly as applied to adults seeking to learn about libraries, it may be useful to review more general literature on learning and teaching. Specifically, we will briefly survey literature on the learning process, learning styles of adults, and some of the literature that deals with teaching strategies appropriate for adults. This includes literature specifically about bibliographic instruction. Later the investigation will center on ways of organizing a course for bibliographic instruction and a description of the writer's first experience.

LEARNING-BEHAVIORALIST TASKS VERSUS CONCEPTUAL UNDERSTANDING

A review of literature on BI suggests that there are two basic orientations that need to be examined. On one hand, and prominent in earlier approaches, is the emphasis on tasks and skill acquisition associated with the behavioralist viewpoint. On the other is an emphasis on conceptual understanding in bibliographic instruction which characterizes the so-called cognitive theory approach.

Aluri and Reichel have written a useful article on the cognitive and behavioral theories of learning as they apply to BI. "The influence of behaviorism on bibliographic instruction has been enormous . . . three of the major products of the behavioral approach (are) . . . behavioral objectives, workbooks, and objective tests" (Aluri and Reichel, 1984, p. 20).

However, it may be argued that BI, undertaken from a cognitive learning approach, is more effective because the knowledge and skills that are acquired are more readily transferable than the kind of rote memorization associated with the behaviorist school.

This transferability has four dimensions: "across time—the individual completes school, begins a career, and throughout life; across place—that is from library to library: across disciplines; and across levels as the individual advances in knowledge and skills" (Beaubien, Hogan and George, 1982, p. 66).

The application of cognitive theory demands that material should be presented using unifying concepts. Some of these concepts for BI include: utilizing systematic literature searching, examining publication sequence and citation patterns, and using primary and secondary sources. Material should be related to what the learner already knows to make it relevant (Aluri and Reichel, 1984). Furthermore, in order to learn concepts, the student must master skills in a hierarchical sequence and Bodi (1984) emphasizes that a variety of experiences must be provided.

Both behavioral and cognitive theories have practical design applications for BI. It is critical that these applications be taken into consideration, according to James and Galbraith, because "a person's learning style is composed of a series of different modalities that together make up each person's unique style. . . . Possible modalities include, but are not limited to the perceptual, cognitive, and emotional and social modes'' (James and Galbraith, 1985, p. 20).

While the individual's mix of modalities varies greatly, there is considerable evidence to suggest a general rule of thumb. One widely quoted survey concludes:

> learners retain about 10% of what they read; 20% of what they hear; 30% of what they see; 50% of what they see and hear; 70% of what they say as they talk, and 90% of what they say as they do a thing. (Fjallbrant, 1984, p. 47)

The author indicates that this order of importance still obtains for different learning styles.

TEACHING STYLES

With regard to teaching styles, there is a fairly clear consensus in the scholarly literature in relation to the style and interpersonal attitudes that are most appropriate and have proven most effective for teaching adults. Sheridan recommends the "power of persuasion, sharing, and example over those of dominance and manipulation" (Sheridan, 1986, p. 165). She further observes that an effective teacher encourages mutual confrontation and collaboration; and discourages destructive comparisons and patronizing attitudes; and perhaps most importantly, allows adults to choose what they need to know.

Knox's (1980) idea of the necessary qualities for teachers are concern and respect for adults with varied backgrounds, and a sense of humor, responsiveness, and flexibility. Gartner (1977) says that the teacher must become a co-learner who adopts a learner role, so that he/she can provide the student with a model of desirable learner behavior.

These writers all point toward a preference for the facilitative and collaborative role as opposed to the authoritative role of teachers characteristically associated with classroom instruction designed for the 18-22 year old traditional student.

We turn now to the more focussed issue of bibliographic instruction for nontraditional students.

A study that deals specifically with adult learners in public libraries was done by Carr (1986) who examined learners as "seeking systems" and observed positive and negative "critical incidents" in over 100 interactions between learners and librarians. Librarians reported on the learner's problem, the librarian's response, and the meaning of the encounter. His conclusions were that a relationship based on collaboration, reciprocity, empathy and trust were critical between the learner and the librarian. Success was determined by the learner's desire and commitment to learn; and the librarian learned to nurture self-discovery in the learner. This kind of assistance is lasting because it changes a person's life. Carr also strongly believes that "however important the information given, it is no more important than the quality of the giving" (Carr, 1986, p. 332).

Sheridan (1986) offers an example of the "learner-centered" approach in describing an instance when the librarian distributed the reference sources to the class and asked for reactions and analysis from students. This established a collaborative relationship because the librarian allowed the students to demonstrate their own knowledge and it showed a willingness to give their opinions credibility. The major disadvantage of this approach is that the librarian may not be able to cover as much material as in a traditional presentation. On the other hand, allowing group discussion can provide support for individual members who are having difficulty acquiring basic knowledge and understanding from lectures, readings, and other methods of presenting information (Watson, 1986).

COURSE CONTENT

Now we move to a deliberation of specific course content in BI. Adams and Morris (1985) advocate organizing a course outline around one of the following five approaches: *the tool approach, the search strategy approach, the discipline approach, types of information approach,* and a miscellaneous category called *"others."* Examination of their conceptualization is helpful because it provides a framework with which to evaluate the multiple and diverse methods of BI encountered in the literature.

The *tool approach* describes use of the various tools such as the card catalog, reference books, indexes, and periodical indexes and abstracts. This is the method used in library school courses; presumably these students have a cognitive understanding of the broader concepts beforehand. This viewpoint stresses that tools must be taught because, regardless of the level of student interest, libraries are organized in this way and students must learn to use these tools in order to access information.

The *search and strategy approach* includes choosing and limiting a topic and locating and using background materials, periodical materials, bibliographies, research reviews, and so on. One well-known example of this type of program was developed at Alverno College and was "designed to interface with the outcome-oriented curriculum of the college" (Krzyminski, 1983, p. 114). This involved the compilation of a bibliography which required the student to understand and formulate an individualized search strategy.

A reminder regarding teaching the research strategy approach through development of a bibliography is asserted by Gratch (1985); "If there is no explicit instruction devoted to evaluating information, then it is inappropriate to place much emphasis on the quality of information cited in their bibliographies" (Gratch, 1985, p. 174). And students are advised that "It is not always easy to know when you have located the most useful sources but there are some signs . . . increasing redundancy and decreasing relevance" (Kuhlthau, 1985, p. 154).

Citation indexes are sometimes used in this category and Clark's (1986) analysis seems particularly relevant;

> How does the student clarify what is being taught? Perhaps by types of materials as librarians do: the student puts all encyclopedias together, all indexes together and learns what type of information is provided by each class of material. However, the student may learn by subject classes, a trail from general classes to specific classes of the subject leading to what is wanted, e.g., an article rather than an encyclopedia. (Clark, 1986, p. 118)

Clark reiterates that the student's motivation depends on his immediate perceived need.

> The student may reject the librarian's presentation of general classes of reference books because he/she wants to select and bring together dissimilar items, directly focussed on immediate requirements. A student may want to go from a subject index to a serial card or entry in a serial list to the volume needed and then to the article found. In that case, he may go on to follow a citation route from article to article. Teaching the understanding of citation indexes should include concepts that can be applied to the use of a citation trail in developing a research strategy. (Clark, 1986, p. 118)

Oberman-Soroka's (1980) "guided design" illustrates yet another search strategy approach. It consists of systematic steps to be followed in locating information in answer to an open-ended question. This method does not name tools but asks the student to imagine an ideal tool to answer his question and then a search is initiated to see if such a tool exists.

Kuhlthau (1985) has written a workbook on the research process which identifies seven basic steps with associated worksheets. A valuable supplement to this work is that it includes observations of the student's thoughts and feelings at each stage of the research process. The emotional stages one progresses through when writing a research paper might typically include: uncertainty about what is expected; optimism; confusion about the topic; gaining a sense of direction; then increasing interest in the project; and finally, a sense of satisfaction or dissatisfaction at the end of the process, depending on how the student feels about the work (Kuhlthau, 1985). Understanding this natural progression helps a student develop a tolerance for ambiguity which allows for the completion of the research cycle.

The *discipline approach* to BI includes an introduction to basic tools, planning a research paper, and then researching in a specific field such as the humanities, social sciences, or sciences. Earlham College instituted the best known project of this kind in 1976. It was sponsored by the National Science Foundation to develop "course-related" library and literature instruction, particularly in the sciences. There were fifteen participating institutions of several types of academic libraries which developed programs for BI in biology, chemistry, engineering, geology, and mathematics.

The *types of information approach* has been used in adult education in public libraries. Adams and Morris's (1985) organization for this approach itemizes: keeping up with current events; finding out about people; finding geographic and travel information; finding facts and statistics; finding consumer information; or finding a good book to read . . . a similar model based on student needs, might be outlined on this basis: finding information for short papers and speeches; researching the long paper; evaluating materials; locating quick facts and statistics; researching a company or career (Adams and Morris, 1985, p. 34).

Two interesting articles have appeared illustrating the types of information approach. The Colorado Commission on Higher Education has been given the authority to demand statements of expected outcomes from public institutions and information skills will be incorporated as one of the outcomes. These outcome statements will contain expectations in terms of knowledge, intellectual capacity and skills. The commission has stated that information literacy is not confined to knowledge of resources, nor should it be confined to searching for library based information. Rather, they emphasize the significance of the available forms and content of information (Breivik, 1985).

The second article mentions using the "Informational Structure of Disciplines" approach as a supplement to the traditional type of BI. It suggests expanding the approach beyond secondary research in library collections and databases. "Students are taught to ask: Who is likely to know about this? From where does information on this subject come from? and, Who pays for this information?" (Trzyna, 1983, p. 1). Students are encouraged to use interviews, telephone calls, and letters of inquiry. This could be interpreted to suggest that access is dependent on personal contacts and the ability to pay for long distance phone calls, but Trzyna disagrees and points to the advantages of a method that allows students to attempt prospective as well as retrospective research. "When students seek out individual articles or short bibliographies, they place an emphasis on facts rather than the relationships that obtain among facts, theories, and the people and organizations that develop these facts and theories'' (Trzyna, 1983, p. 3).

The author illustrates his point with reference to issues surrounding the use of nuclear power.

> While a particular expert's opinion of the safety of nuclear power is a piece of data, the knowledge that there is pro- and anti-nuclear organizations is . . . information about the structure of fact and opinion in that field of inquiry. Often students' papers are unsatisfactory because they fail to show an understanding that such structures exist and that . . . data may have more or less validity, or reliability, or authority. (Trzyna, 1983, p. 3)

The *others approach* in developing BI courses encompasses case studies, self-paced program modules, journals, computer-assisted instruction, worksheets and the like.

Many programs designed to address information handling behavior results in improved library use behavior. ''A half-dozen medical libraries are currently providing instruction in the organization of reprint files as part of their efforts to improve the information handling capability of the clientele'' (King, 1984, p. 54). This example fulfills the requirement of adults choosing for themselves what they want to know.

Other approaches have also included some experiments combining BI and game theory. Reid (1984) devised a game consisting of a series of eight basic tasks to be completed by groups of students. He argues that the advantages of the game format are that games are motivating, encourage understanding, and involve a high level of participation; the students learn from one another while the barrier between teacher and learner is removed. Games provide direct feedback on performance and allow concentration on essentials. On the other hand game playing tends to be time intensive, and it may oversimplify the subject matter. Also there is less control over what is learned; and success can be dependent on a student's prior knowledge.

EVALUATION OF BI PROGRAMS

No discussion of BI is complete without including evaluation, and while a detailed treatment of the evaluation of bibliographic instruction programs is outside the scope of this paper, a brief examination may be appropriate. Werking (1980) affirms the importance of evaluation by pointing to the potential improvements that such reflection can generate; evaluation is also necessary in order to justify funding and other administrative support. It is critical for comparing different methods of instruction as well as an integral part of needs assessment. Furthermore, it is crucial for defining goals and objectives.

One of the major problems of evaluation however, according to Werking (1980), is librarians' lack of familiarity with statistical methodology and research design in user education.

> Social scientists are lacking . . . for the more general field of evaluation research, (and) academics are hard-pressed to measure long-term gains in the mastery of more traditional subjects, . . . (indeed) evaluation is so complex (that) no single tool or method can satisfactorily gauge a program's total effectiveness. (Werking, 1980, p. 164)

One idea is to have some outside, more objective but knowledgeable agency evaluate a library's BI program. In the case of the Brigham Young University Library program, the general education department of their college evaluated the library's program as did the Brigham Young University McKay Institute which specializes in instructional design. This evaluation supported the value of BI and resulted in a one-year grant of $10,000 and an agreement of continuing support for BI in succeeding years.

FAILURE OF BI

The literature notes that there are some common failings and pitfalls of BI. Perkins (1965), for example, cites a study done in 1943 which lamented the fact that students have not acquired specific and detailed knowledge of reference tools such as dictionaries and encyclopedias; have not learned to associate types of questions with types of books most likely to answer them; have not learned to associate authors or editors with types of materials; have not learned to associate topics with general fields of knowledge. (Perkins, 1965, p. 194)

This author would observe that they do not use multiple access points; nor do they think creatively of alternate terms, phrases or key words which describe their subject. Their efforts are further hampered by their disinclination to think across disciplines and their inability to be persistent or systematic in their enquiry.

SUNY EMPIRE STATE COLLEGE STUDY GROUP

Having reviewed some of the themes and issues that are found in the literature of BI, we turn now to a summary discussion and analysis of an experimental study group designed for adult students enrolled at SUNY Empire State College.

SUNY Empire State College is the largest of 14 colleges in the SUNY System. It was founded in 1971 with the specific intention that it would not duplicate existing educational services within the university structure and it was designed to provide adults in New York State with an opportunity to earn a SUNY degree without necessarily having to conform to the traditional class structures. The average age of its students is 37. The college is decentralized in 44 locations throughout the state. For these reasons the college does not have its own library. Its faculty and students have come to rely instead upon the facilities and cooperation of neighboring academic libraries. The study group discussed here emerged out of just such an arrangement between the SUNY Empire State College learning unit in Utica, New York and the library at the SUNY College of Technology.

A group of ten adult learners met in five two-hour sessions, at the library of the SUNY College of Technology, a sister institution within the larger University complex. This facilitated hands-on experience and demonstrations. The students were to use various assigned tools and record their search strategies and findings in a journal. They were also required to submit a bibliography on a topic of their choice. Most were highly motivated in this endeavor as they had been assigned a term paper for a course in which they were concurrently enrolled. The instructional format was conceptualized as an independent study "learning contract." The actual description of the objectives of the study group, as well as the specific assignments were incorporated in the contract which is not dissimilar from a course syllabus. The contract also spelled out the criteria and methods that were used in the evaluation of student work.

This drew on several of the approaches discussed above and included some concern with where things are located and how specific bibliographic tools might be used.

The need for strong library skills on the part of students who are pursuing their educational goals through a series of learning contracts is particularly pronounced because of the nature of the individually planned program. In other words, a nontraditional student's need is more critical than a traditional student's need because "individually planned programs of study have few standard reading lists that could help libraries prepare to meet such student's needs . . . and an independent reading project requires good bibliographic skills or assistance" (Nolan, 1975, p. 17). When Haworth reviewed services available to the independent learner, she stated: "No literature has been found that maintains that the external student is not disadvantaged when compared with his internal peers" (Haworth, 1982, p. 172).

The rapid growth of the adult learner population will very likely lead to a proliferation of academic programs uniquely designed to accommodate their interests and their preferred learning modes. As this occurs, two tendencies will become more evident. First, the development of more interdisciplinary approaches within the curriculum, and second, more programs will emphasize guided independent study as the predominant mode of learning. As one observer has suggested,

> As the lines between the disciplines grow fuzzier, it is obvious that more students will find independent study engaging their interest; when this occurs they will no longer be content with a few standard reference works. Rather, they will begin to

stretch both the library and the librarian to the capacity of their abilities in the search for more unique materials . . . The distinction between independent and dependent learner will disappear and regardless of how or where independent study occurs, its effects will be felt by libraries of all types. (Hover, 1978, p. 548)

CONCLUSION

In summary, this experiment yielded the following notions. First, that while adult students enjoy the opportunity to study independently, like all students, they appreciate clarity and consistency in assignments. By the experimental nature of this project and because the instructor was reading about the efficacy of various techniques in the course of the study group, change and flexibility were key ingredients in the process. Students reported that this was a source of confusion and at times, anxiety.

On the positive side, students reported a much improved confidence in their ability to conduct bibliographic research; several evidently became much more sure of their ability to succeed as independent learners; and most, if not all, clearly acquired a new and broader appreciation of information sources in their fields.

Breivik states that "most studies show that 50%-80% of what is learned in courses is forgotten by students within a year" (Breivik, 1979, p. 230). The acquisition of information handling skills is not a luxury, it is a necessity, because information needs change over the years. By definition, life-long learning implies that the need for information will last a lifetime. This helps to explain why this notion has assumed such prominence in the mission statement of higher education today.

This paper provides a summary of literature in an increasingly important area and it reports on the outcome of a project that attempted, with some success, to implement some of the principles of instruction included in that literature. While much has been learned, clearly more study of this crucial field is warranted by the increasingly significant sector of adult independent learners that comprise the constituents of librarians in all phases of their work.

REFERENCES

Adams, M.S. and Morris, J.M. (1985). *Teaching library skills for academic credit*. Phoenix, Arizona: Oryx Press.

Aluri, R. and Reichel, M. (1981). Learning theories and bibliographic instruction. In C. Kirkendall (Ed.), *Directions for the decade: library instruction in the 1980's* (pp. 15-27).

Beaubien, A.K., Hogan, S.A., and George, M.W. (1982). *Learning the library: concepts and methods for effective bibliographic instruction*. New York: R.R. Bowker Co.

Bodi, S. (1984, January). Relevance in library instruction: the pursuit. *College and Research Libraries, 45*, 59-65.

Breivik, P.S. (1979). The neglected horizon: or, an expanded education role for academic libraries. In R.D. Steart and R.D. Johnson (Eds.), *New horizons for academic libraries* (pp. 229-235). New York: K.G. Saur Publishing, Inc.

Breivik, P.S. (1985, November). Putting libraries back in the information society. *American Libraries, 16*, p. 723.

Carr, D. (1986, Fall). The meanings of the adult independent library learning project. *Library Trends, 35*, pp. 327-345.

Clark, A.S. and Jones, K.F. (Eds.). (1986). *Teaching librarians to teach: on-the-job training for bibliographic instruction librarians*. Metuchen, New Jersey: Scarecrow Press.

Fjallbrant, N. and Malley, I. (1984). *User education in libraries*. London: Clive Bingley.

Gartner, A. and Riessman, F. (1977). *How to individualize learning*. Bloomington, Illinois: Phi Beta Kappa Educational Foundation.

Gratch, B. (1985, Fall). Toward a methodology for evaluating research paper bibliographies. *Research Strategies, 3*, 170-177.

Haworth, E. (1982, July). Library services to the off-campus and independent learner: a review of the literature. *Journal of Librarianship, 14*, 157-175.

Hover, L.M. (1979). The independent learner and the academic library: access and impact. In R.D. Streart and R.D. Johnson (Eds.), *New horizons for academic libraries*. (pp. 545-549).

James, W.B. and Galbraith, M.W. (1985, January). Perceptual learning styles: implications and techniques for the practitioner. *Lifelong Learning, 8*, 20-27.

King, D.N. (1984). Assessing behavior for diversified instructional programming. In C. Kirkendall (Ed.), *Bibliographic instruction and the learning process: theory, style and motivation*. (pp. 49-56). Ann Arbor, Michigan: Pierian Press.

Knox, A.B. (1980). *Teaching adults effectively*. San Francisco: Jossey-Bass.

Krzyminski, C. (1983, Fall). Library instruction in a non-traditional setting. *Wisconsin Library Bulletin, 78*, 113-114.

Kuhlthau, C.C. (1985). *Teaching the library research process: a step-by-step program for secondary school students*. West Nyack, New York: The Center for Applied Research in Education.

Nolan, M. (1975). Library access for students in non-traditional degree programs. *Drexel Library Quarterly*, *11*, 16-33.

Oberman-Soroka, C. (1980). *Petals around a rose: abstract reasoning and bibliographic instruction: a paper*. Chicago: Association of College and Research Libraries.

Perkins, R. (1965). *The prospective teacher's knowledge of library fundamentals*. Metuchen, New Jersey: Scarecrow Press.

Reid, B.J. (1984). Aston intro-active: a library game for new undergraduates. *Research Strategies*, *2*, 108-118.

Sheridan, J. (1986, Fall). Andragogy: a new concept for academic librarians. *Research strategies*, *4*, 156-167.

Trzyna, T. (1983). *The informational structure of disciplines: an approach to teaching research*. Paper presented at the annual meeting of the Wyoming conference on freshman and sophomore English (Laramie, Wyoming: June 27-July 1, 1983). ERIC Document Reproduction Service No. ED 283 004.

Watson, E.R. (1980). Small group instruction. In A.B. Knox *Teaching adults effectively*. San Francisco: Jossey-Bass.

Werking, R.H. (1980, Summer). Evaluating bibliographic education: a review and critique. *Library Trends*, *29*, 153-172.

PART VI:
LIBRARY USE SKILLS: ISSUES RELATED TO MICROCOMPUTERS AND END-USER ONLINE SEARCHING

An Integrated Planning Process for Library Skills: Paper-Based and Computer-Based Instruction

Nancy Allen

SUMMARY. Among new curricular requirements for general education were two elements: computer literacy, and a course called, "The University and Its Libraries." The primary goal of this course was student orientation and retention. The Libraries engaged in an integrated planning process to reach the overall goals of the course while meeting instructional objectives for library skills and support-

Nancy Allen is Assistant Director for Public Services, Colorado State University Library, Fort Collins, CO 80523.

ing computer literacy requirements by offering both paper-based and computer-based instructional modes.

GENERAL EDUCATION REFORM
AT AN URBAN UNIVERSITY

The national picture of the educational and matriculation capabilities of the college freshman is of great concern to higher education, as summarized elsewhere in this volume. But an urban, commuter, research university might possibly represent the most extreme case of the entering freshman retention crisis.

Wayne State University is an urban university drawing heavily on troubled Detroit public schools as well as middle-class suburban public schools for its freshman class. The average student commutes to campus, is working part or full time, is considerably older than students at residential universities, and is self-funded, as opposed to traditional parental funding. The average age of the entire student body is 27, 25-30% are minorities, and 40% of the classes are offered in the evenings or weekends. There is also a growing number of degree students who attend most classes in suburban extension sites.

Although this composite picture of the freshman class might lead one to assume such characteristics as increased motivation, better organizational skills, a higher maturity level, and a greater sense of responsibility, these characteristics, although present in many freshmen, are counter-balanced by impatience with staff, unwillingness to invest time, the endless search for the easy way, and a critical view of learning based on a heightened awareness of the value of the tuition dollar. These characteristics are relevant to the environment in which an examination of the core curriculum took place.

Wayne State University, like many other large research campuses, overhauled its general education requirements two years ago in response to the crisis in secondary schools and in an effort to improve the quality of education for its students. The general education curricular reform emphasized the basics of education, and was in many areas competency based.

Among new requirements were a computer literacy provision. This rather vaguely defined requirement was not necessarily envisioned as a single course, and it was the task of the University's Academic Computing Policy Committee to make a recommendation on exactly how this provision would be met. The library administration was represented on this important committee, which was charged with strategic planning and policy development for all academic computing issues.

UGE 100: THE UNIVERSITY AND ITS LIBRARIES

Another important new requirement was a freshman orientation and retention course called "The University and Its Libraries," called UGE 100 for its place in the University's General Education requirement package.

UGE 100 is a complex course. It is a one-credit course offered the first 8 weeks of a 16-week semester. Its overall structure was based on that of a similar course offered at California State University at Long Beach (CSULB). Even though the title of the course seems to emphasize libraries, the primary emphasis is student retention and orientation to university life.

Students are taught by faculty from all schools and colleges. They meet with faculty in lecture discussion sections a total of 15 classroom hours. Students purchase a package of course readings to support a syllabus addressing such issues as study skills, the relationship of classroom participation to leadership potential, civic responsibilities of the educated, examples of well-known graduates of WSU and discussion of the nature of faculty research contributions to society, and the shift from an industrial to an information society.

In addition to the 15 classroom hours, students must complete 3 out-of-class modules. These are:

1. reading and study skills, which is a self-assessment instrument and brief counseling session;
2. library skills, which is a self-paced program operated by library staff; and
3. a choice between a career counseling self-assessment instru-

ment and a cultural environment program designed to increase the student's awareness of area cultural and student organization opportunities. The career counseling module is computer-based, using a number of microcomputer-based diagnostic tools to help the students assess personal aptitudes and skills.

PLANNING CONSIDERATIONS

Clearly, this is a considerable amount of work for a one-credit course. Because of the concern for the number of hours needed to complete all segments of the course, and because of the desire to create an overall positive attitude toward the university on the part of UGE 100 students, careful planning was required. Considerable pressure came to bear on the planners of the library skills module to:

- make the library skills instructional material fun
- make the content relatively simple
- limit the time requirements for completion
- guarantee success (no failure allowed in a freshman retention course!)

The library segment of UGE 100 was also based on the model developed and used at the Library of California State University at Long Beach, but environmental considerations of Wayne State University had great impact on the progress of planning education for library skills.

The planners of the library portion of UGE 100 felt strongly that library issues should be integrated into the course as a whole, and that libraries should not be relegated to a skills exercise entirely outside the classroom environment. For this reason, readings and discussion on the concept "Information Society" were included in the classroom portion of the course.

Integrated planning for the library skills module was important for many other reasons. Not only were library issues integrated into UGE 100 as a whole, but UGE 100 planning had to integrate many factors about the university and the library system to succeed.

Among these were the nature of the freshman class, as described above, the computing environment (and strategic planning for academic computing), new goals for general education, new requirements for computer literacy, budget considerations, and political realities.

- The computing environment is heavily oriented toward mainframe access student workstations rather than free-standing microcomputers. Relatively few students own their own microcomputers. Fewer than 200 on-campus terminals are operated by the Computing Services Center, and are accessible to all students regardless of affiliation with schools and colleges. Increasingly, schools and colleges, with assistance from the university, are funding their own microcomputer centers, usually linked to the university mainframe.
- At the time UGE 100 planning began, the Academic Computing Policy Committee was still in the process of making recommendations on ways to satisfy the computer literacy requirement stated in the general education curriculum package.
- The management of funding and planning for the only course in the whole university not attached to any one department is highly political. The Libraries' role in planning ranges from ad hoc to official, depending on the issue at hand.
- The goals and objectives of UGE 100 had to be met without placing an undue burden of time on the students enrolled.
- The cost of course development, including computer-assisted instructional design, had to be largely borne by the library. Central university budget sources did assist with travel, consulting fees, and some equipment. And, by the time UGE 100 was first offered, positions had been added to the library specifically for this course.
- UGE 100 would first be required only of entering freshmen. By 1989, however, it will be required of all transfer and extension students as well.
- UGE 100 had to be tested in the summer of 1987, and fully offered by the fall 1987. No delays could be tolerated in course development.

PLANNING FOR PAPER-BASED
AND COMPUTER-ASSISTED
INSTRUCTION

On the basis of these wide-ranging planning considerations, it was quickly decided to pursue both a paper-based and computer-based mode of instructional design simultaneously. A traditional self-paced workbook-based program could be done fairly quickly, as it could be closely based on materials designed and used at the Library of California State University at Long Beach.

The computer-assisted instructional material would take longer to develop, but had a number of clear advantages, documented in several meta-analyses of the overall effects of computer-based education.[1] In addition, a number of the environmental considerations of Wayne State University would be met. Among these advantages were:

- It would be interesting to students;
- It would support the new computer literacy effort;
- It would be easily revised;
- It is interactive and should support the need for students to finish the course with a positive attitude toward the course and the university;
- It is an effective learning tool which lends itself to self-paced programs;
- It could be used in a program designed to be relatively cost-effective in staffing terms.
- It would allow off-campus access for extension students.

Design and writing of the handbook began immediately. Instructional objectives stated in the CSULB model were amended considerably, removing most objectives related to research strategy and composition of search topic. This was due to the fact that the classroom portion of the course had no provision for a library research project, so students would not be applying the information they gained until they had a term paper or other library assignment in a different course. The only connection between the library skills module and the 15 classroom hours is a theoretical unit accompanied by readings on the Information Society. Although thinking about the libraries starts in the classroom, library skills are acquired in the separate, self-paced module.

The content of the library skills module includes instruction on the physical layout of two library buildings, location of library materials, call number systems used at WSU, encyclopedias and general reference sources, card catalog use, online catalog use, printed journal index use, InfoTrac and other end-user online journal indexing, and U.S. government publications and the *Monthly Catalog*.

Since all students in UGE 100, whether they receive instruction via a handbook or via a computer terminal, would need orientation to the library buildings, a separate library tour booklet was prepared to accompany a signage system identifying station stops in the buildings.

A set of four quizzes was prepared. These were designed to reinforce learning and to emphasize certain information, to assess information retention, to ensure that students could talk personally with library staff, and to determine the pass/fail status of the student for the library module of the course.

Personal contact with library staff comes from the procedures surrounding the administration of the quizzes (called "assignments," which is a less threatening word). There are many versions of each assignment, and the student may choose to do a science oriented set of assignments or a social sciences/humanities oriented set. Some assignment questions are based on information gained by touring the buildings. The assignments also include questions designed so that the student must actually use the card catalog, actually do an online catalog search, and actually do an InfoTrac search. In this way, students must learn the difference between the various types of terminals in the reference area, and must see the connections between printed and online access tools. Many of the questions and answer choices are humorously written so that the tone of the quiz process is not intimidating.

Because of the way assignments are completed, no student who takes all the assignments can fail to pass them. Only if a student does not attempt the assignments can the student fail to receive credit for the library skills module of UGE 100.

Each student purchases the printed handbook at the University Bookstore, along with other course materials. As the student begins to read the handbook, s/he sees instructions in a black box at the bottom of the pages. Early in the handbook, the instructions say to go the library's Center for Bibliographic Instruction (CBI) to pick up the first assignment. When the student does this, s/he also fills out a scannable registration form which is used to establish a computer record for the student. When the student completes the assignment, having recorded the multiple choice answers on a scannable answer form, the student returns the form to the CBI. When it is scanned, the computer program checks to see if the student missed more than 5 of 20 questions, or *any* of the questions supporting primary instructional objectives, or key questions. If either of these occurs, the program prints out a "prescription" for action. The prescription and assignment score is picked up by the student, who follows the instructions to re-read relevant parts of the handbook and to try answering the questions again.

This time, the student gives the new answers to a staff member in the CBI, who grades the answers, and if necessary, *tutors* the student in the topics which are confusing. This personal instruction is necessary for about half of the students who do each assignment.

The computer programs also produce reports to the faculty on student progress through the library skills assignments. For course evaluation, there are lists available on demand of the number of times students missed any question on any of the versions of all assignments.

All these procedures were only slightly modified from the model used at CSULB.

ENHANCEMENTS THROUGH CAI

The personal touch is gained through the CBI, but it is very costly to operate. With between 1000 and 2000 students visiting the CBI at least once and often twice for each of four assignments in six weeks, a great deal of staffing is needed. After the first term, CBI staff revised all the assignments in an effort to reduce the percentage of students needing tutoring. One of the most important practical goals of the computer-assisted instructional planning was the development of online concept testing to enable further staff reductions in the CBI.

After a year of development, a set of library skills lessons was mounted on the university mainframe. Students sign on to a terminal, and see a main menu of four lessons. The instructional material in the handbook was used as the basis for screen text, and the chapters were grouped together into the four lessons on the menu. Students can quit at any time. They can go back to the beginning of any lesson or sublesson. They can choose to proceed through all screens or use a fast review mode which goes to screens teaching the main concepts, and skipping over much of the dialog and screen alternatives. They can view an index to the course content, and select any line from the index to go directly to the screen addressing that index topic. They can type "comment" and automatically be put into the electronic mail mode to send the lesson authors evaluative commentary, being returned to the lessons after sending the electronic message.

As many choices as possible were given students using the CAI lessons. Examples illustrating concepts are often optional. Although the order of progress is optional, students are encouraged to go through the lessons in order at first. All lessons have lists of instructional objectives, and students may view these. However, online concept testing is not optional. Directly following instructional text on each of the central concepts are questions testing understanding. Some questions are multiple choice, some are yes/no. The computer responds to the student's answer, and the programs log the student's accuracy. The program also logs the sign-on and sign-off time of each student.

The mainframe version of the library skills lessons is being piloted as of this writing on two sections of UGE 100. For the purposes of this trial, all UGE 100 students in the trial sections complete the same printed assignments as the other students, so that the quiz results of the CAI students can be compared to those of students using the printed handbook. So far, it seems that (as much research has indicated) the test results are almost equal. However, students *like* the CAI better than the handbook, computer sign-on difficulties aside.

In order to effect staff savings, while still providing the "personal touch" of tutoring, it will be necessary to devise a "final" printed assignment for students who have completed the online instruction. Because most concepts are tested online, only one "assignment" is needed, largely as a good mechanism to bring students in to the CBI to talk to a staff member about difficult concepts. This one assignment will reduce the time needed for the student to complete the course, since s/he will need to visit the CBI only once or twice to do the final assignment and if necessary the prescription and tutoring. This one assignment will also include the questions necessitating actual use of the card catalog, online catalog, and printed and online journal indexes.

There is much more that could be done with this mainframe system to create enhancements, especially in the area of administration and record-keeping. However, the programming language, and the nature of the university mainframe system create many limitations. Only very primitive graphics are possible; no screen movement or animation is possible; and bureaucracies and sign-on procedures mandated by the Computer Services Center are cumbersome.

In addition, the number of publicly available terminals is limited. To improve the quality of instruction, and thereby improving the students' attitude toward the instruction and the course UGE 100 as a whole, as well as to increase the number of available terminals, planning has begun to design a set of lesson software for free-standing microcomputers, both for IBM/compatible and MacIntosh equipment. This may more than double the number of available on-campus terminals, while suggesting a broader role for the off-campus extension centers which include two large suburban microcomputer laboratories.

The microcomputer version, as well as the mainframe version will be critical in meeting the need to make UGE 100 available to extension students. Although all students will still have to visit and use the university libraries to complete UGE 100, much of the instructional material will be available on a decentralized basis, since most extension sites have dial access terminals or other equipment connected to the mainframe, as well as free-standing micros.

CONCLUSION

Planning for this course and its library module has been done through integrating library and university-wide goals and environmental considerations. In addition, it is being integrated with other library programs, and has had a major effect on most library operations, ranging from shelving to the tattering of indexes.

- Signage has been upgraded to accommodate the tour portion of the module.
- With online catalog instruction included in the course, all entering students are familiar with basic search strategy.
- All UGE 100 students are required to complete and print out an online catalog search as well as an InfoTrac search. Although this direct comparison assists with the growing problem of computer terminal confusion, it puts great strain on the InfoTrac equipment.
- As almost all students will be familiar with library resources through this required course, fewer instructors will be requesting the traditional orientation tours. Instead, more upper-level course-related bibliographic and research instruction will be offered on subject-specific topics.
- The content of the library module of UGE 100 will affect the courses offered as graduate seminars by library staff.
- As the libraries continue to invest in CD-ROM indexes and other reference sources, UGE 100 can be used as a way to teach all library users the basics on this new technology, allowing detailed searching seminars to be offered to upper-level students in relevant subject departments.
- The nature of printed materials reflects a new base-line of common knowledge.

The effects on other library programs listed here are notably comparable to the effects of a general education program on the university's curriculum. A new base of assumed knowledge is in place, students have been helped to master the basics, and are demonstrated as being competent in the fundamentals of skills needed to complete a program of higher education successfully.

Freshmen entering universities ten years ago had to master the transition from small high school library card catalogs to large and complex university library catalogs and a vast range of journal indexes and other information sources. Today's freshmen must cope with the transition from small high school card catalogs to technology based computer catalogs and indexes.

Two 1984 studies indicated that there is a great percentage of entering freshmen in colleges and universities having some familiarity and corresponding comfort with computers. A study of Pennsylvania public high school curricula showed that over 51% of college bound students had received instruction in computer science courses.[2] And a national survey indicated that just over half of that year's entering freshmen had written a computer program.[3] One could assume that four years later, the percentages are even higher. Students realize that today's college curricula and today's worklife demand a much greater level of "computer literacy."

The relationships between new general education requirements stressing "the basics" and computer literacy requirements are appropriate. It is also appropriate to involve library user education in these new requirements.

The integration of both theoretical and practical library issues into a general education curriculum achieve the user education goals of the university library while supporting the broader goals of the university. Computer assisted instructional design has been a major element in meeting these broader goals.

REFERENCES

1. Hasselbring, Ted S. "Research on the Effectiveness of Computer-Based Instruction: A Review." *International Review of Education*, 32(3), 1986: 313-324. Kulik, Chen-Lin C., and James A. "Effectiveness of Computer-Based Education in Colleges" *AEDS Journal*, 19(2/3) (winter/spring 1986): 81-108.

2. Tellep, Andrew. *Computer Literacy of Entering Freshmen.* ERIC Document 247 970, April 21, 1984, 10 pp.

3. Astin, Alexander W. *et al. The American Freshman: National Norms for Fall 1984.* Higher Education Research Institute, Graduate School of Education, University of California, Los Angeles; Washington, D.C.: American Council on Education, December 1984. 193 pp. ERIC Document 355 106.

Knowledge-Based Instruction
for Lifelong Learning

Judith M. Pask
Dana E. Smith

SUMMARY. Undergraduate students arrive at a research-oriented university or college with varying levels of experience and ability in using libraries or information. The Purdue University Undergraduate Library has designed an instruction program to teach large numbers of students the essential library research skills needed for completing higher education program requirements and for lifelong learning. The major objective of the program is to instill a sense of the value of information utilization to all students without presenting impossible demands on limited library personnel resources.

To meet this objective, the Undergraduate Library Research Skills Program was developed. Through use of several components designed for on-demand, self-directed learning, students obtain instruction on how to logically and efficiently conduct library research. This approach allows students and faculty to satisfy their information instruction requirements based on their personal interest, motivation, and time constraints. The following paper describes the components of this Program and the methodology employed for integrating the content of these components into the existing curriculum. Enhancements to this Program are also described to suggest a process whereby this Program could be adapted to other libraries' instruction requirements.

The tremendous increase in the volume of information accompanied by dynamic technological innovations has become so rapid that no one individual can expect to know everything, even in the most specialized disciplines. As our knowledge-base expands in size and

Judith M. Pask is Reference and Instruction Librarian, Undergraduate Library, and Dana E. Smith is Collection Management Librarian, Approval Services, Yankee Book Peddler, Maple Street, Contoocook, NH 03229.

187

complexity, the ability to succeed in our society is likely to be dependent upon an individual's level of proficiency and competency to make significant and continuing contributions within this expanding environment. The characteristics of the process whereby trained professionals remain current and, therefore, effective will be critical in the rapidly changing environment of tomorrow's workplace.

Many educators believe that preparation for this environment must involve a program of professional education that includes a shift of emphasis from pure knowledge acquisition to practical knowledge utilization. In this respect, instruction in the appreciation and understanding of this knowledge-base — how to gain access to sources of information, how to correlate and assemble it, and how to make accurate judgements from retrieved material — should be emphasized far more than factual knowledge acquisition. These educators contend that the attitudes, habits, and basic skills necessary for a functional process of lifelong learning must be instilled during the professional training period and are as essential as the core of knowledge and practical skills currently acquired to launch an individual along a particular career path.

PREPARATION FOR LIFELONG LEARNING

The Purdue Undergraduate Library opened in May 1982 with a specific mission to provide an appropriate response for the educational challenges and demands of instructors and students preparing for effective involvement in a highly technological, information-based society. This new library provided the library system, consisting of 14 subject-oriented departmental libraries, a place to concentrate on a program for delivery of instruction including basic information literacy skills. In fact, the mission statement for the Undergraduate Library contains the following at the top of its list of programs:

> I. To provide an instructional program to introduce students to library services, resources, and facilities and to develop the bibliographical sophistication necessary to complement lifelong learning through effective library/information utilization.

The Undergraduate Library's Research Skills Program is based on a fundamental premise that within the large research-oriented university, there are significant numbers of undergraduates whose levels of experience and ability in using libraries vary. The Program's instructional design and content reflect specific goals and objectives based on the following presumptions:

1. Most first-year students are unaware of the majority of bibliographic sources available to them.
2. Most freshmen do not yet have the research skills needed to effectively utilize the research library's potential.
3. Some students are intimidated by the complexity and size of a large library system and may be reluctant to ask for assistance.
4. The library is a highly complex system of print and nonprint information. In order to locate pertinent materials, user instruction will be required.

LIBRARY RESEARCH SKILLS PROGRAM

The Undergraduate Library's Research Skills Program has been developed to provide an opportunity for all participants to attain a practical, functional level of sophistication appropriate for their information needs. In this respect, the Program's current four major components: the *Undergraduate Library Research Guide*; a self-guided audio-tour; CAI tutorials; and individual assistance at the Reference/Information desk are intended to complement an individual's unique subject research requirements and nurture the corresponding search strategy. This guided, but self-directed methodology invites the participant to engage in the instructional process in a manner that is personally comfortable, convenient, and effective in helping them at their time of need. All components of the Program are intended to be used according to the type and level of library-related instruction appropriate for their investigative requirements.

Research Guide

Beginning in the fall of 1985, all English 102/Freshman Composition students were required to purchase the *Undergraduate Library Research Guide*. The *Guide* presents a systematic search strategy applicable to any type of library research or information need. It encourages students to articulate their needs, define their topic, and determine the type of information (general, in-depth, specific) they need. The *Guide* not only assists the students, but also provides accurate library information for the English instructors to refer to when teaching the process of writing a research paper.

During the Spring 1988 semester, an instructor's guide for the Program was added in order to assist the classroom instructor in the most effective methods for integrating the Program's components into their specific course outline.

Audio-Tour

The audio-tour provides a general overview of the services and resources available in the Undergraduate Library and where they are located. Students obtain a floor plan of the library on which they identify the locations of library resources or services as they are explained on the taped walking tour. Thus the audio-tour, an alternative to conducting large group tours of the building, provides a feedback mechanism to the instructor that students have familiarized themselves with the facility. This approach has proven useful in reducing the amount of time previously expended by library staff in conducting tours, minimized disruption for other students using the building, and allowed instructors another hour of classroom time they would have used by taking a tour. Students can use their own or library provided cassette tape players at a time of their choice.

Computer-Assisted Tutorials

A computer-assisted instruction program is an ideal approach for an individualized program to teach basic library skills. It provides one-to-one instruction that is interactive, gives appropriate feedback depending on the original response, and allows the student to work at his/her own pace. For the librarian, computer-assisted instruction provides a consistent information source, i.e., each student is given the same information, and performs the basic repetitive skills instruction, while allowing librarians to concentrate on more difficult and involved information requests. CAI is also very flexible. It can be designed to accommodate students' varying skill levels, can be adapted to changing end-user requirements, and can be used at any time the library is open. These programs are also easily transportable and can be made available at sites outside of the library wherever appropriate hardware exists.

On the other hand, CAI-based tutorials can present certain limiting disadvantages. For the most part, these limitations have restricted the widespread growth and use of CAI-based tutorials in library instruction programs. Such tutorials are typically expensive to produce, require readily available program development and revision expertise, involve lengthy preparation time, and can limit personal contact. In addition, there are very few ready-made commercial packages which allow for easy on-site adaptation of program design and content to reflect unique site specific program requirements.

Despite some of these drawbacks, CAI became a part of the Undergraduate Library's Research Skills Program because it offered a practical, and long-term economically feasible opportunity for meeting the instruction demands of a large user population. This approach also offered the level of flexibility for content revision necessary to meet anticipated changing end-user requirements.

The microcomputer-assisted tutorials are available to students in the Undergraduate Library's Independent Study Center. These tutorials can be utilized at any time the center/library is open and are intended to provide a hands-on training experience in periodical index use and analysis, the Purdue Library's specific serials retrieval procedures, and the use of the Undergraduate Library's Books and Media Online Catalog. These tutorials allow students to work at their own pace, and conduct in-depth study on unfamiliar sections, while perhaps moving more rapidly through material they already know. To assist in guiding students through these tutorials, several tear-out pages in the *Research Guide* contain exercises used in conjunction with the tutorials. These pages often become a course assignment and once completed and returned to the instructor, serve as evidence of a students' interaction with the programs. In addition, the online catalog tutorial is designed as a stand alone simulation of the Undergraduate Library Books and Media Online Catalog. It provides instruction about this resource without frustrating other students familiar with search procedures trying to use the limited number of public online terminals.

Reference Assistance

The Library Research Skills Program is further enhanced through individualized assistance offered at the Reference/Information desk. This service is provided 78 hours a week. Here students may receive clarification of a point in the *Research Guide*, additional information about a specific source, or the library system in general, or guidance in what the next step in finding information should be.

The librarians in the Undergraduate Library also provide extended, in-class presentations at the request of instructors. However, with the incorporation and use of the Library Research Skills Program, these classroom presentations are reserved for those classes that have utilized the Program's basic instruction components and now require more advanced presentations in specialized research areas. In this respect, the librarians are able to tailor their presentations to an appropriate level because the students have been previously exposed to the characteristic structure of basic library research skills.

EVALUATION

Since the Undergraduate Library's Research Skills Program was introduced in 1984, there have been significant, measurable effects on the overall quality of student research products and library operational objectives. The evidence of the Program's impact on student learning has been highlighted through feedback from instructors and students. Comments by English Composition (English 102) instructors and students on program evaluation forms completed each semester indicate that the Program has succeeded with some of its goals. Regarding the goal of the Program to reduce the students' anxiety and/or frustration in using a large library system and making them aware of how to obtain help when they need it, instructors have commented that:

— the *Research Guide* ". . . helps to make the library familiar to students and provides them an edge when starting their research projects."

— the microcomputer tutorials ". . . are an immense help to the students. Many were totally unfamiliar with the library; the information presented more than gave them the start they needed."

There is evidence in the literature that students frequently view this instruction as unnecessary, and of little immediate use unless it is received in conjunction with a specific assignment. The Library Research Skills Program is specifically intended to further minimize this perception by allowing students alternative, point-of-need library instruction options. Since 1985, over 3,800 English 102 students have received their introduction to basic library research using the various components of the Program. Ongoing revisions to the Program have increased the students' perception regarding the overall helpfulness of the Program's content.

During the summer of 1986, major revisions were made in the microcomputer tutorials to include more hands-on activities. For example, the first version of the serials tutorial utilized a graphic representation on the computer screen as an example of the Serials Union Catalog microfiche. Feedback from students and course instructors prompted a revision which incorporates the actual use of the microfiche and a reader in completing the tutorial assignment. Student response to these revisions was positive. In the Spring 1986 semester, 42% of student respondents rated the serials tutorial as highly helpful in understanding how to use the microfiche catalog. In the Fall 1986 semester, this figure increased to 62%. Another question on the evaluation form asked how helpful the Program was overall. Sixty-one percent of the students in the Spring 1986 semester rated it as helpful, while 72% gave the same rating in the Fall 1986 semester. The audio-tour, evaluated separately, was rated as helpful by 88% of its users.

During the last three semesters, statistics kept at the Reference/ Information desk have shown an increase in the number of reference questions and a decrease in questions of a purely directional nature. This has been most evident during concentrated periods of instruction and suggests that students have found the Program to be helpful, know when and where they should receive individual assistance, and are acquiring the ability to make more effective use of the library system, and their time spent doing library research.

The impact of the Library Research Skills Program on the operational objectives of the Undergraduate Library has also been positive. Utilizing several approaches provides the necessary flexibility for a limited number of library teaching faculty to interact with a large undergraduate enrollment, including approximately 7,000 new students each year. When the Program was first implemented, library faculty directed students' interaction with the microcomputer tutorials in a classroom setting. The students in each class were assigned in small groups to computer work stations, approximately four to each station, and directed to work through the tutorials during the class period. Librarians answered questions and ensured completion of assignments by the end of the class. This approach, taken at the Program's inception, provided the needed interaction and feedback for changes to the tutorials necessary for the intended future independent study based delivery. In one month, three librarians were able to instruct approximately 1,500 students in the classroom, and still maintain other duties and responsibilities. In addition, the librarians involved in this approach to instruction indicated a much lower sense of "burnout" than previously where the same number of students were provided a personalized, stand-up lecture. This level of instruction activity was maintained over two full academic years utilizing microcomputer equipment originally purchased with approximately $7,500 of building construction/equipment money.

After this initial period of development, experimentation, evaluation and revision of the Program components, the equipment and supporting hardware were moved to the Undergraduate Library's Independent Study Center. This experience has proved to be a cost effective method, freeing librarians to develop more subject specific, course-integrated, and advanced materials for the planned expansion of the instruction program.

In the future, the Undergraduate Library's Research Skills Program will incorporate courses beyond the introductory, heavily-enrolled survey courses now served in this manner. More instructional packages for microcomputers will be developed, particulary as the use of online computer catalogs and the integration of commercial database search services expands. Eventually, the Purdue Undergraduate Library will be organized to allow for more point-of-use, on-demand instructional stations to serve the high volumes of requests for research tutorial assistance when professional assistance is not available. In any event, it is hoped that this type of instruction will afford the professional librarian the latitude to provide extended, specialized, and consultative service at the time it is most needed.

INTEGRATION WITH CHANGING CURRICULUM

The design and nature of the Undergraduate Library Research Skills Program affords potential for application in other disciplines. Since the Program concentrates on a process rather than specific library sources there is a high rate of transferability from the learning situation to other areas of application. In this respect, the Program package is multidisciplinary in scope. A student with a fundamental understanding of the nature and use of information retrieval systems can readily adapt this skill for investigation of available literature in any discipline at the time it is needed.

The variety of requests for use of this Program and the experience acquired from its delivery suggests that future program development should address all potential user groups of academic libraries not just the concerns of undergraduates. The literature regarding future environmental factors beyond the control of libraries also describes its effect on the development and nature of library instruction programs.[1] It is expected that in the future, colleges and universities will have an increasingly heterogeneous group of students including more nontraditional, part-time or evening and international students. These future student populations will be a diverse group whose computer skills and expectations of libraries will vary greatly. The traditional college students of the future, having read less as children, and watched more television may expect professional productions and even "glamorous" user instruction programs. Differences in educational preparation and particularly a student's extent of exposure to both new and traditional library technologies will be pronounced. Students graduating from high schools with new library technologies (online catalogs, CD-ROM indexes, end user searching) will have higher expectations and knowledge of basic library skills than many of their classmates. This will become even more evident as the impact of the technological literacy gap due to the inequitable distribution of school and/or home computing resources becomes manifest.

FUTURE CAI DEVELOPMENT

As the student body does maintain certain similarities in all academic libraries, appropriate instructional packages based on this overall design could be developed for use in other university library systems looking to incorporate similar instruction program objectives. This potential could be further realized if more widespread incorporation of library-related CAI based education was feasible. Many of the current drawbacks for development and incorporation of effective computer-assisted tutorials could be eliminated if programs were designed with operational characteristics to allow for site-specific adaptation of relevant generally accepted program content.

The Purdue Undergraduate Library has developed a computer program of this nature. The "Information Station" program[2] which serves as a computer-assisted extension of reference service has been modified into an authoring software package to allow for wider application through local adaptation of its basic operational characteristics.[3] This program is designed to provide answers to the types of questions that are most frequently presented at the reference desk. The program provides a menu-driven, interactive format for library users to obtain information on such topics as library facilities organization, circulation policies, specific references for subject inquiries, general hints on developing term paper topics, notices of special events and/or workshops, and a listing of the hours for each library in the system. In addition, the program offers a suggestion box and use statistics routine. The information collected through these routines provides a mechanism whereby program design and content can be modified in response to individuals' specific information needs. One additional advantage of the program is that it serves those individuals who do not ask questions at the Reference Desk, and prefer anonymous interaction in this manner.

The features of this program have been incorporated into a software design allowing any library to author their own interactive, unique main menu which then leads users to the corresponding sub-menu selections relevant to specific information screens. The local developer of the program can adjust and design the format of up to 81 screens of main menu, sub-menu, and free text information screens to describe whatever is deemed significant or relative to their library's end-user requirements. This information is then, according to the input design, displayed utilizing the program's automatic processing capabilities. All information that is ultimately presented is determined solely by the local program developer. The development of a working program does not require programming experience and is essentially a fill-in-the-blank process. Editing and/or revisions to the program content are easily accomplished through activation of the screen editing mode in the program. Adjustments to the program to reflect changing end-user and/or program requirements will not disrupt the basic operation of the program and do not require a complete re-write of the original program design.

The programming concepts regarding the development of this software are currently being transferred to the operational design and nature of the Library Research Skills Program components. It is hoped in this process to identify and incorporate the relevant, generally accepted subject content found useful in other libraries so that further site specific refinement of this basic design at the local level can be accomplished as easily as filling in the blank. Since many libraries share in a desire to convey similar concepts in the delivery of their basic library instruction programs, wider application of library related CAI type tutorials to support this process could result through customized programs of this nature.

The flexibility and emphasis of the Library Research Skills Program has assisted the Purdue librarians in working closely with faculty members to provide students with the lifelong learning skills they will need. University of Colorado President Gordon Gee has written,

If, as Robert Hutchins reminded us, "the object of education is to prepare the young to educate themselves throughout their lives," the relationship of our libraries to undergraduate education is clear: We must not only train students to seek the knowledge and wisdom of past generations, but prepare them to use libraries as vital, dynamic resources.[4]

The future development of instruction software needed to complement this library role will make it possible for other institutions to easily create similar but customized instruction programs for their own locations.

REFERENCES

1. Shill, Harold B. "Bibliographic Instruction: Planning for the Electronic Information Environment." *College and Research Libraries*, v. 48(5):433-453, September, 1987.

2. Smith, Dana E. and Steve M. Hutton. "Back at 8:00 AM. Microcomputer Library Reference Support Programs." *Collegiate Microcomputer*, v. 11(4):289-294, Winter, 1984.

3. Smith, Dana E. "QPROMPT: The Reference and Information Authoring Program." *Small Computers in Libraries*, v. 7(10): 24,26, November, 1987.

4. Gee, Gordon as quoted in Breivik, Patricia Senn. "Making the Most of Libraries." *Change*, v. 19(4):44-52, July/August, 1987.

Making Communication:
A Theoretical Framework
for Educating End-Users
of Online Bibliographic
Information Retrieval Systems

Mary M. Huston
Cerise Oberman

SUMMARY. In recognition of the increasing availability of remote database searching, the authors propose an instructional framework for making information retrieval conceptually accessible to end-users. This framework was developed from evidence of information seeking patterns by both experienced and inexperienced researchers. The natural patterns of research must be combined with the conceptual understanding of research as the basis for end-user instruction.

Teaching information retrieval from an electronic format requires a new conceptual framework. This framework must allow students to understand information retrieval in the larger context of their own information universes. The basis of this new framework must be that knowledge retrieval is linked with knowledge creation. Instructional programs must present a framework which links the research

Mary M. Huston is Director, Learning Resources Center and Speech Communications and Women's Studies teacher, Brainerd Community College, Brainerd, MN 56468. She is currently completing her first book, *Making Connections Like a Searcher*, a conceptual guide for end-user searching. Cerise Oberman is Public Services Planning Officer, University of Minnesota Libraries, 449 Wilson Library, Minneapolis, MN 55455. She is currently piloting an end-user gateway project linking an online public access catalog (OPAC) to Bibliographic Retrieval Services (BRS).

process, the research literatures, and the electronic access formats with the innate information seeking patterns of researchers. As such, library instruction must focus on developing a conceptual teaching model appropriate for addressing the unique challenges of electronic information retrieval.

EMERGING INFORMATION ENVIRONMENT

In the last decade, the online industry has come of age. However, only in the last few years has search activity passed from mediated access — i.e., librarians — to direct access — i.e., end-users. This trend has been fed by the increasingly wide availability of microcomputers and their fusion with telecommunications. This combination has allowed information to become more quickly and readily available than ever before. Speed and accessibility, however, are only two of the ways that research is changing. A recent national survey of scholars provides evidence that academic researchers are witnessing rapidly changing methods by which scholars conduct their research. In this study, faculty respondents ranked online database and online catalog access as the most important computer applications not related to word processing (Morton & Price, 1986). This suggests that the microcomputer has gained recognition as a retrieval tool.

Another measure of the growing interest in online retrieval is evidenced in the enthusiastic response to online instruction seminars offered in a number of institutions. At the University of Minnesota, Twin Cities campus, for instance, the Electronic Library Series — which offers courses in how to select an online vendor, how to select database management software, how to construct a search strategy, etc. — are met with overwhelming response. Moreover, as faculty are becoming increasingly knowledgeable and appreciative of online information retrieval, they are likely to require their students to use this method of information retrieval.

Some evidence of this is already apparent. Chemistry, for instance, was an early discipline to embrace online information retrieval as part of the student curriculum. Another example can be found in political science. At the University of Minnesota, for instance, students use the Legislative database as part of their course study. Even in the humanities—where development of databases and, therefore, usage has been slow—interest in online databases is occurring. This emerging interest has been further fueled by The Research Libraries Group (RLG) which has added—or is in the process of adding—a number of humanities-based databases. *Eighteenth Century Short Title Catalog*, the *Medieval and Early Modern Databank*, and the *Modern Language Association (MLA) Research-in-Progress* are among the new files.[1]

A major factor in scholars' awareness of online information retrieval systems is the in-house, online public access catalogs (OPACs) that are now available in most major institutional libraries. For faculty and students alike, the online catalog represents their first direct interaction with electronic retrieval. While their perceived success with using an OPAC is much greater than their actual success (New York University Libraries, 1984), this has not deterred libraries—such as the University of Texas at Austin, the University of Michigan, and the University of California at Berkeley—from offering users direct access to a variety of online systems. These online experiments are simply a prelude to the more integrated information environment which is now developing.

Projected developments at these and other universities suggest that OPACs will become the mechanism for reaching beyond the boundaries of libraries' collections as gateways to a variety of information resources. Several universities are developing switching systems between their OPACs and databases located both on and off their campuses. For instance, Ohio State University has integrated several bibliographic resource files directly into their online catalog; University of Pennsylvania provides a gateway from Pennline to *ABI Info* (a major business database); the University of Minnesota is piloting a gateway between LUMINA, its OPAC, and Bibliographic Retrieval Services (BRS) via the IBM Information Network. According to Rowland Brown, OCLC, "there will be more online catalogs and more publically accessible information databases and services" available in the near future. "More libraries in the university and college community will distribute information by means of personal computers located anywhere on campus" (Gordon, 1987, p. 44).

The combination of microcomputers and online information resources has rightly prompted predictions of the emergence of end-user searching (e.g., Meadow, 1979; Stevenson, 1980). It is equally clear that the full potential for end-user searching has not yet been fully realized (Borgman & Case, 1985). Carol Fenichel, in her review of research on searching databases, attributes this to the fact that "although considerable attention has been focused on the problems of the user . . . in online systems, there has been little substantial research devoted to solutions" (Fenichel, 1980, p. 108). While technological advances have made information *available*, they have not made it necessarily *accessible*.

Many studies confirm the difficulties that end-users experience with formulation and execution of searches (Borgman, 1986c; Fenichel, 1981; Janke, 1984; King & Baker, 1987). Key to strategizing is their mental model of the information retrieval system. Borgman has determined that a mental model represents the structure and internal relationships of the system. An end-user's mental model facilitates understanding of the system — i.e., making inferences about it and predicting its behavior. "It can be helpful (or perhaps even necessary) for dealing with the device" (Borgman, 1986b, p. 48). The challenge, then, for instruction librarians is to develop conceptual teaching models which effectively inform students' model building.

CONCEPTUAL FRAMEWORKS
FOR ONLINE SEARCHING

With roots in the bibliographic instruction (BI) movement, library-sponsored training and education programs have emerged in recent years to support end-users' access. Lacking a user-based theoretical model for online education, efforts have typically been "balancing instruction about the procedural aspects of searching with instruction about the conceptual aspects of searching" (Baker & Sandore, 1987, p. 192).

Online curriculum was initially rudimentary, based exclusively on designers' and instructors' points of view, probably reflective of the discomfort of the instructors (Baker, 1986), who themselves were only just becoming familiar with online search tools. Then, as instructors integrated online tools into their research repertoire, instructional programs began to develop which modeled the intellectual integration of online searching with the search analysts' research skills and processes (Baker & Sandore, 1987, p. 194).

More recently, as librarians' understanding of online retrieval deepened and matured, search analysts and bibliographic instructors alike have employed concept-based instruction built around the characteristics of a database. By explicitly employing concepts, librarians hoped that students would be able to transfer this information to a wide variety of electronic information systems (Lippincott, 1987, p. 183).

Most recently, instructional approaches have incorporated familiar interactions from end-users' lives into instruction. One such approach, which employs references to databases, highlights end-users' life experiences. For instance, these instruction programs include references to automated banking transactions, talking cash machines, mail ordering, and airline and hotel reservations (Baker & Sandore, 1987). Using the database model in instruction allows end-users to draw on their experiences as a means of illustrating "the concept of a database as a collection of records in machine-readable format, accessible in a number of ways by a defined set of commands and protocols" (Baker & Sandore, 1987, p. 201). To date, however, few educational programs have been developed which are based on patterns which people use to access information (Huston, 1988).

THE TACOMA PROJECT

At The Evergreen State College in Tacoma, Washington, an educational program was developed (Huston & Perry, 1987) for adult students who were not conversant with databases. While the curriculum design had its roots in educating students in a manner that engaged their personal conceptual frameworks and developed generic information handling abilities (Oberman & Linton, 1982), it sought to extend its applications for online instruction.

Tacoma curriculum evaluation demonstrated that students are best taught by building on individuals' experiential frameworks and reminding them "of what they do know" (Huston, 1983, p. 186). By explaining the information gathering process with examples from everyday life, individuals seem to be able to transfer their existing knowledge more effectively to the searching of online catalogs, bibliographic databases, and other automated services.[2]

In 1986-87, a research project was undertaken to identify the knowledge used in accessing information by sixty-five culturally diverse, inexperienced researchers and thirty-nine experienced researchers. The novices were students in a research class who were charged with locating information on a subject of interest to them, without any formal instruction. Both online and traditional research tools were available to them. The experienced researchers were both librarians[3] and scholars[4] who were asked to describe their information handling processes. Using an interview methodology, a rich picture was constructed of all participants' information seeking patterns. This was used to classify their activities from their viewpoints (Huston, 1988).

Inexperienced Researchers

Novice researchers characteristically reported that, as one informant stated, ". . . I have a lot of information in myself . . . ." Typically, they identified an important issue from out of their experiences because something in their situations did not make sense to them. They then applied their existing knowledge about where information resided in society to the identification of appropriate sources of information. They generally consulted either informal sources — e.g., friends or co-workers — or institutional sources — e.g., local government agencies or civic associations. In their negotiations with these potential information sources, they generally reported being satisfied with their efforts in navigating their ways through the labyrinths of those communication networks.

As one novice researcher said, "I found out from my research how much information you can obtain yourself." Researchers who gathered information from community and/or government sources, for instance, reported highly informative, interactive experiences between themselves and their informants. Novices' experiences were characteristically generative, as represented by changes in both their lines of inquiry and the meanings they attributed to the information provided.

Their information retrieval events were represented as "alive," "happening," perhaps due to the living, human nature of the information providers who were functioning, in effect, as "interfaces" between the bodies of knowledge and the requestors of information. Or, perhaps, researchers' enthusiasm was attributable to their familiarity with the informal and institutional environments. In any case, the levels of comfort and success reported in their remarks suggest that they felt "at home" in those environments. Novices' interview data revealed a well instilled sense of the structure and organization of society's information sources and an equally well expressed ability to gather information from contextually familiar sources.

While students were very able to obtain information through community and institutional sources, they were less able to retrieve library information through manual or online methods. In the former, students expressed only qualified capability or dissatisfaction in information retrieval. In the latter, none reported success with online information retrieval, despite the availability of available "user-friendly" IR systems. Library and database research were represented as unfamiliar information environments. Unlike their accomplishments in the other two domains, where researchers seemed to feel in control, novices typically expressed either ambivalence or dissatisfaction about any but librarian-guided information gathering experiences. In their interviews, they referred to library tools and scholarly literatures as closed systems which they found to be neither inviting nor hospitable.

Experienced Researchers' Results

Experienced researchers reported using information to "make connections" — i.e., to "amplify their lives" through accessing "provocative lines of communication," creating a "community of the moment," bonding through shared values and ideas. Experiencing their disciplinary literature as "community memory," subject experts satisfied their information needs by connecting with ideas and their originators. Information searching was reported to be a generative, social experience, and an important part of the process by which knowledge was produced. Stated another way, the interconnected thoughts embodied in scholarly discussions were experienced as "intricate threads" which comprised a "networking system." Researchers perceived themselves as part of dynamic informal and formal scholarly communications networks.

The vitality of the knowledge creation process permeated the interview responses. That which was taken to be "knowledge" emerged as a creation of human beings' interacting thoughts, according to which *information retrieval* should be thought of as *information generation*. Experts spoke, for instance, of obtaining new understanding through the retrieval of bibliographic citations from online IR systems. They reported that their responses to particular documents changed both their definitions of other documents and conceptions of what they wanted from future information sources.

The scholarly literature was understood to embody interactions between peoples' ideas. By following the lines of inquiry reflected in footnotes, for instance, scholars identified intellectually antecedent ideas, including their transformations and reinterpretations. Bibliographic control systems, then, provided surrogate representations of disciplines' formal communications and, through retrieval capabilities, enabled researchers to make connections with relevant participants in intellectual communities.

Experts' statements revealed that fundamental to their online searching decisions was an understanding of "what" – i.e., that the "knowledge" represented in the bibliographic database entries is an outcome of interaction among members of intellectual communities who advance ideas in ways particular to their fields and disciplines. Similarly, their search decisions also required an understanding of "why" information is sought, including the role of both formal and informal communication in knowledge creation. Their subsequent logic in strategizing "how" to retrieve online information emerged from what their inquiries imply both substantively and bibliographically – conceptual frameworks which have been elaborated by significant works (McInnis, 1982; Keresztesi, 1982) in this area.

Raymond McInnis, for instance, has suggested that in retrieval, searchers seek either substantive information, the fluid, cognitive content of a body of literature, or bibliographic information, the chronologically fixed published records of research contributions, or a combination of both (McInnis, 1982). His writings underscore expert researchers' observations that the shape of the network of disciplined inquiry, the process of retaining and eliminating substantive material through consensus, occurs as a natural process of the communication process, as does the development of the bibliographic counterpart.

PROPOSED THEORETICAL FRAMEWORK

Through analysis of the Tacoma Project data, a conceptual model of the online retrieval environment emerged which typified "thinking like a searcher" for both inexperienced and experienced searchers (Huston, 1988). This conceptual model suggests that the online search environment functions as a dynamic network. Hine (1977) has characterized this type of dynamic structure as being comprised of three essential qualities. Information networks are (1) segmented, composed of autonomous segments which are organizationally self-sufficient. They are (2) decentralized, connected by horizontal linkages such as overlapping membership. Networks are held together through a fabric of shared values and unified ideas which holds the decentralized segments of a network together in a dynamic pattern of interaction. So, finally, they are also defined by (3) ideological bonds.

These qualities were all present in the reports of both novices and experts. In their descriptions of familiar information environments, all experienced the existence of autonomous segments which are organizationally self-sufficient—e.g., private colleges and local cemeteries (novices) and medical literature and legal case law (experts). They reported that these environments were decentralized, connected by horizontal linkages—e.g., personal referrals (novices) and expert referrals and bibliographic citations (experts). Additionally, through the shared values constituting their respective missions, information producing entities contained in the three domains displayed ideological bonds, the third criteria for networks.

The research results suggest that the communication networks employed in online information retrieval strategizing share commonalities with communication networks among neighborhood friends and invisible college colleagues; people "naturally" participate in a variety of communication networks in gathering needed information. It therefore seems appropriate to acknowledge online environments as a component of the information universe and, in fact, to initiate online instruction with a discussion of everyday information networking.

With the presentation of such a sociologically-based framework, end-users can be confident that, just as their questions originate out of their experiences, so, too, do those of scholars. To make connections with scholarly thinkers, student searchers must understand what kind of ideas are entertained by members of academic communities, including by whom and for whom. They must also be able to distinguish the differences between communication in social communities and those in scholarly communities, including the functions of informal or formal scholarly networks. With this preparation, students could then appropriately be introduced to the particulars of retrieval through the online information network.

Huston's Tacoma Project curriculum design assumed that, by building novices' conceptual awareness through incrementally adding levels of detail to their existent knowledge of communication networks, neophyte searchers can be prepared for online information retrieval. This theoretical approach was assessed through a first level product test of an instructional search guide—*Making Connections—Thinking Like a Searcher*—which synthesizes the communications networks and database model approaches. Twelve informants representing both end-user educators and end-users from law, medicine, science, technology, and education were asked to evaluate the manuscript as to its immediate "usefulness."

Evaluators were in agreement that the conceptual approach could offer important pre-search guidance. Presenting an explanation of online searching through the framework of people's everyday searching experiences produced feelings of intellectual accessibility for evaluators. A technical writer from a *Fortune* 500 corporation appreciated the "authentic sense-making portrayal of how we search for information." A graduate student in special education liked the "idea that a person down the street is struggling through the same process that I, a potential researcher, am struggling through." An instructor of rural Wisconsin end-users applauded the recognition that, with a little supplementary information, readers can learn to "talk right" for a scholarly search and "work the system, rather than let the system work you."

The approach taken in this search guide "will show people how to begin. It will encourage them," said the biomedical researcher.

Then, he continued, they can read a "Grateful Med" manual to find out "what pushing each button [on the keyboard] will give them." He felt that the conceptual nature of the search guide would prepare end-users to search intelligently both now and in the future when gateways and integrated catalogs require a multitude of "logical decisions," including consideration of research queries, knowledge biases, indexing schemas, appropriate databases, document types, and retrieval approaches.

Commenting on the general usefulness of situating online retrieval activities within a model of the human communications network, a librarian educator at a major research university said that such an explanation has "immense educational possibilities for the public and, in academic communities, for students, staff, and faculty." Why? Because unlike "the conceptual underpinnings currently employed to teach the accessing of electronic data" [which are both tool and format specific], this model, "regardless of future formats, serves as a guide to finding information."

CONCLUSION

There is little research in the area of information seeking patterns. The Tacoma Project points to the need to more thoroughly study the process of research patterns, particularly those of inexperienced researchers. The data from such studies should further inform the design of end-user instruction. It should strive to incorporate the information universe of end-users as a foundation for building a solid conceptual understanding of information retrieval in an online environment.

NOTES

1. Research Libraries Group is presently conducting a pilot project which provides direct access to the Research Libraries Information Network (RLIN) and special databases by faculty.

2. The program online education text, *Making Connection — Thinking Like a Searcher* (Huston), has been pilot tested.

3. Bibliography experts who contributed to the study held positions as bibliographic instruction librarians, end-user trainers, information systems designers/planners, professional search analysts, and reference librarians.

4. Subject experts were interviewed from the fields of African-American

Studies, Asian-American Studies, anthropology, artificial intelligence, Chicano Studies, cognitive science, cross-cultural psychology, information science, Native American Studies, social psychology, and technology integration.

REFERENCES

Baker, B. (1986). A new direction for online catalog instruction. *Information Technology and Libraries 5*, 35-41.

Baker, B. & Sandore, B. (1987). The online catalog and instruction – Maintaining the balance on the log. In M. Reichel and M. A. Ramey (Eds.), *Conceptual frameworks for bibliographic education – Theory into practice* (pp.192-206). Littleton, Colorado: Libraries Unlimited, Inc.

Borgman, C. L. & Case, D. O. (1985). University faculty use of computerized databases: An assessment of needs and resources. *Online Review 9*, 307-332.

Borgman, C. L. (1986a). Human-computer interaction with information retrieval systems: Understanding complex communication behavior. *Progress in Communication Sciences 7*, 91-122.

Borgman, C. L. (1986b). The user's mental model of an information retrieval system: An experiment on a prototype online catalog. *International Journal of Man-Machine Studies 24*, 47-64.

Borgman, C. L. (1986c). Why are online catalogs so hard to use? *Journal of the American Society for Information Science 37*, 387-400.

Fenichel, C. H. (1980). The process of searching online bibliographic databases: A review of research. *Library Research 2*, 107-127.

Fenichel, C. H. (1981). Online searching: Measures that discriminate among users with different types of experience. *Journal of the American Society for Information Science 32*, 23-32.

Gordon, H. A. (1987). Online interview: Rowland Brown of OCLC. *Online 11*, 38-44.

Hine, V. (1977). The basic paradigm of a future socio-cultural system. *World Issues 2*, 19-22.

Huston, M. M. (1983). Rethinking our approach for research instruction. *Research Strategies 1*, 185-187.

Huston, M. M. & Perry, S. L. (1987). Information instruction: Considerations for empowerment. *Research Strategies 5*, 70-77.

Huston, M. M. (1988). A theoretical framework and an instructional model for educating end-users of online bibliographic information retrieval systems: A research monograph. Unpublished doctoral dissertation.

Janke, R. V. (1984). Online after six: End user searching comes of age. *Online 8*, 15-31.

Keresztesi, M. (1982). The science of bibliography: Theoretical implications for bibliographic instruction. In C. Oberman and K. Strauch (Eds.), *Theories of bibliographic education* (pp. 1-26). New York, New York: R. R. Bowker.

King, D. & Baker, B. (1987). Human aspects of library technology: Implications for academic library user education. In C. A. Mellon (Ed.), *Bibliographic instruction – The second generation* (pp. 85-107). Littleton, Colorado: Libraries Unlimited, Inc.

Lippincott, J. K. (1987). End-user instruction: Emphasis on concepts. In M. Reichel and M. A. Ramey (Eds.), *Conceptual frameworks for bibliographic education: Theory into practice* (pp. 183-191). Littleton, Colorado: Libraries Unlimited.

McInnis, R. (1982). Do metaphors make good sense in teaching research strategy? In C. Oberman and K. Strauch (Eds.), *Theories of bibliographic education* (pp. 47-74). New York, New York: R. R. Bowker.

Meadow, C. T. (1979). Online searching and computer programming: Some behavioral similarities (or . . . why end users will eventually take over the terminal). *Online 3*, 49-52.

Morton, H. C. & Price, A. J. (1986). The ACLS survey of scholars: Views on publications, computers, libraries. *Scholarly Communication: Notes on Publishing, Library Trends, and Research in the Humanities 5*, 1-16.

New York University Libraries. (1984). *A study of an online catalog from a public service perspective: Final report.* Washington, D.C.: Office of Management Studies, Association of Research Libraries.

Oberman, C. & Linton, R. A. (1982). Guided design: Teaching library research as problem-solving. In C. Oberman and K. Strauch (Eds.), *Theories of bibliographic education: Designs for teaching* (pp. 111-134). New York, New York: R. R. Bowker.

Stevenson, M. B. (1980). Information and the academic community. *Aslib Proceedings 32*, 78-81.

Emerging Microcomputer Technology: Impact on Bibliographic Instruction

Rao Aluri

INTRODUCTION

The basic purpose of library use instruction is to enable the library users, typically college and high school students, to learn how to access the resources that are available in the library. Of course, accessing or retrieving the resources alone is not sufficient. The user should be able to read critically, understand, and make use of information contained in those resources in writing a term paper, thesis, dissertation, journal article or a book. In a typical library use instruction program, the latter aspect is not emphasized for a variety of practical reasons. Critical reading, synthesizing and writing a coherent paper are considered province of the classroom instructors. However, the current microcomputer technology — in terms of both hardware and software — may mean the extension of the scope of bibliographic instruction. The current generation of bibliographic instruction programs should take into consideration the available microcomputer technology and fully exploit it — keeping in mind the basic objective of the library instruction program.

INFORMATION RETRIEVAL

Gone are the days when we have directed hosts of uninterested students to a series of indexes and abstracts, card catalogs, and other resources and told them to copy the relevant bibliographic citations. As librarians, we were absolutely sure that it was the right

Rao Aluri is Librarian, Burr-Brown, 6730 South Tucson Blvd., Tucson, AZ 85706.

213

way of collecting the bibliographic information. What we often ignored is the time it takes to do the bibliographic research, difficulty of understanding the disparate citation styles, jumble of inexplicable abbreviations, and difficulties with separate and often conflicting subject indexing policies of the retrieval tools. The above problems are exacerbated when the tendency on the part of the undergraduates is to postpone the library research as long as possible and then expect the library to miraculously produce all the needed journal articles, books and other resources. In essence, there was always an unresolved conflict between the expectations of library users, instructional librarians and those of the students.

The currently available technology might resolve that conflict in favor of the students. Now many of the information retrieval tools such as indexes and abstracts and library catalogs are available in machine-readable form. For example, many of the significant indexing and abstracting tools are available on-line — e.g., Wilsonline, Dialog, BRS, and ORBIT. Medline, LEXIS and other such services are designed to serve the professional students. On top of that, a significant number of these services are likely to appear in the form of CD-ROM accessible by means of microcomputer-resident retrieval programs — thereby vastly reducing the fear of incurring huge telecommunications and databases charges. With CD-ROM technology, there is no danger in the students making mistakes in their retrieval strategies. After all, they can start over again with the only worry being time. Further, microcomputer-based systems are much more user-friendly and less intimidating than the main-frame-based systems. Adding to these resources is the availability of library on-line catalogs — making retrieval of library materials much easier. There is no longer a need for students, using paper and pencil, to copy down vast amounts of bibliographic data — making numerous mistakes on the way. Now, these information retrieval tools come with printers. In less than half-an-hour, a student can walk away from the computer terminal with an excellent set of bibliographic citations. Note that, in this case, the notion of bibliographic excellence as defined by librarians may coincide with the undergraduates' notion of excellence — relevant papers and books retrieved with minimum effort and time!

Is there something wrong with this situation? Not unless you believe that the students should sweat like we did not too long ago. There is nothing wrong unless you believe that hard work and tension involved in the old ways are good for your soul. After all, this type of thinking is not new. The curriculum of early colleges emphasized Greek and Latin precisely because studying Greek and Latin was supposed to strengthen mental and moral disciplines — many librarians still harbor such views.

Another significant development in the databases is the increasing availability of full-text databases. For example, a number of articles indexed in Magazine Index (File 47) of Dialog system are full texts of articles. Likewise, full texts of articles of a number of journals are also available on-line. In the not too distant future, full texts will migrate to CD-ROM systems.

What is the importance of full-text databases? One of the major problems faced by the library users is the two-step process involved in retrieving books, journal articles or other resources. First, the student searches indexes, abstracts and other such bibliographic tools, copies the information and then tries to locate the actual document. In the case of journal articles, this may involve an additional step — locating the needed journal through another index that lists the periodicals and their holdings that are located in the library. A similar situation may occur in the case of microforms and other such material. What it means is that the library puts a host of hurdles between the user and the document that is sought by the user. Usually, this process discourages many users and they may resort to techniques such as browsing through one or two periodicals or browsing the library shelves, completely bypassing the information retrieval tools. Librarians may frown upon this situation but many students would rather not go through the drudgery of "library research."

DATABASE MANAGEMENT PROGRAMS

Along with the microcomputer came easy to use database management programs to enable the users to compile, edit, sort and print bibliographic citations. While most of the database management softwares were not really meant to handle bibliographic citations, there were some that were designed especially for bibliographic data. One of these specialized database systems is Pro-Cite.

Pro-Cite recognizes over 20 different bibliographic formats—books, journals, conference proceedings, and technical reports. Library users choose the appropriate bibliographic format before entering data into the database. If, for instance, the library user selects conference proceedings, field names that are relevant to this bibliographic format are displayed on the screen. The user, using the screen editing methods, simply enters the data into the appropriate fields—author name, title of the paper, name of the conference, and publisher. The user can prepare an abstract if he or she so chooses and assign subject headings to the bibliographic record. If mistakes were made or additional information needs to be entered into the record, the user can edit the record to make the necessary changes. The user can sort the records, search the records for occurrences of certain words and phrases, and print the entire database, or a selected portion of the databases, depending on the need. The bibliographic records can be printed out alphabetically by author, title, or subject headings. But the most intriguing and exciting aspect of the Pro-Cite is that the bibliographic records can be printed out in any one of a number of citation styles—e.g., APA and MLA. The user can print the database in APA style in one minute and in the next minute can instruct the system to format the record into MLA style. That is, users no longer have to maintain stacks of 3×5 cards with various notations, index terms, and so on. All that drudgery will be handled by the software. The user does not have to succumb to the tyranny of citation styles—one does not have to remember which style requires quotations around the title and which does not, which style requires periods in certain locations and which requires semicolons and so on of these nasty little annoying requirements. On top of that, Pro-Cite would format the record for appropriate style consistently—it does not forget the rules from one minute to another. Again, most people who have ever written term papers would not have any difficulty remembering the terror struck by these citation style requirements. Now, what all users have to worry about is having the author's name, title of the paper or the book, etc. correct and leave the rest to the computer. In other words, the use of this type of microcomputer-based database management system would immensely help the user in maintaining an organized bibliography.

DOWNLOADING

Downloading is the next logical step from online databases and database management programs. If bibliographic data already exists in machine readable form, why re-key all that data into your local microcomputer database? Why not transfer that data directly from the online database or online catalog into your own database? As luck would have it, it is perfectly feasible and this type of downloading was done for a number of years. DIALOG and BRS, for example, can display the bibliographic records in their systems in tagged format. That is, the tagged format identifies each piece of information in the record by a tag. For example, author field can be identified as AU, title field can be identified as TI, etc. As long as the fields are so identified, it would not be difficult to transfer those records field by field into your own database. The downloading is done first by capturing the bibliographic data into a floppy or hard disk file on the microcomputer. In the case of Pro-Cite, the second step is to use an intermediate software that reads the file on the user's computer disk and transfers the data into your pro-Cite database. In the case of other database management systems, different procedures may have to be adopted—but transferring the data is possible and is widely done.

Transferring the bibliographic data into your own database saves enormous time. This is especially suitable for those who need to have an updated bibliography and who can and do search the online catalogs and online databases on their topics at regular intervals. For instance, this is a wonderful way of maintaining updated bibliographies of current interest by reference departments. Usually, however, transferring the records is not always problem-free. If the user is downloading data from multiple database vendors and multiple online catalogs, bibliographic inconsistencies arise. However, if the database system that is adopted by the user has a good editor, editing the records for consistency is much easier than typing in the whole record from scratch.

Another type of downloading that is of immense use is downloading the numeric data into formats that can be used by spreadsheet softwares such as Lotus 1-2-3. For instance, financial data on companies recorded in Compact Disclosure can be downloaded into Lotus 1-2-3. The significance of such downloading is that this numeric data can be further manipulated by the user—e.g., represent that data into a graphic form and verify the accuracy of data. This type of downloading would be enormously appreciated by students and faculties in business management and accounting areas.

WORD PROCESSORS

Now that the student has collected some citations, examined the corresponding documents, thought through what has been read, and taken notes, s/he is now ready to start writing the paper. Everybody knows that word processors come into play here and that they are a hundred-fold improvement over typewriters. Word processors free the users from a number of trivial but exacting details, such as top and bottom margins, left and right margins, numbering pages and so on. Now these things are not as concrete and as threatening as typing a paper using a typewriter. Spelling errors, revisions in text, moving paragraphs, inserting and deleting paragraphs and all such activities do not pose as much of a problem as they did in the days of typewriters. Some word processors allow the students to start from outlines of their papers first and then write section by section. In such systems, if the student wants to move a whole section, all he or she has to do is go to the outline and move the appropriate section heading—the text associated with that heading automatically moves to the new location. Students, in other words, can relax and they can edit and reedit their papers to their hearts' content. It is a great sense of freedom.

Add to the basic features of word processors the more advanced features such as spelling checkers, online thesauri, and grammar and style checkers. With a few keystrokes, students can check spellings of all the words in their papers. They can invoke a thesaurus and look for alternate ways of expressing certain notions, and can command their computers to check their writing for some obvious errors. In fact, word processors really help the classroom instructors to do their job well — suggesting revisions and showing how the suggested revisions improved the paper. This type of revising the drafts could not be realistically done in the typewriter model of writing papers.

The word processing scene is further dramatically altered by the appearance of Microsoft Bookshelf which consists of a number of often used reference sources stored on a CD-ROM disc. Now, the students have, literally at their finger tips, access to tools such as *Bartlett's Quotations*, bibliographies, style manuals, and fact books. Microsoft Bookshelf is only a tip of the iceberg. It is conceivable that other vendors will provide similar access to other reference sources such as encyclopedias, and specialized dictionaries.

HARDWARE RESOURCES

Within a short time, it is possible that every library will have one or more scanners that can scan texts and graphics from a written page and store that data in machine-readable form. This data can then be transferred into a word processor so that the writing can be enhanced by graphics. There are already a number of microcomputer softwares that allow the users to create their own graphics and incorporate them into their word processors. Along with these, the availability of desktop publishing softwares and powerful laser printers with a wide variety of typographical styles can spruce up the average dull academic paper significantly.

INTEGRATING SOFTWARES

What gives enormous power to all these developments is the ability to transfer value-added data from one software to another. For instance, communication software is used to access online catalogs and online databases and store the bibliographic data on a diskette. This stored bibliographic data can then be transferred into a database file. From the database, the user can format the bibliographic records into a standard citation style format and store the formatted bibliographic information in another disk-based file. This file, in turn, can be transferred into a word processing file. Likewise, numeric data can be processed by a spreadsheet program and the results of that processing can be transferred into another word processing file. This type of integration makes the microcomputer a scholar's workstation'' — almost everything can be done from microcomputer.

CONCLUSION

The significance of these developments is the changing notion of library. Libraries are slowly being transformed into electronic document delivery systems and paperless institutions. Users of libraries will discover that the major function of the library is to provide them with information in a form that is usable by them. They will demand document delivery — preferably in an electronic form — rather than being taught about how to retrieve the information. They will demand more and better computer resources so that they can do their work efficiently.

It would be hard to convince the students to learn about the structure of their disciplines. In fact, the electronic revolution is already blurring the distinction between primary, secondary, and tertiary sources. For instance, a full-text journal that is online is a primary source. The indexing attached to it — both machine-created and human assigned indexing — transforms the database into its own secondary source. Anybody who searches for a topic and extracts data from the database is creating an ad hoc tertiary source. Given the fact that even books are stored in electronic formats — prior to printing — there is a good chance that even full-length books will be accessible through online databases or CD ROM systems thereby further blurring distinctions between primary and secondary sources.

Another consequence is that students and teachers can place greater emphasis on areas that matter — for example, developing a coherent and well thought out argument — rather than on trivial details that surround the paper writing ritual. Bibliographies become what they are — means of clearly and unambiguously identifying the sources that were consulted by the student rather than some type of stylistic witchcraft. In that sense, the emerging technology is nothing but a boon.

There are, of course, problems. While the collection and manipulation of information is much easier, there is a danger that the technology is replacing one type of hurdle by another. For instance, now the students have to worry about DOS commands, mastering mouse moves such as pointing and clicking, memorizing commands for a variety of softwares, the danger of accidentally deleting files and plain computer phobia. In addition, there is a danger that, with all the glitter, the student will lose sight of the basic purpose of library research and focus on all other interesting activities such as downloading and massaging the electronically collected data rather than critically evaluating the information, thinking, formulating hypotheses, and writing a well-argued paper.

Another problem is: who should be responsible for teaching all this computer literacy—library, microcomputer center, writing or classroom instructor? As organizers and retrievers of information, librarians should be willing to assist the students in terms of searching online databases, downloading, and designing students' personal databases. Online searching should be much more routine and should be extended to all legitimate users. Having said that, is teaching about designing databases really part of reference librarians' jobs? If it were, we are adding another responsibility to the ever growing list of reference librarians' responsibility—not to mention about changing printer ribbons and papers, and troubleshooting with computer equipment. If the responsibility of teaching about computers is taken over by classroom faculty, they may not place as much emphasis on library information resources and they may not demonstrate as effectively as they should the interrelationships between library resources and writing of the paper. Likewise, people working for microcomputer centers tend to be more technology-oriented rather than application-oriented. They would rather discuss how to do certain things with as few keystrokes as possible rather than focusing on information gathering, assimilation and the writing process itself. In any case, providing appropriate computer hardware and software training to the students would be a problem for some time.

In the end, there is no guarantee that, with all this availability of information resources, computer technologies, and assistance from librarians and other professionals, students will be able to write a "better" term paper in terms of content. The papers may look better in terms of techniques but they may still suffer from the same old term paper problems.

Microcomputers
and Bibliographic Instruction

Betsy Baker
Susan Swords Steffen

SUMMARY. In recent years, bibliographic instruction librarians have begun to explore appropriate applications of microcomputers in user education activities. This paper highlights three microcomputer instructional projects which provide a glimpse of the possibilities ahead for enhancing user education services through microcomputer technology. Implications of these activities for library users, librarians, and libraries are discussed.

The widespread use and availability of microcomputers throughout our society challenges academic librarians to make optimal use of these new and powerful tools. As microcomputers become mainstream resources outside the library, they can no longer be regarded as alternative resources within the library. Across the country, librarians are experimenting with using microcomputers to accomplish old tasks more efficiently and exploring the new horizons which microcomputers open to us. The library literature abounds with reports of library applications of commercial and locally developed software. But, it has only been in recent years that bibliographic instruction librarians have begun to explore appropriate applications of microcomputers in user education activities. In this paper, we will highlight three projects undertaken at Northwestern University, which provide a glimpse of the possibilities ahead for

---

Betsy Baker is Head, Reference Department, 1935 Sheridan Rd., Northwestern University, Evanston, IL 60201. Susan Swords Steffen is Head, Schaffner Library, 339 E. Chicago Ave., Northwestern University, Chicago, IL 60611.

enhancing user education services through microcomputing technology.

Approaches to adopting new technology vary among institutions according to the resources available and to the level of interest of the librarians involved. Many use microcomputers primarily to support existing instruction programs with word processing and records management applications.[1] Others use microcomputers to facilitate end user searching and instruction programs.[2] Some look to microcomputers as tools which will help ease the burden of providing bibliographic instruction to large numbers of students by using computer-assisted instruction methods.[3] A few libraries are beginning to expand their instruction programs to include broader information management issues. Finally, other innovative librarians are assuming full responsibility for teaching computer literacy skills campus-wide.[4]

Librarians at Northwestern University are among those exploring the uses of microcomputers to enhance instructional programs. Northwestern has a long history of experimentation with library automation beginning in the early 1970s with the in-house development of NOTIS (Northwestern Online Totally Integrated System) and more recently with two large scale research efforts: the Online Public Access Project and a Council of Library Resources funded project entitled "Educating the Online Catalog User."[5] Experience with these projects has led instruction planners at Northwestern to believe future bibliographic instruction efforts should focus, not on further online catalog instruction, but rather on building students' skills in information retrieval which can be used to access a variety of information technologies. We believe that microcomputers provide an exciting medium for furthering this aspect of instructional services. Not only are students able to gain experience in using microcomputers for information retrieval and skills which may be useful in other contexts, but they are beginning to value computer-based information technology as playing a central role in the research process. As an important by-product of this work, librarians are increasing their understanding of the capabilities of microcomputers which will benefit not only the Northwestern University Library but the profession as a whole.

Our early explorations have focused on three major program areas: (1) interactive instructional technology as a means of educating users about library automation; (2) development of teaching software by Brian Nielsen Assistant University Librarian for Branch Libraries and Information Technology to be used with a microcomputer to demonstrate online information retrieval in the classroom and; (3) the establishment of the Schaffner Library, a branch library located on Northwestern's Chicago campus, as an "electronic library laboratory."

First, as an off-shoot of the "Educating the Online Catalog User" project, the viability of developing a computer-assisted instructional package for the LUIS online catalog was explored. The appeal of a computer-assisted module for instructing students in the use of LUIS was viewed as a potentially attractive addition to existing instructional services in the Library. With the assistance of a Council on Library Resources/University of Michigan Graduate Library School of Library Science Intern some progress was made in producing an interactive instructional program for the online catalog that could be packaged for self-instructional use.

The instructional design was developed on an IBM PC with the IBM version of PILOT (Programmed Inquiry, Learning or Teaching). PILOT provides a system for producing software for instructional purposes that is individualized, using the interactive capability of the computer. The instructional computer modules developed during the project were based on specific learning objectives outlined in the earlier online catalog project.[6]

While microcomputers seemingly place such CAI within the reach of instructional librarians, the staff time still required for useful software development hinders its use. This was the case at Northwestern where we found the staff time to be of such significance that it was difficult to justify the heavy expenditure of time for something that was to be only one facet of an instructional endeavor. This is not to say that CAI has lost its appeal for us, but, rather, we look forward to the introduction of new instructional design software that might not require so much programming to continue development work in this area. Although we did complete one instructional module, we have held back on devoting time to this work. Fully developed, such an instructional program would prove especially useful for staff training, particularly training of student assistants. It may be with this goal in mind we complete the programming in the future.

Our next effort led us outside the library to cooperate with another major computer literacy effort on campus. Over the course of two terms, the Head of the Reference Department presented lectures on bibliographic retrieval systems to the Microcomputer Literacy courses offered by the Program on Computing in the Arts and Sciences. These lectures were intended to alert students to the growing importance of large bibliographic databases and other information retrieval systems as tools for research. That is, their purpose was to broaden the students' understanding of the capabilities of computer information resources rather than to teach the use of a specific retrieval system. The instruction included a description of the NOTIS system, discussion of the function of the country's major bibliographic utilities and a review of the public policy problems associated with the growing trend toward the commoditization of information.

To conduct the instruction, an IBM-PC attached to a large video projector was used to display examples of NOTIS (staff made) and DIALOG records, to demonstrate LUIS interactively, and to illustrate other points made in the presentation. Since the classroom for the lecture was not equipped with a telephone and a modem, screen images of records from DIALOG, NOTIS and RLIN were created. The text to serve as visuals for the lecture was also incorporated into the computer software. An MS-DOS batch file was used to sequence and project these screen images. By using a terminal emulator to access the Library's computer via the hardwired campus computer network, LUIS was also demonstrated interactively in the classroom. By combining the lecture outline, a series of 24-line text screens similar in content to transparencies usually used with an overhead projector, and an interactive online catalog demonstration, a cohesive and effective instructional program was presented. The recent addition of an LCD display unit in the Library to interface screen displays from a microcomputer to an overhead projector offers increased opportunities for clear display of microcomputer screens for training and instructional programs.

During the fall of 1986, we took the development of the teaching software package further by developing a new version to incorporate online searching skills as well as conceptual knowledge. The new software has been used for both Knowledge Index and LUIS online catalog demonstrations and instruction. We are able to take instructional programs to classrooms not equipped with telephone lines and to make copies of the disk to place on course reserve. Not only does this make our instruction more portable, but it also allows librarians to have more control over the content of instruction because they do not have to rely on the availability of a particular online system. In addition, we are also able to place the software package on reserve so students are able to review independently examples presented in the classroom and an abbreviated version of our lecture notes.

Even when dial-access is an option, the approach described here is our teaching preference. This method, a logical sequence of screens, purposefully created to illustrate specific features and show specific examples permits the instructor to have more control over the content of the class and eliminates the hazards of telephone line problems or other unexpected problems that interfere with the flow of the lecture. This approach also shows the librarian/instructor in control of the hardware as well as the subject matter. By actually using the technology about which we are teaching, we demonstrate its accessibility and ease of use first hand to students. Finally, a prepared package also allows for consistency in teaching when such teaching is shared among many librarians. There is still ample opportunity for individual teaching style to emerge, but the content is established. At this point in time, when there is still confusion and uncertainty among many of us about how to effectively present information retrieval skills, pre-arranged or "packaged" support gives librarians the confidence to try their hand in this new area. Since most of us have had to make such a fast transition to these new tools with very little background or training in this area, we are probably better able to appreciate the value of such support for our colleagues.

Third, because implementing change in any large organization is difficult, we have established a branch of the University Library as a site for innovation and experimentation. The need to find a new way to provide library services to adult students attending evening courses on Northwestern's Chicago campus, University College's interest in providing its students with experience with information technology, and the University Library's need for a "library laboratory" serendipitously coincided. Beginning in 1985, the Schaffner Library, located on the Chicago campus, received supplemental University funding to become an "electronic library laboratory" where we could experiment with new technologies while developing new library services for University College and the Kellogg Graduate School of Management. Once applications of technology are proven successful in this small and controlled setting, they can be shared with colleagues in the Main Library and adapted for use there on a larger scale.[7]

We began our renewal efforts at Schaffner by integrating microcomputers into as many of our library operations as possible. During the project's first three years, we developed an online book on-order system which supplements NOTIS, databases to keep track of corporate annual reports and serial orders, and an intracampus borrowing system, various circulation and reserve applications, and internal bookkeeping systems.[8] Now, we are applying the knowledge and expertise gained from these activities to our instructional and public services programs.

In conjunction with University College's Introduction to Computers course and in workshops offered outside of class-time, we have taught over 300 adult students the basic elements of online computer searching or remote bibliographic systems, using DIALOG's Knowledge Index. After a two hour classroom session, each participant conducts a Knowledge Index search on a topic of his or her choice, outside of class and without charge. This exercise not only enables students to build useful bibliographies for other class work, but also gives them experience with using Boolean logical operators to retrieve items from large bibliographic databases. Students also learn to manipulate a microcomputer to meet their information needs: logging on, conducting search, and downloading and printing their results.

We have also used microcomputers to expand our end user searching and instructional programs to a wider range of students. We provide access to and informal instruction in using Business Periodical Index on WILSONDISC and other Wilson databases on WILSEARCH to students enrolled on the Chicago campus. We were a beta test site, along with the main campus, for a project to introduce graduate business students to DIALOG's BUSINESS CONNECTION, and now, this program has become a regular part of several graduate management courses. Recently, cooperation between the Library's Reference Department and Schaffner Library has resulted in specialized instruction to graduate journalism students in the use of Datatimes software to access the *Chicago Sun Times*.

Most recently, we have been using our new expertise with microcomputers to increase the involvement of librarians in the activities of the microcomputer lab located in the Library. Owned by the Kellogg Graduate School of Management and supervised by the Library, this microcomputer lab contains 20 Zenith microcomputers and a variety of software packages for the use of graduate management students. Librarians and library science student interns provide informal instruction in the use of Lotus 1-2-3 and other software and in microcomputer operation. The Library is building a collection of books to support the applications used in the lab. We are beginning to regularly contact faculty about software assignments in their courses just as we do about library assignments. Each quarter a librarian attends a session of the required Introduction to Microcomputers workshop to discuss library services, and a self-instructional tutorial for WILSONDISC is included in workshop materials. As Kellogg Graduate School of Management expands its use of microcomputers throughout its curriculum, librarians are taking an active role in identifying instructional needs and suggesting appropriate instructional methods. In the future, we hope that librarians will be able to participate more formally in microcomputer and information management instruction within the Kellogg Graduate School of Management.

The location of the microcomputer lab within the Library allows us to closely coordinate the activities of both units and has proved to be quite beneficial for students and for librarians. By applying our library expertise, our experience with bibliographic instruction, we are able to help students use the lab more effectively. With librarians, software, and print materials flowing freely between the lab and the library proper, students do not perceive the lab as distinct from the library. They view microcomputers and computer-based information as preferred information sources, and are more receptive to new information technologies. By integrating the operation of the lab into library operations, we are able to explore new roles for librarians as microcomputer and information management consultants and instructors. Helping students with microcomputers and providing instruction in the use of spreadsheet software have more in common with reference and bibliographic instruction than may be apparent at first. We are finding that each activity informs and enriches the others.

We are now in the process of transferring knowledge gained from these experiences from the Schaffner Library to the Main Library. The Main Library Reference Department now offers end user online searching to Evanston campus University College students. The end user instruction software package is available to all librarians teaching on the Evanston campus. Experience with this program has prompted some rethinking of previous ideas about the role and place of online searching in a large research library, as well as discussion about the reconfiguration of reference department space and service design. We look forward to applying knowledge gained from the librarians' involvement in Schaffner's microcomputer lab to staff development, to the microcomputer lab located in the University Library, and to the information management education activities of the Reference Department. In addition, we are actively soliciting ideas for future innovations from a variety of Main Library public services units.

Although we have only begun to experiment with microcomputers, we have made a good beginning and eagerly look to the future. We are confident further experimentation with microcomputers in the coming years will benefit students, librarians, and the Library as a whole.

As the educational and research processes rely more on computers, it is essential that user education programs teach the technological skills and related conceptual issues that are becoming more important in our society. Based on what we have learned from our explorations about what students need to learn and about which methods are effective for teaching them, we will expand our programs of formal and informal bibliographic instruction in online information retrieval. As we do this, we expect this instruction will become a natural and integral part of bibliographic instruction at Northwestern. Through our programs, we hope students will gain a clearer insight into new information technologies and their value as library research tools, and that these skills will be transferable to other situations.

As a by-product of the instruction, librarians are increasing their competence and confidence about information technology. As this occurs new technological horizons are opening to them which will enable more creative approaches to service delivery in the coming years. They will feel freer to experiment with microcomputer applications. Librarians will be better able to take a leadership role in planning for the next wave of technological change in the library.

The library, as a whole, will benefit from this large group of professionals who are able to think and speak competently about information technology. In this era of rapidly changing computer and information technology, libraries need a broad base of knowledgeable and confident professionals to plan for the services our users will demand. Too frequently in libraries, knowledge about technology is concentrated in one or several individuals, or perhaps in one department or division, and more often than not, reference and instruction librarians are not in the center of this concentration. Rapidly changing technology will soon require all of us to make many decisions about how to employ it. It is imperative all areas of libraries participate in this decision-making and planning. Our work with microcomputers is helping to prepare reference librarians at Northwestern to participate in and set direction for these crucial decisions.

REFERENCES

1. Tippet, Harriet. "Word Processing and Record Management Applications." *Reference Services Review* 12 (Winter 1984): 73-75. Sugranes, Maria R. and Snider, Larry C. "Microcomputer Applications for Library Instruction: Automation of Test and Assignment Scoring and Student Record Keeping." *Microcomputers for Information Management: An International Journal of Library and Information Services* 2 n.3 (September 1985): 171-188.

2. Friend, Linda. "Identifying and Informing the Potential End-User: Online Information Seminars." *Online* 10 n.1 (January 1986): 47-56.

3. Arnott, Patricia and Richards, Deborah E. "Using the IBM Personal Com-

puter for Library Instruction." *Reference Services Review* 13 (Spring 1985): 69-72. Nipp, Deanna and Straub, Ron. "The Design and Implementation of Microcomputer Program for Library Orientation." *Research Strategies* 4 (Spring 1986): 60-67. Fitzgerald, Patricia A., Arnott, Patricia, and Richards, Deborah. "Computer-Assisted Instruction in Libraries: Guidelines for Effective Lesson Design." *Library HI-Tech* 4 (1986): 29-37.

4. Piele, Linda J., Pryor, Judith, and Tuckett, Harold W. "Teaching Microcomputer Literacy: New Roles For Academic Librarians." *College and Research Libraries* 47 (July 1986): 374-378. Rader, Hannelore B. "Teaching Library Enters the Electronic Age." *College and Research Libraries News* 47 (1986): 402-404. Tawyea, Edward W. and Shedlock, James. "Teaching the User About Information Management Using Microcomputers." *Medical Reference Services Quarterly* 5 n.2 (Summer 1986): 27-35.

5. Nielsen, Brian, Baker, Betsy, and Sandore, Beth. *Educating the Online Catalog User: A Model for Instruction Development and Evaluation, Final Report.* ED 261 679. 1986.

6. Baker, Betsy. "A Conceptual Framework for Teaching Online Catalog Use." *Journal of Academic Librarianship* 12 n.2 (May 1986): 90-96.

7. Pickett, Mary Joyce and Nielsen, Brian. "Library Development as a Catalyst for Continuing Education Innovation in a Major Research University: A Case Study." In *Proceedings of the Off-Campus Library Services Conference II: Current Practices-Future Challenges.* Mt. Pleasant, Michigan: Central Michigan University, April 18-19, 1985. 151-160.

8. Steffen, Susan Swords. "Living With and Managing Change: A Case Study of the Schaffner Library." *Illinois Libraries* 69 n.2 (February 1987): 126-129.

PART VII:
OTHER CONSIDERATIONS
FOR INTEGRATION
OF LIBRARY USE SKILLS

Bibliographic Instruction
and Critical Inquiry
in the Undergraduate Curriculum

Barbara MacAdam
Barbara Kemp

SUMMARY. There is a growing commitment among educators to establish a core curriculum at the college level capable of imparting to students the basic knowledge and skills commensurate with general education. Undergraduates enjoy possibly the single best opportunity in their education to develop the joys of scholarly exploration and the critical thinking skills that characterize the independent, self-motivated, life-long learner. Based on the belief that skilled and inquisitive use of libraries can enrich the academic and personal lives of students, bibliographic instruction can be instrumental in

Barbara MacAdam is Head, Undergraduate Library, The University of Michigan, Ann Arbor, MI 48109 and Barbara Kemp is Head, Humanities/Social Sciences Libraries, Washington State University, Pullman, WA 99164.

233

developing the information-handling, thinking and writing skills that form the foundation of the academic experience.

THINKING SKILLS AND THE CORE CURRICULUM

In almost any discussion of the undergraduate curriculum in the United States today, one hears about the wave of educational reform sweeping through colleges and universities. After the relative anarchy of the 1960s, in which general education or core curriculum requirements were reduced or even eliminated, there is a growing call to return to a common, core curriculum, which will impart to all students basic knowledge and skills. While there are different opinions as to what constitutes "general education," the President's Commission on Higher Education is quoted as defining the phrase as ". . . a term that has come to be accepted as those phases of nonspecialized and nonvocational learning which should be the common experience of all educated men and women." The Commission also has indicated that general education "focuses on concepts and principles rather than facts," and "has an integrative function."[1] Ernest Boyer adds that "the core program must be seen ultimately as relating the curriculum consequentially to life."[2]

Some of the basic skills receiving renewed attention as part of a general education are those aggregate skills often referred to as "critical thinking." Like "general education," "critical thinking" is a phrase frequently used, but there does not seem to be a commonly accepted definition identifying what constitutes critical thinking. Just as the theorists and practitioners differ in defining "critical thinking," they also use different terminology to identify similar or overlapping aspects and concepts of thinking. Some of the most commonly occurring terms used in addition to "critical thinking," are "analytical thinking," "reasoning skills," "problem solving," and "higher order thinking." This lack of a precise definition and the proliferation of terms and concepts increases confusion and debate. However, some of the components often mentioned as being involved in critical thinking are the abilities to formulate questions, to reason logically, to analyze and evaluate information effectively, and to solve problems. Regardless of terminology and definition, however, one feature of critical thinking is usually stressed: the skills involved should be transferrable and able to be applied in a variety of situations. A 1984 National Institute of Education report concludes

> that a college education should enable students to adapt to a changing world and that successful adaptation requires "the ability to think critically, to synthesize large quantities of new information."[3]

A second prominent theme seen in contemporary curricular reform is that of writing across the curriculum. This and other similar movements are

> based upon the recognition that too much teaching is directed at getting students to learn content and the moral reward structure of the teacher rather than the essential skills they need to become life-long learners in a rapidly changing world.[4]

The assignment of responsibility for the teaching of writing to the English department now is seen as having several negative consequences, including the lack of opportunity to practice necessary skills, the separation of the process of writing from both content and context, low student involvement and motivation and "a perception that writing is not central to the other, more important parts of the curriculum . . . ." Both writing and critical thinking are viewed as social processes, enhanced by active learning. Proponents of writing across the curriculum argue "that writing is a *central* basic skill, but is even more important as a central *learning* skill in all fields and at all levels."[5]

Many of the theories of critical thinking and writing across the curriculum obviously are very similar or highly complementary. Most of the ideas outlined above certainly are not new to any bibliographic instruction librarian. Conceptual learning rather than rote memorization, analysis and evaluation of information, and the transferability of skills across disciplines are familiar themes long espoused in the theory and practice of library user education.

BIBLIOGRAPHIC INSTRUCTION
AND CRITICAL INQUIRY

The perception of bibliographic instruction as being fundamentally concerned with teaching conceptual models researchers could use to formulate search strategies and to build information handling skills has been in the literature for a long time. Oberman and Strauch, Beaubien et al., and Kobelski and Reichel as well as Tuckett and Stoffle did much to dispel the simplistic version of bibliographic instruction reduced to library orientation, laundry list bibliography, or the ubiquitous pathfinder. Kirk proposes:

> Bibliographic instruction can be more than providing directions on how to use library resources to complete a specific assignment. It can also make a significant contribution to the aims of liberal education

and goes on to delineate critical thinking skills as one of the foundations of the educational experience:

> One of the most important functions of a liberal arts program is to develop those abilities and qualities that characterize the rational mind. This includes the ability to solve problems by asking questions, critically analyzing the information, and then answering the questions.[6]

As a sophomore in college, one of the authors foolishly (or so it seemed at the onset) elected a senior graduate student summer term class on the History of the Roman Empire. At the first class session, aghast to find a room full of obvious intellectuals sporting attache cases and rimless glasses, she concluded that a quick exit was her only salvation. Then the professor said something recalled many times in the twenty years since, in essence:

> You're going to be asked to critique the works of some reputable scholars on the subject of the Roman Empire and you'll ask yourself how you're ever supposed to do this when they are the experts and you know nothing about the subject. What you must learn to do is to say to yourself "Did they ask the right questions," or the best questions or even all the ques-

tions, or are there questions that occur to you that they did not pose. Concentrate on the *question*, not the answers, and you'll be surprised at your ability to analyze what you read.

How often she has shared that thought with students intimidated by the terrifying icons of scholarship that, in their eyes, seemed to dwarf their attempts at original thought. And how that experience presaged question analysis as a paradigm for search strategy in bibliographic instruction.[7]

The nature of library research is to gather information, but all information is not equal. While the nature of research is fundamentally inquiry, it is inquiry — especially for the average undergraduate — with a specific object in mind: generally a paper, an assignment to complete, a speech to prepare. Further, it is inquiry with an implicit standard against which the results (or information gathering) will be judged: a grade, teacher expectations, even the student's own sense of validity or "rightness." At its best, bibliographic instruction can and should give a student the wherewithal to formulate the research problem, translate this into the basic inquiry to be investigated, establish a standard or set of measures by which all information gathered will be accepted or rejected based on that standard, and finally, be able to articulate a defense and justification for the entire character of this process. The student learns in essence to think, to think in a new way, and to question, challenge, keep, discard, and analyze information. These are skills that are crucial and intrinsic to the self-directed, life-long learner. This process is also a key preliminary to effective and well argued writing, described by some as a process of pre-writing.[8]

Constance Mellon related the design of successful library instruction programs to Perry's theory of intellectual and ethical development. In this model, students must extend their thinking from "What is the right answer," through acceptance of more than one perspective on a problem, and finally to,

> . . . become aware that there are few areas in which things can be known absolutely and thus recognize the necessity of supporting information to back up opinions. They accept the need for perception, analysis and evaluation in forming judgments.[9]

RESEARCH PATHS AND INTELLECTUAL COURAGE

What are the components of bibliographic instruction that transmit these analytical and critical thinking skills? In his excellent article on library use and development of critical thought, Plum proposes the discipline-centered model as a structure for bibliographic instruction and describes topic selection, the nature of evidence, use of citation, structure of reference tools, and formulation of research strategy. The question analysis model for formulating a search strategy also suggests posing the initial question "what discipline is associated with this topic?" Presented correctly, a student should begin to consider the following:

- —Who thinks, writes, talks about this idea? Philosophers, psychologists, mathematicians, highway safety engineers?
- —If, as is likely, several "disciplines" explain this idea, what angle is of particular interest to me? e.g., a psychological perspective, economic, medical?

Plum suggests that students should recognize that

> Research methods, or the principles behind criticism are not universally accepted within the discipline. A variety of critical approaches to a single work can legitimately arrive at different, yet valid, interpretations and criticism.[10]

But even further, the cogent point is that by isolating a disciplinary approach to a topic, the student learns that he/she creates a gateway, opening onto a path taking the student along on a scholarly exploration, following other researchers who have explored the concept or topic before. Again, the process of selection/rejection is a conscious one in which the student makes the first analytical choice, and takes the intellectual controls of the information-gathering process. Not only is the student's critical ability formed (the ability to distinguish from things equally "right," the approach that is "right" for what the student wants), the student can also see his perspective as something he has every right to choose and he shares this right with every other researcher who has considered the topic before. As Oscar Handlin expresses it, the shear contemplation of the wide range of possibilities represented by the wealth of resources available in a research library should inspire confidence that:

> . . . not all the correct answers are known; not all the right questions have ever been asked. There is still the opportunity for involvement in the long process of asking and answering of which these collections are evidence.[11]

Intellectual courage is the first attribute requisite for critical inquiry. If bibliographic instruction can give the student courage, that student will be willing to investigate and exercise his/her critical judgment.

THE POWER OF "NAMES"

If bibliographic instruction librarians had a dollar for every time they explained Library of Congress or any system of subject headings, they'd have handsome bibliographic nest eggs. Defining terms, establishing vocabulary and clarifying unfamiliar terms are basic steps in question analysis. Bibliographic instruction with a premium on thinking skills can enable a student to see that the names we give to things often determines or reflects their destiny: a basketball player named "Magic," children alternatively called "exceptional," "learning disabled," or "mentally impaired." Subject headings in one index may refer to "disabled," another may refer to the "handicapped." Why, expecting to find World War I in the catalog do we have to use European War 1914-1918? Because the heading creators were not prescient; World War I and World War II as terms carry an emotional, cultural, and historical baggage just in their mere expression. The thought process a student might follow:

- What do people call this idea, what "names" do they give it?
- What do scholars call it, people whose job it is to study it, take it apart, talk about it?
- What names/terms fit most closely with the names I would give to this idea?
- What does it mean when the same "idea" has different "names?"

Again, by selecting a subject heading to search under, the student has made a choice, and this choice will open additional gateways. The student also learns that names express values; information is not necessarily objective, or neutral. Even the fact that no heading or precise vocabulary exists for a topic can make a student begin to ask why, and explore the reasons no one has given the idea a descriptive vocabulary. And finally the student can extrapolate: the lack of a vocabulary may consign an idea to languish undiscovered, undiscussed, and inaccessible to those who seek for it. Thus vocabulary has power to impart or withhold life to an idea. Did women poets exist before "Poetry—Women Authors"? Of course, but a subject heading can say volumes about the status of an idea in our everyday consciousness or fabric of our culture.

CRITICAL INQUIRY AND INFORMATION VALUE JUDGMENT

Bibliographic instruction in an academic library must impart the distinction between popular and scholarly literature. In doing so, students need to learn that scholarly literature is not arbitrarily good and popular literature bad, but that they represent two different species of communication. Sometimes interspecial communication takes place when, for example, a newspaper article attempts to tip the public off to the latest dangers in coffee, as gleaned from a peer-review medical journal. Newspaper coverage of an anti-abortion rally may have equal "validity" with a medical article describing related medical procedures. The articles are about the same subject, but they are not at all the same thing, and their respective appropriateness depends upon their match to the "standard" the researcher has defined.

Students tend to think that citations are about plagiarism. Bibliographic instruction, in teaching the very concept of bibliography, shares with the student the idea that knowledge does not, generally, advance in quantum leaps. It advances by inches, and a literature review is really a yardstick that measures who has inched how far. The very concept of bibliography is yet another opportunity to instill intellectual courage and confidence, because a student should recognize that when he cites, he is saying:

—I fit here, my work comes here.
—Even if my idea only adds another quarter inch—it has a right to exist.

The ultimate recognition on the part of the student is that the yardstick isn't, in fact, straight. Ideas zigzag back and forth and the fundamental matter of inquiry is to question, refine, or readjust the status quo whatever that may be.

As Oscar Handlin suggests, the critical thinker needs to unlearn mass-consumer attitudes and resist the impulse to go for the latest, shiniest model:

> Above all every scholar knows—or should know—that not all knowledge is cumulative, that the latest book is not necessarily better than an earlier one, and that some new subjects simply dress the old corpus up in flashy but insubstantial raiment.[12]

As students begin to analyze and establish their measures for "good" information in their context, they have many options: current or retrospective, scholarly or popular, the quoted opinion of an expert versus published research findings. In any case, they ultimately must impose value judgment on the information they find and assess the quality of the information. One of the final pieces in measuring quality is *questioning* the authority or trust level of the writer as opposed to accepting everything one reads. Bibliographic instruction encourages students to extend their critical inquiry to the source itself:

—Who is this author and why should I trust him/her?
—Might the author have any reason to minimize or exaggerate the truth?
—Do I want to know what this person thinks or try to determine what a lot of people think on this subject?
—How might this person or group benefit if readers accept what they say?

The enhanced ability of the student to formulate a search strategy and retrieve information in general permits investigation of these questions as a sub-piece of a larger research question.

CONCLUSION

Librarians' response to the ever-expanding universe of information has been to impose layer upon layer of "control." Tools to identify other tools exist in an array, though far from entropy, initially as confusing to the average student as the original untrammeled universe. The best education enables a student to set a course and steer it steady and true, with confidence and intellectual satisfaction, through unfamiliar territory or to stop and linger over the sights as interest and need compel. Good education is never easy, and the realities always fall short of expectations if those expectations are high. The most ambitious, committed and visionary bibliographic instruction program in the world cannot, within a curriculum, *assure* realization of the life-long, independent thinker, learner, speaker, writer, but the college curriculum without such instruction will find the realization impossible.

REFERENCES

1. A. Smith and Clements, *Meeting the Changing Needs*, 25-6.
2. Boyer, *College*, 91.
3. McMillan, "Enhancing College Students' Critical Thinking," 3.
4. B. Smith, Writing Across the Curriculum, 1.
5. Ibid., 1-3.
6. Thomas G. Kirk, "Concluding Remarks," In Kirk, *Increasing the Teaching Role*, 96.
7. Beaubien, Hogan, and George, *Learning the Library*, 75.
8. Parsigian, "News Reporting."
9. Constance A. Mellon, "Information Problem-Solving: A Developmental Approach to Library Instruction," In Oberman and Strauch, *Theories of Bibliographic Instruction*, 75-89.
10. Stephan M. Plum, "Library Use and the Development of Critical Thought," In Kirk, *Increasing the Teaching Role*, 25-33.
11. Handlin, "Libraries and Learning," 216.
12. Ibid.

BIBLIOGRAPHY

Beaubien, Anne, Sharon Hogan, and Mary George. *Learning the Library*. New York: R.R. Bowker, 1982.

Boyer, Ernest L. College: *The Undergraduate Experience in America*. New York: Harper & Row, 1987.

Cash, D. Michele. "Scrutiny of the Bounty or Teaching Critical Thinking in Library Instruction." Paper presented at the Indiana Library Association Meeting, October 15, 1985. ED 270 128.

Friedman, Sarah L., Ellen Kofsky Scholnick, and Rodney R. Cocking, eds. *Blueprints for Thinking: The Role of Planning in Cognitive Development*. New York: Cambridge University Press, 1987.

Griffin, C. William. *Teaching Writing in All Disciplines*. New Directions for Teaching and Learning, 12. San Francisco: Jossey-Bass, 1982.

Grinols, Anne Bradstreet, ed. *Critical Thinking: Reading and Writing Across the Curriculum*. Belmont, Calif.: Wadsworth, 1988.

Handlin, Oscar. "Libraries and Learning." *The American Scholar*. 56, no.2 (Spring 1987): 205-218.

Heiman, Marcia and Joshua Slomianko. *Critical Thinking Skills*. Washington, D.C.: National Education Association, 1985.

Keller, Phyllis. *Getting at the Core: Curricular Reform at Harvard*. Cambridge, Mass.: Harvard University Press, 1982.

Kirk, Thomas G., ed. *Increasing the Teaching Role of Academic Libraries*. New Directions for Teaching and Learning, 18. San Francisco: Jossey-Bass, 1984.

Kobelski, Pamela and Mary Reichel. "Conceptual Frameworks for Bibliographic Instruction." *The Journal of Academic Librarianship*. 7, no.2 (May 1981): 73-77.

McMillan, James H. "Enhancing College Students' Critical Thinking: A Review of Studies." *Research in Higher Education*. 25, no. 1 (1987): 3-29.

McPeck, John E. *Critical Thinking and Education*. New York: St. Martin's Press, 1981.

Mellon, Constance A. "Process Not Product in Course-Integrated Instruction: A Generic Model of Library Research." *College & Research Libraries*. 45, no. 6 (November 1984): 471-478.

Oberman, Cerise and Katina Strauch. *Theories of Bibliographic Education: Designs for Teaching*. New York: R.R. Bowker, 1982.

O'Hanlon, Nancyanne. "Library Skills, Critical Thinking, and the Teacher-training Curriculum." *College & Research Libraries*. 48, no. 1 (January 1987): 17-26.

Parsigian, Elise K. "News Reporting—Method in the Midst of Chaos." Ph.D. diss., University of Michigan, 1986.

Paul, Richard W. "Critical Thinking: Fundamental to Education for a Free Society." *Educational Leadership* 42, no. 1 (September 1984): 4-14.

Perry, William G. *Intellectual and Ethical Development in the College Years: A Scheme*. Cambridge, Mass.: Harvard University Press, 1970.

Rudolph, Frederick. *Curriculum: A History of the American Undergraduate Course of Study since 1636*. San Francisco: Jossey-Bass, 1977.

Smith, Al and Clyde Clements, eds. *Meeting the Changing Needs: Undergraduate Curriculum and Instruction*. Port Washington, New York: Associated Faculty Press, 1984.

Smith, Barbara Leigh, ed. *Writing Across the Curriculum*. Current Issues in Higher Education, no. 3. Washington, D.C.: American Association for Higher Education, 1984.

Tuckett, Harold and Carla Stoffle. "Learning Theory and the Self-Reliant Library User." *RQ* 24, no. 1 (Fall 1984): 58-66.

General Education, Graduate Education, and Instruction in the Use of Libraries

William Miller

SUMMARY. Libraries have an important role to play in the general education process, even at the graduate level. An infusion of education about library resources can help to lessen the insularity which characterizes so much of graduate education in the U.S., and could help to break the cycle which perpetuates the lack of communication between academic disciplines. Various roles suggested for academic libraries in this regard include an approach through disciplinary instruction, a "handmaiden approach" to assisting individual graduate students, and a specific general education role for libraries which cuts across disciplines, through the use of seminars and other general education activities. Computer database searching may be a useful fulcrum, in any of these approaches, to broaden the perspective and the interdisciplinary awareness of both graduate students and faculty.

General education and graduate education, as practiced in America today, appear to have little to do with each other. General education is associated with undergraduates whose knowledge base and perspectives are being formed and broadened. Graduate students, on the other hand, are "attempting to gain in-depth knowledge of a specialized field and to prepare for a career in which research is a basic element."[1] Graduate education is thus viewed as a narrowing process which focuses the mind on a discipline in order to create

---

William Miller is Director of Libraries, Florida Atlantic University, Boca Raton, FL 33431-0992.

specialists who can research and publish and thereby advance the state of the art within that one discipline.

It is widely assumed that the average graduate student has already received a healthy dose of general education, and it is widely pronounced that such dosage is both good and necessary. A statement in 1952 by the American Association of Law Schools, for instance, affirms that "there is no professional curricular substitute for the minimum basic exposure to human experience that is called a liberal education."[2] Indeed, as far back as 1915, the American Association of University Professors issued a statement that the three purposes of a university should be to "promote inquiry and advance the sum of human knowledge," to "provide general instruction to the students," and "develop experts for various branches of the public service."[3] Implicit in such a statement is the idea that both general and specialized education are essential in the university environment.

However, there is considerable evidence that general education, which indeed began as a reaction to the overspecialization of graduate schools in the 1920s, has taken a perennial second-place to such overspecialization to this day. In universities with major graduate programs, the general education component of that three-part mission has tended to erode over time. As a matter of human nature, such erosion is probably inevitable, given the culture of academia.

INTEGRATION AND SEGMENTALISM

Rosabeth Moss Kanter has commented in her book *The Change Masters* on the opposing principles of "integration" and "segmentalism," the former representing a "willingness to move beyond received wisdom, to combine ideas from unconnected sources, to embrace change," while the latter emphasizes "uncrossable boundaries."[4] Clearly, graduate education today is characterized by segmentalism. Faculty loyalty is to their discipline rather than to any integrative urge. Even in the undergraduate program, the ideal student is likely to be a budding specialist interested in emulating the professional career of his or her instructor, rather than the novice sampling the field, with no particular intention of entering it. The reward structure of academe does not encourage attention to such generalists, or indeed to any undergraduate students, because faculty who teach undergraduates tend to be "distracted from teaching by the demand of research and publication necessary for professional advancement and tenure."[5]

The fragmentation which is fostered by such specialization is reflected in the kind of assistance in the use of libraries which is generally available in universities. Knowledge is highly partitioned and artificially apportioned among academic departments (whereas in small colleges there is likely to be more interchange among departments, and even hybrid departments, e.g., Anthropology-Sociology). Because library use and library instruction both tend to be course-dependent, university undergraduates are not taught about the structure of knowledge, in general, but rather about the subset of that structure which will enable them to complete a particular paper or assignment in a specific disciplinary course. Nor do university undergraduates mind such artificial narrowing; the evidence is that they welcome it. The costs of their education and the emphasis on career training encourage a "practical" approach rather than a theoretical one. What seems practical, however, entails the wearing of blinders to avoid being distracted by extraneous information while rushing to finish one's assigned race.

GRADUATE STUDENTS AND LIBRARY KNOWLEDGE

Many of these undergraduates eventually become graduate students. Lacking any theoretical feeling for the creation of knowledge in any field, such students will rapidly forget both the general concepts and the particular tools which they may possibly have been exposed to as undergraduates. If they become graduate students in the field of their undergraduate major, they may perhaps recall having used one or more of the major research tools within that discipline. In general, however, instruction in the use of libraries for graduate students has not differed greatly from instruction for undergraduates. Librarians are well aware of the reality of graduate student library expertise. As Beaubien, Hogan and George put it, "one is much more likely to overestimate the research sophistication of users than to underestimate it."[6]

Faculty, on the other hand, are either unaware of this lack of skills or would prefer not to acknowledge what they know.[7] They presume that general education has transpired, that their students are well-rounded intellects, and that they should already know how to use libraries in a sophisticated fashion. Graduate faculty do not accept a burden for instruction in the use of libraries.[8] If their students do not know how to operate within a library, the graduate faculty member is likely to feel that the onus is on the student, who should be motivated to learn on his or her own. Graduate faculty members do not perceive that libraries are difficult places to learn how to use. Nor do they generally perceive librarians as important partners in this learning process, though that situation has probably improved slightly during the past five years.

LIBRARIANS AND GRADUATE EDUCATION

Librarians have allowed themselves to be coopted into this narrowing process of graduate education, because they do not perceive that they have much of a choice. Instead of being able to broaden the approach which graduate students take to knowledge, librarians (where they are allowed to enter into the dynamics of graduate student library use) are generally limited to the role of reference work or the teaching of discipline-specific tools for a particular research assignment, in much the same way that they would teach an undergraduate one-hour stand.

It is unfortunate, from the students' perspective, that librarians occupy such an insignificant place in their graduate training. Graduate faculty in effect have placed the burden for instruction in library use on undergraduate instructors, who in turn have assumed such instruction to be the burden of a freshman workbook program or a high school where no significant instruction can really have taken place. Leaving the librarian out of the equation only reinforces the notion that the purpose of graduate study is to learn to emulate or be a clone of the major professors, and tends to limit the students to the tools and techniques which these professors themselves learned as graduate students. Graduate students trained through such a process step out into the world as faculty members who simply perpetuate the process and the preconceptions.

The other unfortunate effect of the subordinate role for librarians is that the disciplines themselves are kept unnecessarily narrow, along with the training of the specialists and the growth of the field and its literature. Graduate students are not taught to seek for information, but rather for information as published in particular journals. If one looks at the citations in the cohort of journals devoted to the teaching of specific disciplines (e.g., *Teaching Sociology, Teaching History, Teaching Philosophy, Teaching Political Science*), it is amazing to note how little cross-fertilization there is; it is as if presumably interesting information, if presented in the journals of other fields, is by definition either invalid or irrelevant. The disciplines seemingly have little to say to or learn from each other, even in closely related fields which share methodologies.

A New Role for Librarians

What can librarians do to address this situation? Clearly, they cannot be the tail which wags the dog, in terms of insisting upon an immediate and radical revamping of graduate education in this country. The relationship between the instructor and the student will continue to be the primary one, with librarians usually playing at best an ancillary role. Still, there are things which have been done at particular institutions, and still more things which could be done to ameliorate this situation. We must try to eliminate the narrowing effect of both undergraduate and graduate education, and of library instruction in support of such education, because such narrowing cannot contribute to the goal of creating an educated citizenry, capable of discovering information for itself and engaging in continuing educational renewal.[9]

TOWARD A NEW ARTICULATION POLICY FOR GRADUATE STUDY AND LIBRARIES

Few would dispute, at least in the abstract, the relevance of general education and skill in library use at the undergraduate level. As E. Gordon Gee put it during the recent Arden House Conference at Columbia University,

If . . . "the object of education is to prepare the young to educate themselves throughout their lives," the relationship of our libraries to undergraduate education is clear: We must not only train students to seek the knowledge and wisdom of past generations, but prepare them to use libraries as vital, dynamic resources.[10]

At the graduate level, however, there are clearly many who would argue that a narrowing focus is entirely appropriate, and that general instruction in library use is a function most appropriately carried out at an earlier stage in students' education. There is no question, moreover, that it should be easier to integrate such general instruction into the undergraduate curriculum than it would be to integrate it into the graduate curriculum. On an ideal level, therefore, it would make sense to work toward a new "articulation" policy regarding library use competence between graduate programs and the undergraduate programs which supply them. Such agreements would be not unlike the articulation agreements which colleges more and more have with high schools regarding minimal acceptance requirements.

Such an articulation policy is an ideal which probably cannot be realized at most institutions. As a practical matter there would be many difficulties involved in formalizing an expectation that graduate students come to their programs with some minimal level of competency at general library use, especially at a time when graduate schools are dropping foreign language requirements. A further complication is that academic libraries must stand ready to provide extensive opportunities for undergraduates to develop such competence before graduate schools can reasonably be expected to require it. Few university libraries are staffed and equipped to handle a meaningful instructional program on a universal scale for undergraduates, nor do we appear to know how to carry out such a program. Freshman workbook programs do not accomplish the task because they are superficial and have demonstrated no long-term effectiveness.

To institutionalize, as an undergraduate general education requirement, the ability to use libraries and understand how knowledge is disseminated and made accessible is a wonderful idea whose practicality is better discussed elsewhere in this volume. How likely it is that such a requirement will ever exist on a grand scale one might well question. However, it would be much more likely to exist at a liberal arts college than at a major university, and it would be much more likely to exist at the undergraduate level than at the graduate level. At a time when general education course requirements themselves seem to be more than many an institution can handle, given fiscal and staffing constraints, perhaps the best to be hoped for at the graduate level would be to work more modestly to improve graduate education through broadened library competence for students in particular programs, and at particular stages of their careers. Such efforts could help to break the cycle of intellectual poverty which currently characterizes so much graduate student library use and training.

The Disciplinary Approach

It is probably the case that the disciplines which could most benefit from an infusion of multidisciplinary library instruction are the very ones least likely to put aside their "segmentalism." But librarians could not attack every discipline simultaneously anyway, and while there are those disciplines which will probably always resist any encroachment, there are others which should be very open to library instruction as an integrating force. We could ameliorate the current situation by beginning with such disciplines, and with selected faculty in other disciplines who give evidence of interest in broadening their teaching or research perspectives. There is at least some evidence within the literature of almost every field to support the notion that interdisciplinary background, general education, or the ability to use libraries and/or do research independently are positive goods. Even in fields such as pharmacy, law, and medicine, the literature is replete with articles extolling the value of the humanities to practical work in the field.[11]

Furthermore, most universities have interdisciplinary departments and programs (e.g., Environmental Chemistry, American Studies) and dual-degree programs (including those involving the MLS!) which by their very nature invite the librarian to suggest an instructional role of a multidisciplinary kind. The kinds of involvement need not be belabored here, but could range from the traditional one-hour stand to an extended, course-integrated role, either in a research methods course, another course or cluster of courses, or in some more general departmental or program role, including satisfaction of some non-course requirement. The onus is necessarily on librarians to take the lead in suggesting their own involvement to the faculty and departments involved. Success will be in large part a function of personal interactions and the perceived qualifications and performance ability of the librarian.

The Handmaiden Approach

Closely related to the disciplinary approach is the "handmaiden approach" which has traditionally been suggested in library literature.[12] Various authors have delineated stages in the graduate study process (course work stage, proposal writing stage, dissertation research, dissertation writing) at which librarians can be useful to students as counselors and advisors. Ideally, in this process the librarian becomes a long-term ally or mentor for an individual student, and assists that student not only in the basics of library use but also in alternative approaches which could certainly offer possibilities of which the instructor is unaware.

The General Education Approach

Instead of approaching individual students or instructors, it is possible for libraries to take a pan-disciplinary role which is also a general education role within the university, though it is probably outside the realm of formal requirements. Certainly we have already seen elements of such a program in the faculty and graduate students seminars or workshops (the terminology varies) offered by various libraries.[13] These tend not to focus on a particular discipline, but rather to focus on a cluster such as "Computer Database Searching in the Social Sciences."

In offering such pan-disciplinary instructional sessions, librarians have stumbled across what is probably one of the most attractive options for a proactive role in the general education process as it involves graduate study. The teaching of computer searching simply enhances the possibilities for this mode of instruction to support the general education function. Although an immediate weakness might appear to be the lack of close course relatedness for the students, most of those attending such a session will probably have a topic in mind which could easily be run across the databases of various disciplines, with surprising and useful results. The generation of a relevant citation from outside the narrow disciplinary literature makes an immediate impression far more valuable than any which could be made by talking in the abstract about reference tools or other materials which the audience has never seen or used.

This general education approach is attractive because it avoids the labor-intensiveness of the handmaiden approach while presenting the librarian in a positive instructional context which students respect and seek out voluntarily. It offers students and faculty from multiple disciplines the opportunity to meet together in the same room and interact, and it also offers librarians a good forum in which to encourage exchange of ideas. As an opening gambit, then, this approach has much to recommend it. If it could be expanded into a full-blown instructional program, it could perhaps offer academic libraries that place in the educational scheme of things which they have long sought. Without a formal place in the catalog for such a program, however, continuity becomes difficult and efforts wane over time. In any case such a program is likely to be institutionalized only as a complement to more traditional reference work assistance and course-related instruction.

POSSIBILITIES FOR THE FUTURE

Nothing discussed in this paper outlines a radical blueprint for greater involvement of libraries in the general education or graduate education processes. Such increased involvement may in fact never occur. The onus for such increased involvement falls equally on the library community and on the higher education community, and it certainly remains to be seen whether or not either community will accept the challenge and the responsibility. Certainly efforts such as the recent Arden House conference, work by the Association of College and Research Libraries' Professional Association Liaison Committee, and the success of associations such as the Association for Integrative Studies will all have some bearing on the possible increased involvement of libraries in the graduate education process at an integrative level. Meanwhile, librarians need to demonstrate unequivocally that they have much of value to add to the process, and the higher education community as a whole needs to recognize the value of one of its most untapped assets. The research skills and interdisciplinary vision of librarians could potentially add much to the graduate education process. Through stress on their ability to contribute to this process, librarians could enrich higher education and foster the generation of knowledge while at the same time actualizing much of the potential inherent in their own education and training.

REFERENCES

1. Connie R. Dunlap, "Library Services to the Graduate Community: The University of Michigan," *College & Research Libraries*, 37 (May 1976), p. 248.

2. Cited in Bruce A. Kimball, "Legal Education, Liberal Education, and the Trivial *Artes*," *JGE: The Journal of General Education*, 38, No. 3 (1986), p. 182.

3. American Association of University Professors, *Report of the Committee on Academic Freedom and Tenure*, cited in *American Higher Education: A Documentary History*, II, ed. Richard Hofstadter and Wilson Smith (1961; reprint ed., Chicago: University of Chicago Press, 1968), p. 866.

4. New York: Simon and Schuster, 1983, pp. 27-31.

5. Michael Bisesi, "Professional Specialization and General Education: Organizational and Professional Realities," ASHE 1984 Annual Meeting Paper, p. 7 (ED245609).

6. Anne K. Beaubien, Sharon A. Hogan, and Mary W. George, *Learning the Library: Concepts and Methods for Effective Bibliographic Instruction* (New York: Bowker, 1982). p. 56.

7. See Denise Madland, "Library Instruction for Graduate Students," *College Teaching*, 33 (Fall 1985), pp. 163-64, which states that "while many teachers assume that graduate students have mastered the art of using the library, there is evidence that graduate students do not know how to find the information they need."

8. See the survey results in Richard A. Dreifuss, "Library Instruction and Graduate Students: More Work for George," *RQ*, 21 (Winter 1981), pp. 121-123.

9. Bruce O'Connell, "Where Does Harvard Lead Us?" *Change*, 10 (Sept. 1978), pp. 35-40, 61.

10. Quoted in Patricia Senn Breivik, "Making the Most of Libraries," *Change* 19 (July/August 1987), p. 48.

11. See for instance Maria J. O'Neil and Patricia Wilson-Coker, "The Child

Welfare Specialist: An Interdisciplinary Graduate Curriculum,'' *Child Welfare* 65 (March/April 1986), pp. 99-117; Jurate A. Sakalys and Jean Watson, ''Professional Education: Post-Baccalaureate Education for Professional Nursing,'' *Journal of Professional Nursing* 2 (March/April 1986), pp. 91-97; John J. Kirk, ''Education for a Better Environment,'' *Mazingira* 8 (1985), pp. 6-7, 9-10; and Kathleen K. Colby and others, ''Problem-Based Learning of Social Sciences and Humanities by Fourth-Year Medical Students,'' *Journal of Medical Education* 61 (May 1986), pp. 413-415.

12. See Dunlap, op. cit; Anne Grodzins Lipow, ''Library Services to the Graduate Community: The University of California, Berkeley,'' *College & Research Libraries* 37 (May 1976), pp. 252-256; Susan M. Pickert and Adele B. Chwalek, ''Integrating Bibliographic Research Skills into a Graduate Program in Education,'' *Catholic Library World* 55 (April 1984), pp. 392-394; and Bill Bailey, ''Thesis Practicum and the Librarian's Role,'' *Journal of Academic Librarianship* 11 (May 1985), pp. 79-81.

13. See Linda de Wit, Agnes Haigh, and Julie Hurd, ''Library Seminars: Keeping Faculty Informed,'' *College & Research Libraries News* 42 (October 1981), pp. 326-327; and Pamela S. Bradigan, Susan M. Kroll, and Sally R. Sims, ''Graduate Student Bibliographic Instruction at a Large University: A Workshop Approach,'' *RQ* 26 (Spring 1987), pp. 335-340.

Impact and Implications of a Library-Use Integrated Education Program

Afton McGrath Miner

SUMMARY. The reactions to a Graduate Council recommendation for the removal of professional librarians from scheduled duty at the reference desks are reported and the effects of its implementation on reference-related activities, such as bibliographic instruction, are explored. The genesis and development of a pilot program of course-integrated bibliographic instruction for the College of Education at Brigham Young University are described as is the impact the program has already had on the library. Plans for future directions of the program are discussed and the implications for the library are considered.

A Graduate Council review of the library program at Brigham Young University in 1985 caused reverberations still being felt by public services librarians. After weeks of study, the Council determined, among other things, that the subject librarians should no longer be scheduled at the reference desks. Instead, they should spend significantly more time working with faculty members in collection development and assessment, and become more involved with faculty and students in bibliographic instruction and committee work.

RESTRUCTURING OF REFERENCE SERVICE

Many of the librarians who had worked for years in public services were upset about the recommendation concerning discontinuance of professional librarian service at the reference desks. But the

---

Afton McGrath Miner is Education Librarian, Harold B. Lee Library, Brigham Young University, Provo, UT 84602.

Council recommendations had been approved by the university administration and were allowed to stand. The subject specialists, most of whom considered themselves reference librarians, reluctantly turned the reference desk duty over to student reference assistants and paraprofessional staff. Patrons needing more specialized assistance were to be referred to the subject specialists in their offices.

In addition each subject specialist was scheduled for ten hours per week and three or four hours one night a week as a resource person to back up nonprofessionals working at the desk and to help patrons needing more in-depth assistance. Professional librarians continued working at the General Reference Desk and one reference specialist, responsible for training students and "maintaining the quality of reference service," was appointed for each subject reference desk. So when professional help was needed, it was still available. Actually, under the new arrangement patrons referred to a subject specialist for help might fare better than under the old system as the librarian could devote time to them exclusively without being distracted by other patrons.

In spite of some dire predictions made by the public services librarians at the time the changes were initiated, the library reference services have not collapsed. Subject librarians are not completely convinced that reference desks are operating as efficiently and accurately without them, nor are they sure that all patrons who could use their assistance are referred to them, but most have long since become involved in other non-desk, reference-related activities in support of the library and the university and feel good about the contributions they are making.

One such activity has resulted in the genesis and development of an integrated bibliographic instruction program for the College of Education at Brigham Young University.

A NATION AT RISK

In March 1985, the climate was right for approaching the dean of the College of Education concerning bibliographic instruction needs for preservice teachers, principals and counselors. Following the 1984 appearance of *A Nation at Risk*, the government report describing alarming weaknesses in American public schools, a great deal of soul-searching was taking place in colleges of education across the nation. Minutes of faculty meetings during that period chronicled innumerable far-reaching proposals for improving pre-service teacher education. College of education-public school district partnerships were formed in an attempt to identify and remedy weaknesses in the preparation and induction of teachers and scores of ad hoc committees were appointed, devoting thousands of meeting hours to topics concerned with educational excellence and renewal.

The education librarian had expressed willingness to serve on committees if needed, thinking she could make a contribution to the committee charged with studying campus services, which included the library. She was asked, instead, to serve on the college committee focusing on field experiences of preservice teachers. At first the focus seemed irrevelant in terms of her background and expertise, but through the months of weekly deliberations, this committee service proved to be extremely valuable for many reasons. From the beginning she provided documentation for discussion topics and helped professors locate further information needed for their own committee assignments, thus becoming a contributing member early on. And by keeping up on the literature of the discussion topics, she was able to give meaningful input. Incidentally, this committee evolved into one of the most influential of all the ad hoc committees, lasting long after the others were dissolved. The committee members were given the charge to develop the "key school" or "partner school" concept and plan for its implementation in the partnership formed by the College and five school districts. The many hours of productive committee work helped earn the education librarian the respect of her education colleagues and created opportunities for the discussion of library concerns.

LIBRARY LITERACY FOR PRESERVICE TEACHERS

It was during this period of openness and searching that the education librarian at Brigham Young University approached the dean of the College of Education and commented that in all the meetings she had attended and the proposals she had read, she had found nothing concerning the importance of preparing prospective teachers for ongoing self-renewal in terms of life-long learning.

In the productive conversation that ensued the dean and the librarian discussed, among many other things, the importance of pre-service teachers being prepared to keep up-to-date on trends and developments in education. They agreed that preparation for an effective teacher should include training and experience in locating and using educational research and the findings and experiences of other educators; that innovative ideas for successful teaching and solutions other teachers have found to common educational problems are indeed readily available to those prepared to use the appropriate access tools and strategies.

The dean assured the librarian of his willingness to consider any and all concrete proposals for program improvement, whether from committees, faculty or education librarians—and there the conversation ended.

Bibliographic Workshop Foments Interest

The announcement of a "Course-Integrated Bibliographic Instruction Workshop" to be presented by Earlham College and Willamette University librarians and faculty members at Willamette, Oregon, arrived at an opportune time. The librarian lost no time in proposing to the dean that the college have a faculty library representative attend the workshop which she also planned to attend. The dean decided not only to fund the attendance of a faculty representative from the Department of Curriculum and Instructional Science but also encouraged the chairmen of the departments of Elementary Education and Secondary Education to attend.

The busy professor and administrators who had been thus drafted were good sports, though not excited at the prospect of spending three days talking about library instruction. Librarians who have attended Evan Farber's Earlham presentations will probably guess that the attitudes of the three professors on the return trip were somewhat different from those expressed on the flight to Willamette. The workshop was extremely motivating with participants learning of not only the highly acclaimed program at Earlham but of the successful program adaptations made at Willamette.

The flight home was spent enthusiastically discussing how the College of Education could adapt this program at BYU. An initial decision—to take a low-key approach—has turned out to be the most important decision made. The program would begin with a few pilot classes, and if these proved successful, a college-wide integrated program would be undertaken. Otherwise the demands on the education librarian, who would be working with each instructor in tailoring a program for each course, would be overwhelming.

The education librarian had been working for years with the various graduate programs in the College of Education. She also cooperated with the English Department in presenting discipline-oriented junior-level library-instruction sessions at research paper time. Most of the students in these classes had attended freshman-level research strategy sessions but few of them had used the library enough to remember much that had been presented. It seemed obvious that the only way students would really master the use of the library would be through the assignment of on-going course-integrated activities. But first it was important to ensure that all students received good introductions to research strategy while freshmen, and introductions to discipline-related research, along with a review of strategy, while juniors.

Inter-Departmental Cooperation

On the trip to Willamette, the librarian had learned of some innovative ideas being tried in the College of Education. For example, faculty members in the Department of Elementary Education were concerned about the training prospective teachers were receiving in the junior-level English classes. They considered it vital that the future classroom teachers not only learn to write well themselves, but that they learn how to teach their students to write well. The Department of Elementary Education had, therefore, negotiated with the English Department to teach a special composition course for elementary education students, English 313, Critical Writing for Elementary Education Majors.

For years the library had encountered difficulties in ensuring the attendance of junior-level English students at supposedly required library orientation sessions. The chairman of the Elementary Education Department invited the librarian to attend his next meeting with the English supervisor and the teachers assigned to the special sections. At that meeting, it was decided that bibliographic instruction was indeed important to the Elementary Education Department. It was therefore agreed that rather than expecting their students to individually attend one of the regularly scheduled library instruction sessions, teachers of each special section would bring their classes to the library as a group at the time their students needed the instruction to complete library research assignments. The education librarian and the English teachers could also work together to tailor the class to meet the needs of the students and the teaching style of the instructor.

The English instructors have been most cooperative and have extended great effort in their work with the prospective teachers. For example, one instructor decided to work a few hours a week as a research assistant for a doctoral candidate in education to gain the experience she felt that she needed in educational research. She now feels that she better understands the problems which her students are sure to encounter. During the first week the students are working on research papers she spends her office hours in the library so she can be of assistance to them.

Another of the English teachers worked on a research paper, along with her students, to familiarize herself with educational research tools and strategy.

Extra Dividend for Good Work

The relationships established with the English instructors have paid off handsomely in terms of improved library instruction for prospective elementary school teachers. Not only have the students been doing better research, but many are being prepared to work as research assistants for education professors and graduate students. The English teachers have recommended students who have done exceptionally well on research and writing to the education librarian who has followed up with them to be sure that they are well-grounded in working with education research strategies and tools. Now, when professors inquire about a competent research assistant they are given a list of twice-recommended (by English teacher and education librarian) students from their own department.

Although the Secondary Education Department does not have special English classes for their students, the professors of English

377, Secondary Teaching Procedures, and English 378, Teaching Reading, have cooperated with the education librarian to provide the same advantages for prospective secondary teachers who would like to work as research assistants.

Teachers of other subject-oriented secondary education classes, such as Vocational Education, Foreign Language Education, Home Economics Education, Social Studies Education, and Art Education have also made arrangements for discipline-related library orientations.

CAMPUS-WIDE BIBLIOGRAPHIC INSTRUCTION WORKSHOP

With the introductory and discipline-oriented overview classes for education students now functioning, the four who had attended the Willamette workshop decided to introduce the College as a whole to the concept of "Course-Integrated Bibliographic Instruction" (CIBI). The dean was pleased with what had happened thus far and was ready to finance an Earlham workshop for the College of Education. However, library administrators, who had been closely following developments, were also interested in an Earlham workshop to introduce other university departments to the concept of course-integrated bibliographic instruction. So it was agreed that the College of Education and the University Library would co-sponsor a two-day workshop to which all faculty members in the College of Education and all library faculty would be invited. All English teachers who were working with the special elementary education classes were also invited and urged to attend. In addition, each subject librarian was encouraged to invite a faculty library representative, a department chairman, or other interested faculty member from the colleges or departments with whom they worked.

The workshop began with a general meeting held in the College of Education to which the whole campus was invited. After the dean of the college and the library director gave brief welcoming remarks, Evan Farber, of Earlham, introduced the concept of course-integrated bibliographic instruction and one of the three professors he had brought with him briefly shared his "conversion" story and titillated the audience with hints of what was to come in later sessions.

The workshop was well attended, thanks to the written invitations from the dean and library director. Evan Farber and his colleagues soon generated a contagious enthusiasm among those in attendance. It was not just enthusiasm, however, that influenced this knowledgeable group. The ideas made sense, and the librarians and professors saw how they could work together to prepare students to become proficient library users of the literature in their disciplines.

The entire workshop was planned to give ample opportunity for faculty and librarian interaction with the guests, with each other, and with colleagues from other colleges and departments. And interact they did. The workshop sessions were informal and quickly adapted to meet the needs of the participants. Meals and frequent breaks also provided opportunities for discussion and socializing. The wrap-up session late on Friday afternoon was as motivating as the first session had been. The workshop successfully provided the impetus to implement the next phase of the overall plan.

Several professors who had attended the workshop expressed an interest in integrating a library assignment into their classes. These early efforts would have to be considered course-related rather than fully course-integrated, but were considered a step toward the objective of course-integrated programs.

Foundations Class as Pilot Program

One of the most effective of these efforts is that developed by Elementary Education 310R, Introduction to Learning and Teaching, required of all entering elementary education majors. With strong encouragement from their department chairman, the professors who team teach this class of 100 to 150 students per semester worked out a library assignment in which each student was required to take a teacher aptitude test and then assigned to do some research in the areas in which the instrument had identified weaknesses. The students then had to write papers discussing what could be done to improve their levels of competency in the weak areas. This assignment was definitely related to course objectives and, except for the difficulty the students experienced in identifying appropriate search terms for the concepts included in the locally-produced teacher aptitude test, could be considered a meaningful and positive library experience.

This past semester the education librarian worked with the professor of educational foundations to create a course-integrated library module for Elementary Education 310R. Based on the library research strategies learned in a two-hour introductory session, an assignment, and a one-hour follow-up session at the beginning of the semester, the module requires each student to research an educational philosopher, his ideas, and the influence he has had on education. The librarian had provided a model philosopher search, with copies of the pages consulted in each reference tool. After following the step-by-step search she performed in class, most students appear quite competent in performing their own searches. Speaking from a mid-semester vantage point, the module appears to be working well.

The education librarian and a professor of children's literature worked cooperatively on a lesson introducing the students to the important book reviewing sources for children's literature. In a three-year study carried out with the many sections of this class, it was discovered that the great majority of students selected books based primarily on teacher recommendation or the recommendation of their peers. Unless the prospective teachers learned to be more independent in identifying and selecting good books, it was feared that they would continue to recommend only the books which they had heard about in their classes, becoming more and more outdated.

The initial class was taught by the education librarian, but the children's literature professor has now incorporated this segment into her own teaching.

PLANS FOR SURVIVAL

Numerous other professors have requested classes to meet specific needs and the education librarian has worked with them to develop appropriate presentations and assignments. However, it now appears that the time for retrenchment is rapidly approaching.

The program goal was, and is, to ensure that everyone who graduates from the College of Education is library literate. Ways have opened up to make this goal appear possible, but it is now time to plan additional options for reaching all of the students as the program has already become almost too much for one librarian to handle.

Compounding the work load in Bibliographic Instruction is the library's recent acquisition of ERIC on CD-ROM. The Education Librarian was buried in requests for classes and individual introductions to the system. Fortunately, one of the instructional science professors has developed a users' guide and the library training officer is now working on a training program for the CD-ROM systems. Again, department-library cooperation is paying off.

An active Library Bibliographic Instruction Committee has wisely concluded that only so much can be taught in the freshman-level and junior-level classes already described. The committee is now leaning toward optional classes on the use of the automated catalog and various CD-ROM systems, to be taught by the training officer or subject librarians as appropriate.

The fifty-minute freshman-level introductory strategy classes and the fifty-minute junior-level discipline-oriented strategy sessions are firmly in place and the Elementary Education 310R class library module is functioning as a course integrated review for those students just coming into the elementary education program and as a discipline-oriented library introduction to transfer students and others who, for whatever reason, have not taken the freshman and junior English classes.

Since the need for bibliographic instruction has now been clearly established by the College of Education, supported by the university library and acknowledged by the faculty, more work must be done to ensure that individual professors and teaching assistants are able to handle more of the responsibility for a successful program. In too many cases the librarian is still doing most of the planning and presenting, primarily due to lack of the time necessary for cooperation. So much progress has been made, though, since the initial efforts in 1985, that optimism appears justified. The education librarian has recently obtained a number of class syllabi and is working to prepare a few library assignments which will fulfill course objectives at the same time they enhance the planned development of library skills. It is hoped that these examples will help to suggest other ideas for successful class library experiences to the professors.

Cooperative planning of truly integrated assignments can do much to enrich classes and provide the experience needed by the students if they are to master the tools and strategies of successful educational research and make life-long learning a real part of their personal and professional lives.

In retrospect, the fears experienced by the subject librarians when they were banned from scheduled hours at the reference desk appear groundless. Never has their expertise been in greater demand. Exposure to throngs of students in discipline-oriented bibliographic instruction classes has assured them of immortality (or at least of student and faculty contact). When students need special help with research in education (or history, or political science, or biology, etc.) they know exactly where to go and whom to see. Hours when the librarian is available are announced in the classes and students are encouraged to call for appointments, if needed, at other times.

While most public services librarians acknowledge the vital need for bibliographic instruction they also understand that the impact of any type of program can be devastating on a department unless plans are made to relieve the librarians of some of their other responsibilities during the heavy involvement periods. This is one of the reasons that most of the subject librarians at Brigham Young University have finally come to view their exile from the reference desks with relative equanimity.

Course-related, and particularly course-integrated classes require much more time initially and an unwavering commitment to good librarian/professor relations. However, in the final analysis, a successful program of course-integrated bibliographic instruction is a contribution worthy of the most dedicated and service-oriented academic librarian and is well worth the required expenditure of time and effort.

Term Paper Counseling:
The Library's Tutorial

Lizabeth A. Wilson
Joyce C. Wright

SUMMARY. Term paper counseling has emerged as the library's solution to the instructional limitations and constraints of the reference desk and the bibliographic instruction classroom. Term paper counseling uses the tutorial method of instruction to provide students with individualized assistance. Paralleling the four major tutoring structures, term paper counseling has been provided as standalone tutoring, course tutoring, emergency tutoring, and structured tutoring. This paper details tutoring as an instructional method, term paper counseling as tutorial, and successful models for term paper counseling.

Any reference librarian who has faced lines of eager students awaiting assistance with their research papers at the reference desk has felt the frustration of not being able to offer more than superficial assistance due to lack of time or staff. In a noble attempt to help the students, the reference librarian tries to juggle the questions, getting one student started with a periodical index, the next with the online catalog, and another with a recently published bibliography. Then it's back to the reference desk to field another wave of questions, making rapid-fire judgments based on staccato reference interviews as the telephone rings and the caller asks for help in deciphering a garbled proceedings citation.

Likewise, bibliographic instruction librarians involved in class-

---

Lizabeth A. Wilson is Assistant Director for Undergraduate Libraries and Instructional Services, and Joyce C. Wright is Assistant Undergraduate Librarian and Coordinator of Reference Services, Undergraduate Library, University of Illinois, 1408 W. Gregory Drive, Urbana, IL 61801.

room teaching can provide anecdotal evidence which illustrates the inadequacies of group instruction. The instruction librarian is challenged to effectively address the divergent levels of student research expertise and experience within the confines of the hour-long presentation. Most instruction librarians have had the experience of having a student in class appear anxious about the impending research paper but too intimidated or overwhelmed by the amount of information presented to ask questions. Or take that student with the glazed expression. Was the presentation totally irrelevant, too basic, or too accelerated for the withdrawn student?

While the limitations and constraints of the reference desk and the bibliographic instruction classroom may be quite different when it comes to meeting students' research demands, reference and instruction librarians do share the common concern that they often cannot adequately help the individual student solve specific research problems in an efficient, productive manner. Term paper counseling has emerged as a common solution to the limitations of both reference desk service and formal classroom instruction. Term paper counseling serves both as an extension of the reference desk and a supplement to classroom instruction. Term paper counseling has become the library's tutorial. This paper will discuss tutoring as a teaching method, term paper counseling as tutorial, and successful models for term paper counseling.

TUTORING AS A TEACHING METHOD

Tutoring is a method of instruction in which a student or a small group of students receives individualized assistance from a teacher. The teacher may be a paid instructor, a volunteer, the student's parent, a peer, a teacher's assistant, or even a machine. The teacher is called, not surprisingly, a tutor and the student receiving the personalized instruction the tutee.

Tutoring is often used to provide supplemental or remedial instruction to students who haven't been successful learning by traditional classroom methods or for some reason are prevented from participating in a regular educational program. Tutoring can result in highly productive dialog between the tutor and tutee. The most successful tutoring allows the student to discover and develop new ideas. During this discovery process, the tutor provides the help and support vital to building student confidence. Tutoring permits the teacher and student to follow through a process or idea, turning generalities and abstractions into individual strategies and answers. The tutor can address specific student deficiencies and solve problems as they present themselves. Tutoring facilitates independent learning and fosters critical thinking. Tutoring as a teaching method allows for the individual differences among students to be effectively addressed, enabling the tutor to become conversant with an individual student's weaknesses, strengths, and uniqueness as a person.[1]

Tutoring conjures up colorful and varied images. Hollywood depictions of Anna educating the Siamese king's children in *The King and I* or Reginald Johnston instructing and counseling Pu Yi in *The Last Emperor* vividly illustrate the dynamic one-to-one educational relationship of tutor and tutee. There exists a tutorial relationship between every parent and infant as the child begins to talk. The child tries out a sentence. Although the verb might not agree with the subject, the meaning comes through. The parent gently and routinely corrects the grammatical mistake without a second thought. The child repeats the correction and the tutorial dialog continues. Then there is the volunteer tutor working in the community literacy program, encouraging the middle-aged reader with praise and positive feedback as he struggles through the first paragraph. From the royal companion to the proud parent to the volunteer, each tutor illustrates the essence of the tutorial — the immediacy and flexibility of one-to-one teaching.

TUTORING STRUCTURES

While the essential ingredient of tutoring remains the directness of the teaching method, tutoring can be structured in several ways. The four major types of tutorials include: standalone tutoring, course tutoring, emergency tutoring, and structured tutoring.[2]

Standalone tutoring occurs when instruction is only available through the tutorial. The tutorial is the class. Standalone tutoring often exists when conditions prevent the student from participating in the established educational structure or the needed instructional program doesn't exist. The segregation of royal children from mainstream society resulted in standalone tutoring. Contemporary examples of standalone tutoring include the university professor who hires the international student to teach him basic Mandarin before an upcoming lecture tour of Beijing or the community literacy program volunteers who teach fellow adults to read at the local library.

In course tutoring, the tutor provides the tutee supplemental assistance directly tied to material covered in a course. The role of the tutor is to clarify and review course material, to encourage the student, and to provide immediate feedback on the student's progress. Course tutoring is often used in support of skill-based courses such as mathematics or writing courses. In the case of writing courses, the tutorial is commonly referred to as the writing conference.[3]

Emergency tutoring is tutoring provided to students who need quick and immediate assistance because of tomorrow's final, a personal crisis, test anxiety, or impending deadlines. Informal emergency tutoring goes on in every residence hall the night before an examination as the magnanimous senior helps the forlorn freshman review the essential points of the course. Emergency tutoring is often provided spontaneously by professors when a panicked student shows up during office hours. The commercial firms which offer cram courses promising students improved GRE scores specialize in emergency tutoring.

In structured tutoring, the tutor and student make use of computer structured materials and programmed learning. In some cases, the computer or tape recorder becomes the tutor. For the student enrolled in an Italian course, the tutorial transpires in the language laboratory where the student completes the drills provided on tutorial tapes. With the advances in recent years in computer-aided tutoring and interactive video programs, there is increasing utilization of computers as tutors.

GUIDELINES FOR SUCCESSFUL TUTORING

Regardless of the structure of the tutoring, successful tutoring is dependent upon the quality of the relationship between the tutor and tutee. While there is no sure-fire prescription for successful tutoring, there are some general guidelines to follow concerning the role of the tutor in establishing a quality tutor-tutee relationship.

The tutor plays numerous roles in the tutorial relationship. The tutor must be at once coach, commentator, counselor, and listener. As coach, the tutor guides the student, identifies problem areas, evaluates progress, and suggests areas for further attention. As commentator, the tutor serves to provide the student with the larger picture, broadening the student's cognitive domain. The tutor-as-commentator helps the student draw on past knowledge and current experience, providing the student with a framework for learning. As counselor, the tutor must look at the student as a whole person. Often motivational problems, low self-esteem, learning or physical disabilities or personal problems make it difficult if not impossible for the students to be academically successful. For many students, the tutorial setting is the only environment in which they feel comfortable enough to expose the conditions stifling their progress. As listener, the tutor shows interest in the student while trying to decipher what the student needs. The tutor-as-listener attempts to make an accurate needs diagnosis.

The attitude of the tutor can positively or negatively affect the learning environment. The tutor should create an atmosphere of trust in which the student feels free to ask questions and express hesitations. The tutor should be positive and nonjudgmental in providing assistance. It is essential that the tutor articulates the goals of the tutorial as well as the roles of the tutor and the student. Clearly established goals and objectives reduce ambiguity and serve to focus the session.[4]

Given the great educational benefits of the tutorial, it is not surprising that many libraries have developed term paper counseling services based on the dynamics of one-to-one teaching. The remainder of this paper will detail term paper counseling as tutorial, the librarian as tutor, and four models for term paper counseling.

TERM PAPER COUNSELING AS TUTORIAL

Term paper counseling has emerged as an accepted institutional solution to the limitations of reference desk service and the bibliographic instruction classroom. Term paper counseling goes by many names: term paper assistance, research consultations, term paper clinics, and tutorial instruction. Regardless of the name, the various individualized term paper programs share several elements and advantages characteristic of the tutoring method of instruction.

Term paper counseling typically involves one-to-one instruction between a student and a librarian much like the relationship of a tutor and a tutee. Students who avail themselves of term paper research counseling receive personalized research assistance which is tailored to their individual paper topics. When James Rice outlined the advantages of term paper counseling clinics, he could just as well have been writing about tutorials:

1. They focus the instruction on a real need rather than on something the librarian perceives as a need.
2. They automatically correspond to a utilization of materials and an application of learning.
3. They communicate to the student a willingness to help.[5]

Term paper counseling responds to students' instructional needs for one-to-one instruction in a way that reference service or classroom instruction cannot. Term paper counseling can provide supplemental, remedial, or follow-up instruction, can be adjusted to the student's level of research expertise, and can allow the librarian to respond to the diverse learning styles of heterogeneous learners.

TERM PAPER COUNSELOR AS TUTOR

Term paper counselors are indeed tutors. Several essential elements must be addressed to insure that term paper counseling based on the tutorial model is successful. First, informed decisions need to be made concerning who will tutor. Second, adequate tutor training and preparation are needed for a solid tutorial program. And finally, the term paper counseling sessions need to be properly structured to provide the greatest benefit for the student.

Typically, reference librarians have served as the counselors or tutors in term paper counseling settings. In Northern Illinois University's term paper clinic described by Eileen Dubin et al. in 1978, reference librarians spearheaded an early attempt at small group tutorials in the library.[6] Reference librarians from both the Undergraduate Library and the Humanities Reference department at the University of North Carolina-Chapel Hill joined forces to offer Library and Research Consultations (LaRC) as detailed in 1978.[7] Gillian Debreczeny has reported on the continued use of reference librarians at UNC in providing undergraduates with individualized term paper consultations as well as computer enhancements to the tutorials.[8] Similarly, the term paper counseling offered at the University of Ottawa uses solely reference librarians as counselors.[9] The Term Paper Assistance Program (TAP) at University of Michigan's Undergraduate Library is staffed by undergraduate reference librarians.[10]

Less often, technical service librarians join reference personnel in serving as term paper tutors. For the past fifteen years, librarians from both traditionally public service units and technical service units have volunteered to serve as tutors at Term Paper Research Counseling offered in the Undergraduate Library of the University of Illinois at Urbana-Champaign.[11] The advantages of bringing librarians from diverse professional backgrounds together to instruct students are detailed in Lois Pausch and Carol Penka's discussion of reference and technical service cooperation in library instruction.[12]

In some instances, teaching or graduate assistants have served as counselors. Tutorial library instruction offered as part of the freshmen program at Berea College uses both librarians and instructors from the teaching departments on its tutorial staff.[13] At the University of Illinois, graduate students enrolled in the Graduate School of Library and Information Science join librarians in volunteering their time and expertise in assisting the hundreds of students who annually seek out help at the term paper counseling table.[14]

Given the enthusiasm for peer tutoring in many fields, it is interesting to note that term paper counselors to date have been limited to librarians, librarians-in-training, and teaching associates. Respective of the ever-increasing demands on the limited staff resources of the library and of the success of peer tutoring programs, it may be beneficial for libraries to investigate using peer tutors for term paper counseling. During a staff workshop on international students and the library held at the University of Illinois at Urbana-Champaign during the summer of 1987, keynote speaker Catalina

Diluvio, a doctoral student in library and information science from the Philippines, remarked that international students often seek out a more experienced foreign student to show them the ropes of the library attempting to avoid asking for help at the reference desk. Diluvio suggested that some students avoid asking for help because of fear of appearing inadequate, being unable to explain themselves sufficiently in English, or lack of familiarity with reference services. Diluvio proposed that some international students become the "gatekeepers" to the library and are actively sought out by anxious and unsure library users. Librarians may do well to invite these gatekeepers to participate as peer tutors in a program of term paper counseling.

Regardless of who tutors, the attitude of the counselor is of paramount importance to the success of term paper counseling as tutorial. The counselor must be able to coach, comment, counsel, and listen. Since tutoring is a one-to-one instructional method, the term paper tutor must feel comfortable with entering into an active dialog with the student.

Often, the training of term paper counselors consists of a one-hour orientation for volunteers or discussion about the aims of the program at a weekly reference meeting. It is important that the term paper counseling administrator provides counselors with a solid foundation in the aims, goals, and objectives of the tutorials as well as an opportunity to discuss and evaluate the program. Term paper counselors are well served by receiving a needs profile of the students who take part in term paper counseling. If term paper counseling is supplementary to classroom instruction, the counselor must be acquainted with the course content, the course text, and the goals and expectations of the instructor. Perhaps most importantly, the counselor needs administrative support, professional backup, and a knowledge of area resources in the event that a referral is necessary to help the student with personal problems which may surface in the tutorial which are outside the librarian's expertise.[15]

The term paper tutorial session should be structured to allow for diagnostic time, instructional time, and evaluation time. A typical session lasts thirty minutes, a reasonable timeframe in which to diagnose, instruct, and evaluate the student's immediate needs. Term paper counseling should be structured to facilitate and encourage students to make repeat tutorial visits. A tutoring record can be kept by the student or the tutor through the use of a checklist or a research log. A tutoring or research record ensures that each subsequent visit will build on the work completed in the previous tutorials.

If attention is paid to the selection of the term paper counselors, the training and preparation of the tutors, and the proper structuring of the tutorial itself, the essential elements of a successful term paper counseling program will be firmly in place. No two term paper counseling programs are identical because each must respond to the needs of the local student body, the administrative constraints, the available staff resources, and the established need for a particular tutoring structure.

MODELS FOR TERM PAPER COUNSELING

The major models for term paper counseling parallel the four types of tutorials: standalone tutoring, course tutoring, emergency tutoring, and structured tutoring. The choice of a particular tutoring structure for a term paper counseling program is guided by the instructional needs of the students being served and by the existing instructional structure. In order to illustrate how each tutoring structure can be effectively implemented in libraries, successful term paper counseling programs will be discussed as models for the library's tutorial.

Term Paper Counseling
as Standalone Tutoring

Term paper counseling as standalone tutoring provides a model where the tutorial is the primary instructional mode. Standalone term paper counseling is often developed when no other bibliographic instruction components have been established. In other cases, the standalone term paper counseling model is selected in lieu of other bibliographic instruction modes because of the personalized instruction afforded through one-to-one tutorials. Two successful examples of the standalone tutorial model are Berea College's tutorial library program and University of North Carolina at Chapel Hill's Library and Research Consultations (LaRC).

Berea's tutorial library program was developed in the mid-1970s as its exclusive method for mass library instruction on the freshman level. After five years of ongoing implementation, Hughes and Flandreau report that it "has proven to be a practical and effective alternative for instruction of large numbers of students."[16] The tutorial library program was predicated on the following beliefs:

1. The ability to search for and retrieve information is one of the competencies of an educated person. Instruction in these skills must systematically and effectively reach all students before their graduation from college.
2. The distinguishing purpose of an undergraduate library is to ensure that this instruction occurs. Such instruction should be the first priority and mission of a college library.
3. To the greatest extent possible, if not exclusively, library instruction should take place in the library and in a hands-on mode. Learning should most effectively occur directly and actively with the library tools to be manipulated rather than indirectly and passively in the classroom and/or with media substitutes.
4. To be effective, library instruction must occur at the time the student has the specific need for such instruction. In addition, it should be offered within, and be an integral part of, existing courses, not something artificially imposed in a separate course.[17]

Berea's premises reinforce the fundamentals of tutoring: systematic instruction; active learning; hands-on experience; and, individualized instruction.

Librarians and teaching associates participated in an intensive training program prior to the tutoring. Through the training all tutors strived to achieve an indepth knowledge of basic search strategies and library tools. The librarians and teaching associates learned about the ingredients for successful tutoring — active learning on the part of the tutee and the role of the tutor as listener, questioner, and coach.

The Berea library tutorial program offered all freshmen two hours of individualized instruction in the library. The tutor detailed the objectives of the sessions and the roles of tutor and tutee in the initial session. Each of the two conferences was structured for effective tutoring allowing for diagnosis, instruction, and evaluation. During session one, the first ten minutes were devoted to an informal diagnostic discussion during which the tutor attempted to ascertain the student's level of research sophistication. The bulk of the tutoring session focused on hands-on instruction in search methods during which the tutee did all of the active work. The tutor questioned, suggested, and guided the student where appropriate, resisting the temptation to take over the student's work. The conference concluded with an evaluation of what had been accomplished, particularly focusing on whether the topic was feasible to research given the available resources. A second tutorial was scheduled approximately two weeks later. During the intervening two weeks, the student was expected to complete the full topic search.

The second tutorial followed a similar pattern of diagnosis, instruction, and evaluation. The sessions began with a review and discussion of the student's working bibliography. Depending on the condition of the bibliography, the remaining time was devoted to working with resources missed in the student's independent search or to information not covered during the first session due to lack of time. The session concluded with the tutor once again evaluating the student's progress. If the tutor determined that the student had compiled an appropriate bibliography, the library tutorial program was concluded; if further work is needed, a third session was scheduled.

Hughes and Flandreau report that the library tutorial program proved to be successful on several fronts including strengthened library competencies by freshmen, increased student interest in the library, and demonstrated evidence to student and faculty of the library's instructional commitment.[18]

While Berea's term paper counseling is geared to standalone tutorials for undergraduates, the LaRC program of the University of North Carolina provides research tutorials for graduate students. Since there was no formal bibliographic instruction specifically directed at graduate students, the reference departments at North Carolina responded to this gap in library service by organizing a tutorial program to meet the instructional and research needs of graduates.[19]

The LaRC was designed as a standalone tutorial providing one-to-one, uninterrupted consultation away from the frantic pace of the reference desk. As Ishaq and Cornick so aptly described:

> It is not always easy for librarians to shift mental gears and immediately recall the best sources of information on twelfth-century Spanish manuscripts after spending time on questions dealing with black English or Chinese-American foreign relations.[20]

Graduate students signed up for a consultation by filling out an appointment form detailing the research topic and stage of the project. A librarian would do some pre-consultation preparation on the specific topic before the LaRC tutorial. During the thirty to forty-five minute tutorial, the librarian worked with the tutee to identify and use appropriate sources. The librarian strived to appear unhurried, hoping to provide an atmosphere in which the student felt inclined to ask questions, following one of the basic guidelines for successful tutoring.

Students were uniformly positive on the tutorial service for graduate students whether their research project was a thesis, paper, or dissertation. Among the numerous laudatory comments from students, one highlighted the effectiveness of tutorials being tailored to very specific needs:

> . . . pleased to be treated with respect and consideration. This, I feel, reflects highly on your department's vision of clients as individuals with specific information needs.[21]

Term Paper Counseling as Course Tutoring

Term paper counseling as course tutoring provides a model where the tutee receives supplemental assistance directly tied to material covered in a class. Course-tied term paper counseling most often emerges in a mature bibliographic instruction program where a strong classroom component is already established. Course tutoring allows a library to offer one-to-one instruction which further articulates the content of classroom bibliographic instruction. Course tutoring allows for more detailed and individualized instruction following a bibliographic instruction session. In term paper counseling modeled on course tutoring, the term paper counseling becomes, in some ways, the "office hours" of the bibliographic instruction librarian.

At the Undergraduate Library of the University of Illinois at Urbana-Champaign, term paper counseling is based on the course tutoring model. When term paper counseling was originally implemented at Illinois in the early 1970s, the counseling was closer to the emergency tutoring model. But, as the Illinois classroom bibliographic instruction program continued to expand and become fully course-integrated, the focus of term paper counseling changed from emergency tutoring to course tutoring.

The bibliographic instruction program at Illinois' Undergraduate Library is course-integrated, directed at the research needs of undergraduates enrolled in the university's required freshmen composition course.[22] The program operates on three major premises: (1) that students be instructed in a cognitive approach to research skills; (2) that the student body is heterogeneous and every attempt should be made to address individual research experience and learning preferences; and, (3) that instruction needs to be offered at the student's time of instructional need.

In order to address these three key premises, nine unique bibliographic instruction programs for distinct groups of learners have been developed. The mode and type of instruction varies with the group. The instructional components include a required research text, orientation tours, pre-research skills instruction, tool-specific workshops, research skills instruction, subject seminars, team-teaching, and term paper research counseling. Term paper research counseling is a vital component of the program, allowing the library to offer one-to-one instruction to a large student body.

Illinois' term paper research counseling supplements the material presented in all the numerous bibliographic instruction components offered to students. During classroom presentations, students are encouraged to avail themselves of term paper research counseling as follow-up much in the way they would utilize a professor's office hours.

Term paper research counseling is offered for four weeks each semester during the peak periods of bibliographic instruction classes and reference desk activity. Staffed by volunteer librarians and graduate students enrolled in the Graduate School of Library and Information Science, the tutoring is offered on a drop-in basis with no prior appointment necessary. Over 300 students use term paper research counseling in a typical semester, many making multiple visits to the tutoring table.

In an orientation training session for the tutors, the coordinator of term paper research counseling instructs the volunteers in the goals and objectives of the tutoring, profiles the students who will be coming to the counseling, discusses tutoring techniques, and informs tutors about the content of the other bibliographic instruction components in which the students will have already participated. The tutors view the same videotape the students will have seen in their classes, receive a desk copy of the required textbook, and review the printed aids which were distributed in class. In essence, the training session prepares the tutors for the demands of course tutoring.

By using volunteer librarians and graduate students as tutors and by providing appropriate training, the Undergraduate Library is able to temporarily increase its staff to allow it to offer this intensive one-to-one tutorial service at a large university. Term paper research counseling is viewed by both librarians and students alike as dynamic, individualized course tutoring which supplements and enriches classroom bibliographic instruction and reference desk service.

Term Paper Counseling as Emergency Tutoring

Term paper counseling as emergency tutoring provides students with assistance when needed because of an impending deadline (i.e., a term paper due date) or research intimidation. Because of the pressure of deadlines or library anxiety, many students eagerly take advantage of term paper counseling structured to provide emergency tutoring. Two excellent examples of emergency tutoring are the University of Michigan Undergraduate Library's Term Paper

Assistance Program (TAP) and the University of Ottawa's Term-paper Counseling (TPC).

Michigan's TAP began in 1979, designed to provide students with special, one-to-one assistance on research papers from a reference librarian. Students made appointments for research assistance by filling out a research form. Librarians screened the forms to determine which students could be helped at the reference desk and which needed the one-to-one tutorial. During the tutorial, the student participated actively in the physical retrieval of materials while learning the process of a search strategy.

Bergen and MacAdam report that they harbored numerous concerns about the practicality of offering a program of tutoring:

1. Does the reference staff have time for this program without jeopardizing other services, such as reference and classroom bibliographic instruction?
2. How would such a program mesh with reference and classroom library instruction, and would interest in these services decrease among users?
3. Even if staff were able to begin such a program, what would happen if every student wanted an individual appointment? In large academic institutions, which may have even a freshman enrollment of several thousand, is such a service prohibited from the start?[23]

Their fears turned out to be unfounded. Demand for bibliographic instruction classes did not waiver and reference didn't decrease. The number of students participating in TAP reached a stable plateau of 100-150 annually.

An emergency tutoring program called TPC was implemented at the University of Ottawa. Designed specifically for graduate students, TPC attempted to respond to a student's immediate need with an individualized service. Schobert's description of how TPC differed from instruction seminars and reference desk service highlights the immediacy of emergency tutoring:

It differs from ordinary instruction in that it is given on a one-to-one basis, and can be tailored exactly to the student's topic, and the goal is not basic orientation — the students are expected to find out about the card catalog and library services on their own. It differs from the typical reference encounter in that the librarian is able to spend more time with the client than would ordinarily be possible for a reference question.[24]

At the appointment desk, the tutee and the librarian went through a diagnostic discussion of the student's research needs. During the session, the librarian reviewed the goals of the service as an assistance program. After a diagnosis of research needs, the librarian and student worked together identifying sources and retrieving materials. Students responded positively to TPC although Schobert cautions that:

Evaluating a project like this objectively is nearly impossible. There is a built-in bias in its favor: where there was nothing, suddenly there is an individualized instruction program; the responses are bound to be positive. Indeed, such was the case.[25]

Term Paper Counseling
as Structured Tutoring

Term paper counseling as structured tutoring makes use of computer structured materials or programmed learning. Structured tutoring allows the tutee to proceed at his or her own pace, learning incrementally with a follow-up evaluation. Libraries are beginning to take advantage of computer-aided tutoring as term paper counseling. The SourceFinder computer-assisted term paper tutorial program developed by Mary Beth Allen and Joyce Wright at the Undergraduate Library at the University of Illinois at Urbana-Champaign is an example of term paper counseling using the structured tutoring model.

Illinois' SourceFinder is a computer-assisted instruction program which guides students through a cognitive framework for bibliographic research.[26] SourceFinder encourages students to work through the research framework as a reinforcing follow-up to a bibliographic instruction session or as an individualized tutorial when no reference librarian or term paper counselor is available.

Through the support of an instructional grant, the Undergraduate Instructional Award from the Office of the Vice-Chancellor for Academic Affairs at the University of Illinois, Allen and Wright spent the summer of 1987 writing specifications for a computer tutorial which would provide structured tutoring as term paper counseling. With the assistance of graduate student Julia Schult, they authored a software package designed for independent student use. SourceFinder is written in dBASE III Plus and runs on an IBM Personal System 2 model 30. Once the software was completed, the database constructed, and the hardware secured, SourceFinder made its debut during the fall of 1987, resting near the reference collection in easy view of the reference desk in the Undergraduate Library.

SourceFinder guides a student through a cognitive research process, asking the student to make decisions about each step of the research process (e.g., What is the subject focus of your research? What kind of information do you need? Do you want contemporary or retrospective materials? etc.). When the student answers each hierarchically structured question, SourceFinder provides the student with a list of sources which fills his or her need simultaneously reviewing the characteristics of each information type.

SourceFinder has been received positively by all concerned. Students like the easy-to-follow instructions and the individualized attention of the program. Librarians from throughout the library system have expressed interest in having SourceFinder available at more library locations. Undergraduate librarians view SourceFinder as a computerized term paper counselor, always available, eternally patient, and ready with a list of sources tailored to the individual student's interests.

CONCLUSION

Over the past two decades, term paper counseling programs have emerged to fill those student instructional needs which cannot be adequately handled in the bibliographic instruction classroom or at the multi-purpose reference desk. Term paper counseling allows libraries to offer one-to-one tutoring and research consultations to individual students, often at quite large universities. While all term paper counseling programs are based on the vitality of the one-to-one interaction between librarian and student, four major models have proven to be successful and enduring. Paralleling major tutoring structures, term paper counseling has been provided as standalone tutoring, course tutoring, emergency tutoring, and structured tutoring. While the choice to use a particular tutoring structure is dependent on numerous institutional factors, all term paper counseling programs share the same goal and purpose: to provide students with personalized, individualized assistance at the student's time of instructional need, ultimately encouraging independent and informed retrieval and use of information. Term paper counseling is indeed the library's tutorial.

REFERENCES

1. For general discussions of the benefits of tutoring as a teaching method see: Sidney Rauch's *Handbook for the Volunteer Tutor* (Newark, Delaware: International Reading Association, 1985); Muriel Harris' *Teaching One-to-One: The Writing Conference* (Urbana, Illinois: National Council of Teachers of English, 1986); and, Stewart W. Ehly and Stephen C. Larsen's *Peer Tutoring for Individualized Instruction* (Boston: Allyn and Bacon, Inc., 1980).

2. F.J. Medway, "Tutoring as a Teaching Method," in *The International Encyclopedia of Education: Research and Studies* (Oxford, England: Pergamon Press, 1985), pp. 5315.

3. For a discussion specifically on the use of tutorials as writing conferences see Harris pp. 3-25.

4. Harris, pp. 46-47.

5. James Rice, Jr. *Teaching Library Use: A Guide for Library Instruction* (Westport, Connecticut; Greenwood Press, 1981), p. 65.

6. Eileen Dubin, Jitka Hurych, and Patricia McMillan, "An In-Depth Analysis of a Term Paper Clinic," *Illinois Libraries* 60 (March 1978), pp. 324-333.

7. Mary R. Ishaq and Donna P. Cornick, "Library and Research Consultations (LaRC): A Service for Graduate Students," *RQ* 18 (Winter 1978). pp. 168-176.

8. Gillian Debreczeny, "Coping with Numbers: Undergraduates and Individualized Term Paper Consultations," *Research Strategies* 3 (Fall 1985), pp. 156-163.

9. Tim Schobert, "Term Paper Counseling: Individualized Bibliographic Instruction," *RQ* 22 (Winter 1982), pp. 157-162.

10. Kathleen Bergen and Barbara MacAdam, "One-to-One: Term Paper Assistance Programs," *RQ* 24 (Spring 1985), pp. 333-339.

11. Virginia Simpson and Lizabeth Wilson, "Selling a Free Service: Term Paper Research Counseling in the Undergraduate Library," in *Marketing Instructional Services*, ed. Carolyn Kirkendall (Ann Arbor, Michigan: Pierian Press, 1986), pp. 94-98.

12. Lois Pausch and Carol Penka, "Reference/Technical Services Cooperation in Library Instruction," in *Library Instruction and Reference Services*, ed. Bill Katz and Ruth A Fraley (New York: The Haworth Press, Inc. 1984), pp. 101-108.

13. Phyllis Hughes and Arthur Flandreau, "Tutorial Library Instruction: The Freshmen Program at Berea College," *Journal of Academic Librarianship* 6 (May 1980), pp. 91-94.

14. Lizabeth Wilson and Lori L. Arp, "An Overview of the Undergraduate Library Instruction Program," *Research Strategies* 2 (Winter 1984), pp. 12-15.

15. In her article, "The Self-Management Lab: Responding to Personal Needs," *Wilson Library Bulletin* 62 (January 1988), p. 12, Joyce Wright discusses the development of a self-help information and referral center established in the University of Illinois at Urbana-Champaign Undergraduate Library to help students address pressing personal issues and concerns.

16. Hughes and Flandreau, p. 91.

17. Ibid., pp. 91-92.

18. Ibid., pp. 93-94.

19. Ishaq and Cornick, p. 168.

20. Ibid., pp. 169-179.

21. Ibid., p. 175.

22. For a detailed discussion of the Undergraduate Library program see "Large Scale-Bibliographic Instruction: The Illinois Experience," *Research Strategies* 2 (Winter 1984), pp. 4-44.

23. Bergen and MacAdam, p. 335.

24. Schobert, p. 157.

25. Ibid., p. 160.

26. For a discussion of the cognitive framework used, see David F. Kohl and Lizabeth A. Wilson, "Effectiveness of Course-Integrated Bibliographic Instruction in Improving Coursework," *RQ* 27 (Winter 1986), pp. 206-211.

Fifteen Ways to Meet Your User: Public Relations and Outreach Suggestions for Bibliographic Instruction

Laurene E. Zaporozhetz

SUMMARY. Current reports and publications from government agencies and professional organizations emphasize the changing populations entering higher education programs. Predictions indicate the current majority of traditional college students—those students entering immediately after high school, attending full time, and being between the ages of 17 and 22—will be in the minority by the year 2000. In addition, college and university programs are becoming more diverse and new programs are continually developing. This is most evident in the numbers of new specialized journals that appear each year. As libraries are developing and maintaining bibliographic instruction programs, the balance of meeting the needs of newly identified user groups as well as newly developing programs becomes more of a challenge.

In this brief article, I suggest fifteen alternatives that can be used to assist some our new users and new disciplines. This list is to be considered a beginning point, and needs to be adapted to the unique and individual characteristics of each campus community.

The fifteen ways are organized in three broad groups: before the users enter the campus; entering the library building; and outreach on campus.

BEFORE THE USERS ENTER THE CAMPUS

1. *A clear library logo.* The purpose of a logo is to be instantly identifiable to your users. Meet with the public relations officer on

---

Laurene E. Zaporozhetz is Director, Tampa Campus Library, University of South Florida, Tampa, FL 33620.

289

your campus and discuss options for developing a unique logo for the library. The library logo should complement the college/university logo. Decisions should be made for reproducing the logo in black and white as well as full color, and multiple masters in varying sizes for different purposes should be developed.

2. *Admissions*. Library services and collections should be featured as one of the criteria to consider in selecting a potential arena of higher education. Have a current set of photographs of users in the library, representing the variety of users on your campus. Offer to write the paragraphs describing the library. Many campuses offer tours to prospective students. Send over a brief script highlighting library collections and services that can be used by the students giving the tours.

3. *Continuing education*. Offer a special library orientation for those returning to campus for only one course. Advertise the offering in the continuing education brochure. Work with the staff in the continuing education office to identify the unique needs of the students.

4. *External campuses*. As campus offerings go off the main campus or are televised, make sure library services follow. Offer packets of information to faculty members teaching off campus. These packets should include basic information such as the location of the library — very clearly — for every possible driving direction that could be used. Parking locations and their proximity to the library should be clearly identified. Circulation procedures, length of borrowing period, renewals, fines, should be outlined. Have "trailers" following televised courses listing library hours, "read more about it" generic ads and so on.

5. *Hours*. Hours the library (and branch libraries) are open should be posted in a very visible place. Handouts listing hours should be available for users. Variations in standard hours should be as consistent as possible — i.e., intersessions should be the same, holidays as consistent as possible. Bookmarks indicating changes in hours should be available a couple weeks in advance. Consider a telephone line and an answering machine with a tape enumerating the library hours.

ENTERING THE BUILDING

6. *Signage*. Walk into your library building as if you had never been there before. What is the first thing you see? Due to security systems in most larger facilities, the first thing is probably a turnstile, and possibly a circulation desk. What directs the user to a basic information point? to the collection? to the reference desk? to a specialized collection?

Develop a set of policies to implement a set of procedures for signs. Include size, color, variations, number (don't oversign) and other needs unique to your facility. In developing signage, think of yourself in another service or educational institution, such as a bank or a museum. How to you feel when you first enter the facility, how do you know where to go, who to ask? The sign should come where it will provide the most impact, i.e., location directories should be near the catalog, all terminals that provide access to the catalog, all elevators and stairs.

7. *Publications*. Publications need to be visible in two areas, a centralized area to increase overall awareness and at the service point-of-point of use. Equipment and supply catalogs offer a variety of solutions for displaying these types of materials. Have both a visible centralized location for library publications (guides, hours, reference handouts) and appropriate equipment to post point-of-use information for heavily used sources. Consider color coding the publications, i.e., overall information could be white, locational/directional could be yellow, business sources could be green, education sources could be blue, science source could be orange and so on.

8. *Suggestion Board*. Have a place for users to ask questions, comment on services, complain about whatever. Answers to all should be posted within a reasonable time period, and prior suggestions/answers should be removed within a similar time period.

9. *New Book Shelf/Display cases*.

a. New book shelf. An area, with space for seating and browsing should be available to emphasize the growth of the collection. Materials should be cleared and sent to the collection on a predictable calendar, i.e., every Wednesday. Signage should indicate that the materials can circulate, and that the materials represent new additions to the library (versus recent publications only) that have been added to the collection within the past week (or appropriate time period).

b. Display cases. Display cases can be used to complement events on campus and emphasizing the relationship of library materials to campus events. Displays can highlight commencement speakers, symposia, and other special events using books covers, actual books, copies of articles, and so on.

10. *Instruction*. In addition to traditional course related instruction, many options exist.

a. Computer-assisted instruction. Some packages are available for heavily used sources. This option will allow users to learn at their own pace. Many campuses have used locally developed programs to make the instruction unique for their campus.

b. On demand instruction. Place sign up sheets near new CD-ROM products to offer on demand instruction for those users who may not have taken a class where detailed instruction was offered.

c. Office hours. Make it clear that librarians can offer extended assistance in addition to that offered at the reference desk. Appointment and office hours can be designated. One campus offers a "one to one" service designating a specific librarian for each graduate student.

d. Term paper clinics. Offer extended services during term paper time. Often called "term paper clinics," these services review the basics in how to use the library, how to begin a paper and are often done in conjunction with a teaching faculty member and a member from the counseling center (who talks about stress).

e. "Difficult topic." Have periodic "difficult topic" nights, with brief presentations on how to tackle interdisciplinary topics, or problems in narrowing large topics.

f. Tracking. Keep track at public service points such as reference, reserve, and circulation, of difficult questions, questions hard or impossible to answer, problem assignments, and so on. Review on a weekly basis and decide if follow-up is required.

OUTREACH ON CAMPUS

11. *Administration.* As campus issues arise, assign an administrative liaison to check with upper level administration to see if additional information can be provided. This can be as simple as reading the campus paper and seeing that faculty are concerned about merit pay. A quick search can be run in a database such as ERIC, merely to offer an example that possibly other campuses are dealing with the same problem. If the results are useful, procedures can be made for a more thorough search, and follow-up with copies of the actual items. This assistance will give concrete evidence that the library exists not only to support the academic disciplines on campus, but the administrative needs.

These services are not limited to upper level administration. There should be a close working relationship with the alumni office, the fund raising office and the grants offices on campus.

12. *Faculty.*

a. Departmental meetings. Library liaisons should periodically attend meetings of each department to explain services, book and journal ordering procedures, new services, and to solicit information regarding their needs, and perceptions of quality as well as areas of concern regarding library services. This probably is a natural for the person responsible for collection development and/or bibliographic instruction.

b. Course work. Library liaisons should work with teaching faculty in making the study of the library attractive in their courses. This is most appropriate at the upper level courses such as seminars or independent study courses. Some examples: have the economics department study the problem of escalating costs of serials; have the criminal justice students study why theft and mutilation of periodicals so often occurs in university libraries; have the art/interior design students help design a color scheme to nonverbally indicate areas of quiet study, areas for noise; your campus needs will identify disciplines most appropriate for this type of outreach.

c. Faculty senate. Follow issues raised in faculty senate, and in campus wide committees. As with service to the administration, offer small "tempting searches" as a preview of what other sources exist in the library. For example, many campuses are struggling with retention of students, and have established committees to look at this problem. A quick search in ERIC would offer some preliminary ideas. Sometimes committees forget that others are struggling with similar problems.

13. *Student services.* There are many areas offering services to students related to course work that could use library materials. Again, they may not have thought of the library as a resource. Some ideas follow:

a. School paper. Ask for a reporter to do the "library beat"; offer a range of options for stories on a periodic basis. Involve all areas of the library, not just public service areas. Users need to know about cataloging, preservation, complexities of ordering out of print titles, and so on. One campus paper sent a reporter over to the library during extended hours of finals week to interview the students who were studying in the facility in the wee hours of the morning.

b. Dormitories. Contact the residence hall advisors and ask to speak at one of the orientations, or to send brochures, especially brochures indicating hours.

c. Financial aid. Offer a bibliography of sources for scholarships and other sources of funding in reference materials.

d. Placement. Offer a bibliography of how to locate information on a company prior to interview.

e. Academic advising. Offer a bibliography on career sources available in the library.

f. Counseling. Many campus counseling centers, in addition to helping students through the stresses of college now offer courses for spouses of college students. Offer to co-sponsor a "basics" course for spouses on how to locate a book, a journal article, etc. so they can feel comfortable when they are sent to "fetch" something from the library.

g. New student orientation. Make sure the library participates with tours for new freshman, more intense training for new graduate teaching assistants. Discuss the differences between orientation and instruction.

14. *Student groups.* The college/university community offers a variety of opportunities for students to gather. Student organiza-

tions revolve around many points of similarity, described in one campus catalog in the following way: academic/departmental, coordination/government, honor societies, international, political/social change, professional recognition, religious/inspirational, residence halls, service/resource, sports/recreation & social.

Each of these areas can be brought on as a "cheerleader" for the library, if they are taught the appropriate ways to use library materials. The key is to personalize the information to the organization. For example, student organization groups could be shown how to locate information to run more productive meetings, sports groups could be shown how to locate information to improve their technique. Service groups could be encouraged to take on the library as a project. For example, last year a fraternity group, as a service project, cleaned all the gum off the bottoms of study tables in one university library.

Work with the campus person responsible for students with special needs. Make sure entrances accommodate wheelchairs, crutches, easily. Are there services for the hearing impaired, the visually impaired? One library places the blind study room in a beautiful corner windows area, so that the dog who accompanies the user can also enjoy the library.

15. *Involve the entire staff.* Use employees at all levels in the outreach and bibliographic instruction program of the library. Students can do initial tours, all staff can spend some time at an information desk to answer directional and general information questions. To help with users who speak little English, keep a list of language specialties within the library at public service points.

Common arguments against a full-blown outreach public relations/bibliographic instruction program follow:

a. Just WHO is going to do this? A very legitimate question. One person should be designated as a coordinator to make sure attempts are not duplicated. This person should also work with a publications coordinator to see that all publications follow a standard format, use the library logo and so on. The main point in any outreach public relations/bibliographic instruction program is that the ENTIRE STAFF PARTICIPATES. Your library may have a golfer in serials processing who could work with the golfing group on campus; a member of a campus wide committee on retention in the Director's office, a collector of matchbooks in reference who could work with popular culture studies, a cataloger who regularly attends theatrical productions. The importance is the personal contact with someone in the library to initially get the user in the door, and direct them to the area needed. Every staff member should be a walking talking advertisement for the library.

b. This type of a program will just increase use! True, no argument. It is also one of the main reasons for a campus to have a library—so that the materials and services will be used. Study after study have shown that the majority of users of our college/university libraries come ill prepared, and often do not use the library during their college career.

c. What am I going to drop to do this—I already have too many responsibilities! The administrative team at your library has to constantly monitor workload and decide what is the most efficient and effective use of time. Not every outreach project will have to be developed from scratch, i.e., outreach to residence halls may consist of a telephone call, lunch and sending over copies of the list of hours for posting in all the dormitories.

The main reason to start or enhance an already existing public relations/bibliographic instruction outreach program is to build on the uniqueness of your campus. There *IS* a reason it exists—that either the legislature (if state funded) or a governing board approve, or the institution would not be funded from year to year. Seeing that library facilities are visible and relevant to all aspects of the campus makes basic political sense.

One area of concern. Be careful not to fall into the trap of making each user group an entity. Each "group" consists of individuals with individual strengths, weaknesses and interests. Stereotyping of any group (i.e., "You know those librarians") is offensive and unlikely to produce results.

In conclusion, to implement a program, start with a small group of individuals who are interested in this concept, work with library administration to develop policies, approve any additional funding for items such as photographs and duplication of materials. Then enjoy being in the business of advertising the library—and the special services and collections it offers.

Alternatives to the Term Paper:
An Aid to Critical Thinking

Craig Gibson

SUMMARY. The inadequacies of the traditional term paper are well-known to reference and instruction librarians. Term papers often fail to develop appropriate and mature research habits in undergraduates. Unless carefully monitored by teaching faculty, students procrastinate, do not formulate appropriate search strategies, fail to think critically about library sources consulted, and, in some cases, engage in academic dishonesty. Librarians can offer teaching faculty alternative assignments to the traditional term paper, assignments that encourage better use of library materials, stimulate student interest, develop a more holistic perspective on the artificial divisions of academia, and perhaps most important, facilitate growth in critical thinking.

Robert Ennis' critical thinking goals are offered as a foundation for planning alternative library assignments — goals that include such behaviors as focussing on an issue, analyzing arguments, asking clarifying questions, evaluating reliability of sources, and examining assumptions. Alternative library assignments should be designed with these overarching goals in mind, so that students are challenged to grow intellectually. Library assignments that encourage critical thinking will foster multiple perspectives on "real world" issues, increased awareness of the assumptions used by various academic disciplines, and a questioning, thoughtful attitude toward printed information. Librarians who develop such assignments will contribute greatly to the current movement to revitalize undergraduate education.

Ask any reference or instruction librarian about the challenges of working with teaching faculty, and you will often hear such com-

Craig Gibson is Head, Library User Education Program, Libraries, Washington State University, Pullman, WA 99164-5610.

297

ments as "they really don't understand how useful librarians can be to them" or "they give the same assignments year after year." This latter remark is likely to be heard most often near the end of the semester, when desperate students have bombarded the reference staff with pleas for help in completing their term papers on topics such as euthanasia, abortion, or capital punishment.

The term paper itself is a time-honored exercise, a "rite of passage" for most college freshmen that often lacks any real meaning as a learning experience. Some freshmen, of course, may have been required to write term papers during their high school years; these assignments, however, are often little more than research reports — a stitching together of information from several basic reference sources, with little real effort at synthesis and evaluation of such information.

College instructors and librarians alike are familiar with this "term paper syndrome," and know, too, that these research habits of high school students often persist well into their college years. Unless challenged by talented and innovative instructors and librarians, students continue their superficial research habits; they may graduate believing that they have used a library effectively and are perfectly competent writers of research papers. Students have been conditioned by high school library experiences to expect "more of the same" in college: a passing acquaintance with *Encyclopaedia Britannica* or the *Americana*, a general familiarity with the card catalog, and the practice of using *Readers' Guide* with the assumption that it contains a comprehensive listing of periodical articles suitable for any research project assigned in college.

Undergraduate students' research papers therefore are often formulaic, reflecting their arrested understanding of research, of library organization and materials, and, in general, of the purpose of undergraduate education. Of course, students should not be blamed for using formulaic approaches; after all, such strategies are often rewarded with at least passing grades. To depart from the formulaic approach would simply not occur to most students, unless they are given explicit instructions to use other sources and search strategies.

Many instructors continue to assign the traditional term paper out of sheer habit, or because they believe that a lengthy "period of incubation" allows for time for students to develop their critical thinking skills, with a paper submitted at the end of the semester as proof of such critical thinking (Meyers, 1986, p. 71). Of course, reference librarians know that the hoped-for "period of incubation" gets short-circuited because of students' procrastination, poor study skills, complacency, and lack of motivation — a whole complex of unfavorable attitudes and dispositions. The desperate student who pleads with a librarian to solve his research problems at the last minute is undoubtedly a familiar figure; even with adequate help, the procrastinating student will probably not produce a quality paper — and he or she will certainly not develop critical thinking abilities.

The result, then, is a shoddy piece of work. The student follows the practices he learned in his secondary school experience and hastily stitches together yet another research report, with little or no critical analysis, synthesis, or evaluation of the sources used. Other students, less honest but more resourceful in avoiding academic work altogether, rifle fraternity files or buy research papers from term paper companies. These abuses associated with the "term paper syndrome" are familiar to everyone in higher education, and are justifiably condemned. However, the hastily written term paper, written out of boredom, poor research skills, and procrastination, is just as surely an abuse of the process as the previously mentioned practices. Out of sheer inertia, professors, librarians, and administrators often continue to tolerate the "term paper syndrome" — a complex of attitudes, dispositions, and practices that, to anyone who seriously cares about learning, should be intolerable.

A ROLE FOR REFERENCE
AND INSTRUCTION LIBRARIANS

How, then, to change this situation? One group in higher education who possesses an often overlooked opportunity to diminish the "term paper syndrome" is reference and instruction librarians. Reference librarians often see inadequate or faulty learning occurring in students' preparation of term papers, but consider themselves powerless to effect real improvements in students' research habits because of the nature of the assignments given the students. Faculty autonomy prevails, and students continue their formulaic research habits. However, reference and instruction librarians possess the training and experience to develop other types of assignments that encourage real learning. Many librarians have a background in education or instructional design; and certainly all reference librarians have a constantly reinforced knowledge of weaknesses in students' research abilities. Obviously, too, reference librarians know their own reference collections and can think of ways that underutilized or poorly utilized sources might be used more effectively.

Reference and instruction librarians can become agents for change in higher education in several ways; one of the most significant involves adopting an active role as developers of alternatives to the term paper and as facilitators of critical thinking through such alternative assignments.

Alternative library assignments have been used in some innovative library instruction programs for a number of years. Under the direction of Evan Farber at Earlham College, librarians and faculty members have developed a set of creative assignments that stimulate student interest and often make better use of library resources than does the traditional term paper (Farber, 1984). Farber's discussion of these assignments includes some examples, and suggests in a general way many possibilities for cooperation between librarians and teaching faculty in improving student learning. The alternative assignments developed at Earlham also suggest the possibilities for expanding librarians' role in creating innovative library projects, especially ones that encourage critical thinking.

Some might question whether librarians should be involved in critical thinking — after all, isn't teaching of thinking ability a more natural role for regular faculty? The response should be: librarians are already involved in critical thinking. The reference interview allows many opportunities for encouraging students to think better. If a reference librarian suggests alternative sources to a student who might otherwise obtain a limited perspective from a single source, the librarian is facilitating better thinking. If a librarian encourages a student to consider an author's reputation and expertise, he or she is, again, facilitating critical thinking. Better yet, if librarians engage students in active dialogue concerning their assumptions and prejudices about a topic, about authorities, or about varying perspectives on an issue offered by different disciplines, they are mov-

ing the students toward what Richard Paul calls "dialogical thinking" — growing beyond narrow or egocentric thinking into more
relativistic perspectives (Paul, 1987). More generally, if librarians
instill in students a questioning attitude toward printed information,
they will enable them to transcend their submission to the supposed
infallibility of the printed word. Undoubtedly, many reference and
instruction librarians have been encouraging at least some levels of
critical thinking in students for many years; but as Mona McCormick observes in regard to critical thinking, "the sights for library
instruction may not be set high enough" (McCormick, 1983, p.
339).

THE BENEFITS OF CRITICAL THINKING
TO LIBRARY INSTRUCTION

The critical thinking movement has much to offer reference and
instruction librarians in designing alternative library assignments.
Definitions of critical thinking abound, but surely one of the best is
offered by Robert Ennis of the Illinois Critical Thinking Project:
"Critical thinking is reasonable reflective thinking that is focused
on deciding what to believe or do" (Ennis, 1987, p. 10). In a list of
goals for a critical thinking curriculum, Ennis includes twelve critical thinking abilities. Some of the most important ones for library
instruction are: focusing on an issue or question; analyzing arguments; using questions of clarification; determining the credibility
of a source; making judgments of value; defining unclear terms; and
locating and examining assumptions (Ennis, 1987, pp. 12-14).

To some extent, Ennis's critical thinking goals reflect Bloom's
taxonomy of educational objectives (Bloom, 1956). Like Bloom,
Ennis emphasizes the "higher order" thinking skills of analysis,
synthesis, and evaluation, though he notes the vagueness of these
concepts in Bloom's scheme, and questions their usefulness because of lack of criteria for determining if these three activities are
being performed correctly (Ennis, 1987, p. 11). Ennis's own list of
critical thinking goals is sufficiently detailed to include such criteria, and is organized in such a fashion as to present a learning continuum — from most basic skills through most advanced abilities.

Ennis's critical thinking continuum contains elements that should
prove useful to librarians in designing alternative library assign-

ments. Perhaps the most significant point about Ennis's list is its developmental nature, the fact that it is a continuum. Critical thinking abilities do not develop quickly, but constitute a developmental sequence; in college students, these abilities continue to expand and develop, as suggested by William Perry's stages of intellectual and ethical growth (Perry, 1970). Because critical thinking abilities develop sequentially, library-based assignments intended to increase such abilities should themselves be sequenced, the initial ones focussing on discrete thinking skills from the "early" part of Ennis's continuum, and with later ones developing the more sophisticated thinking abilities.

CHARACTERISTICS OF EFFECTIVE ALTERNATIVE ASSIGNMENTS

Taking Ennis's critical thinking goals into account, librarians can design valuable alternative assignments that facilitate growth in critical thinking. Chet Meyers, in *Teaching Students to Think Critically*, discusses some features of effective critical thinking assignments. He specifies careful sequencing of assignments to build critical thinking, focusing on real-world problems, and providing clear instructions for each assignment (Meyers, 1986, pp. 72-73). To these characteristics might be added other features suggested by Ennis's critical thinking goals: development of specific objectives for each assignment; building in the necessity for clarifying assumptions and definitions; encouraging multiple perspectives on an issue or problem, with an attendant tolerance for ambiguity; and eliminating irrelevant or useless information, leaving only what is appropriate or relevant for a given decision or task.

Examples of Alternative Library Assignments

The assignments that follow have been successful in stimulating faculty interest in the library, and in facilitating student growth, at Lewis-Clark State College. The instruction librarian developed these assignments as part of a "casebook" of alternative assignments, with several goals in mind: to make students more aware of the variety of library resources available to them; to increase faculty awareness of how an undergraduate collection can be better used to support the curriculum; to demonstrate to faculty and administrators alike that librarians can make contributions in revitalizing undergraduate education; and, of course, to use the assignments for a goal beyond themselves — enhancing student sophistication as critical thinkers, as "consumers" of information in a time when such sophistication is more crucial than ever.

Multiple Perspectives

The following assignment challenges students to use library resources in a critical way, on a significant contemporary issue.

Changes in the Soviet Union

Identify three leading contemporary experts on the Soviet Union. Write an essay describing their positions on the issue of change in the Soviet Union under Gorbachev's leadership. Draw comparisons and contrasts among their positions. Is there at present a consensus among these experts about this issue, or are their views so divergent that no commonalities emerge? The second half of the assignment should be a brief essay discussing the qualifications of the three experts selected. Consider such matters as academic backgrounds and subject specializations, foreign service/diplomatic experience, and books and articles written.

Critical thinking abilities aimed for here include considering multiple perspectives on an issue, and evaluating authorities. In completing such a project, students come to realize that experts and scholars disagree, and that one responsibility of a thinking citizen is thoughtful consideration—with judgment suspended—of clashing viewpoints.

Another example of an assignment requiring analysis and evaluation of varying perspectives is the following:

Impact of the Hanford Nuclear Reservation

Identify the main viewpoints concerning the impacts (environmental, economic, social) of the Hanford Nuclear Reservation upon the Northwest. Where possible, identify the groups and spokesmen associated with each. Then write a five-page report discussing the different perspectives on the merits and disadvantages of the Hanford Plant.

The objective of this assignment, again, is to consider multiple perspectives and viewpoints. This type of assignment, given often enough, should help students grow beyond mere multiplistic awareness into a more mature relativistic state. Additional advantages of the Hanford assignment include brevity, and the necessity of finding information both inside and outside the library. Students' critical awareness expands when they are required to complete library-based projects that point to information sources and contacts beyond the library itself. Students also begin to realize that information collected from different sources (journal articles, environmental impact statements, newspaper articles, interviews) must all be subjected to critical scrutiny, and that printed information is not infallible.

Comparative Studies

Somewhat similar to assignments facilitating multiple perspectives are ones requiring students to consider how various academic disciplines differ in their treatment of an issue.

Social Science Perspectives

Take one of the following developments and find out how it is being treated/discussed in two of the fields listed below. Write a bibliographic essay (five-six pages) discussing, comparing, and evaluating the key works in each field that deal with the topic you have chosen.

Topics:

— the increase of political activism among religious fundamentalists
— the transformation of the U.S. economy from an industrial base to an information/service base
— the increase of two-career marriages in the U.S. since World War II
— the decline of political participation (as indicated by low voter turnouts) in the U.S. since 1970

Fields: anthropology economics
psychology theology/religious studies
sociology political science
history

In completing this assignment, students learn to identify and think about assumptions and leading paradigms that various disciplines employ in examining reality. Ideally, students will learn to think critically about the unique strengths and limitations of each discipline examined. An assignment of this type would be especially appropriate in interdisciplinary or integrative seminars for more advanced students. They will have to struggle with fragmented information scattered throughout a wide variety of sources, and synthesize and distill this information so that they attain a more critical, holistic perspective on the artificial divisions of academia.

Real-Life Case Studies

Another possible alternative assignment is the open-ended "real-life" professional project. Although obviously appropriate for pre-professional courses, this type of assignment can be used to stimulate critical thinking, where appropriate, in the general education curriculum as well.

The Home Health Care Nurse and AIDS

Your first job as a professional nurse involves working for a home health care agency. During your first two months, you discover that one of the patients you work with, who had earlier been diagnosed as having a severe case of mononucleosis, has since tested positive for the AIDS virus. Naturally, you are concerned about potential health risks both to members of the patient's family and to yourself. You decide to discuss the matter with your supervisor. He suggests that you do some research on current practices in caring for AIDS patients in large city hospitals around the country and, based on this research, prepare for him and other staff members a set of model guidelines for home health care of AIDS patients.

List the steps you would follow in doing this research, and briefly explain the importance of each step.

Open-ended assignments such as this one can serve as valuable heuristic exercises. Requiring students to explain their thought processes — making explicit the steps they would take in gathering the information — is often more important than focusing on the "product" (information presented in a typical research paper). A related benefit of this particular assignment is its departure from the formulaic or generic search strategy; students very quickly learn that they cannot find information on AIDS in an encyclopedia, handbook, or other standard reference source; and that the evolving research on the disease requires rigorous scrutiny of new information, careful sifting of evidence, and, in many instances, suspension and deferral of judgment. Students need not be medical researchers or health care experts to understand that new information must be treated with skepticism and suspension of judgment simply because it is new.

The Critical Thinking Spectrum: Definition, Analysis, Synthesis, Evaluation, Integration

A final type of assignment engages some of the most significant critical thinking abilities. It is an expanded version of a traditional library exercise known as the "pathfinder."

The "Mini Guide-to-the-Literature"

Prepare a "mini guide-to-the-literature" for a limited topic such as one of the following: (12-20 pages)

- the psychological impact of Alzheimer's Disease upon family members of the patient
- the influence of stress upon sleep patterns
- the influence of psychosocial development during adolescence on career choice

Your "mini guide-to-the-literature" should contain the following:

a. a brief discussion of the background, importance, and relevance of the topic, with all potentially confusing terms defined.
b. a discussion and evaluation of reference books (general and

subject encyclopedias, subject dictionaries, handbooks and manuals) containing articles or entries specifically appropriate for the topic. Identify special features of each source.

c. a division of the topic into its most important subtopics, with a brief discussion of each subtopic followed by an annotated listing of books, magazine and journal articles, and newspaper articles discussing the subtopic. Each subtopic, with its bibliography, should comprise a major section or "chapter."

d. a brief discussion and evaluation of the usefulness of various indexes, abstracts, and other bibliographies and guides to the literature for this topic.

e. a brief section discussing the most important audiovisual materials, if any are available, for this topic.

f. a brief discussion of computerized databases useful for this topic.

g. a conclusion analyzing research trends for this topic and other closely related topics.

This assignment requires careful focusing on an issue or problem, clear definitions of terminology, analysis of the topic into subtopics, selection and evaluation of sources, and synthesis and integration of all the information into a coherent whole. Like the traditional "pathfinder," this assignment develops knowledge of a wide variety of library materials in a logical search strategy order; its more in-depth requirements, however, encourage students to think critically about what information sources would be most helpful in this small "guide to the literature." Packaging information in this format avoids the formulaic research strategy associated with the traditional term paper, and allows students to gain a coherent perspective on research.

THE ALTERNATIVE LIBRARY ASSIGNMENT AND ITS ROLE IN THE GENERAL EDUCATION CURRICULUM

In *College: The Undergraduate Experience in America*, Ernest L. Boyer writes, "In a complex, interdependent world we simply cannot afford to graduate students who fail to place their knowledge and lives in perspective'' (Boyer, 1987, p. 91). Entirely too often, undergraduate students are not given opportunities for perspective, but are simply "processed" through a minimum number of general education courses. Students memorize a miscellany of facts, names, and theories which they regurgitate on tests or in term papers; such information is usually promptly forgotten in their preoccupation with their preprofessional coursework.

A revitalized general education curriculum needs a critical thinking component. In becoming critical thinkers, students learn to see connections between disciplines, to focus to significant questions, to sort out the genuine from the spurious, and to examine their own assumptions and limitations. They also gain a crucial perspective on academic coursework and its connection to the "real world" of work. They learn that general education courses, with their emphasis on perspective, can contribute to their preparation as future professionals, who obviously more than ever need perspective and critical thinking abilities. The general education curriculum, integrated and strengthened with overarching critical thinking goals, can become an invaluable preparation for professional life.

Reference and instruction librarians can help renew the general education curriculum by developing resource files of critical thinking assignments for teaching faculty. The assignments should be designed to stimulate student interest, to make effective use of library resources, to develop a variety of thinking abilities, and to meet the instructional objectives of faculty. If librarians become active partners in revitalizing the curriculum, students and faculty alike will benefit; and librarians will add a fuller dimension to their own professional lives and to the life of the academic communities of which they are an essential part.

In "The Rock," T. S. Eliot wrote,

> Where is the wisdom we have lost in
>   knowledge?
> Where is the knowledge we have lost in
>   information?

Through efforts at improving critical thinking in the general education curriculum, librarians can help restore some of the real knowledge, as opposed to mere information, in the minds of students and faculty. And if librarians persist in championing a critical thinking curriculum, perhaps their respective institutions will be enriched with more wisdom as well.

REFERENCES

Bloom, Benjamin S., ed. *Taxonomy of Educational Objectives*. New York: David McKay Co., 1956.

Boyer, Ernest L. *College: The Undergraduate Experience in America*. New York: Harper & Row, 1987.

Ennis, Robert H. "A Taxonomy of Critical Thinking Dispositions and Abilities." In Joan B. Baron and Robert J. Sternberg (Eds.), *Teaching Thinking Skills: Theory and Practice*. New York: W. H. Freeman and Co., 1987.

Farber, Evan. "Alternatives to the Term Paper." In T. Kirk (Ed.), *Increasing the Teaching Role of Academic Libraries*. San Francisco: Jossey-Bass, 1984.

McCormick, Mona. "Critical Thinking and Library Instruction." *RQ*, 1983, *22*(4), 339-342.

Meyers, Chet. *Teaching Students to Think Critically: A Guide for Faculty in All Disciplines*. San Francisco: Jossey-Bass, 1986.

Paul, Richard. "Dialogical Thinking: Critical Thought Essential to the Acquisition of Rational Knowledge and Passions." In Joan B. Baron and Robert J. Sternberg (Eds.), *Teaching Thinking Skills: Theory and Practice*. New York: W. H. Freeman and Co., 1987.

Perry, William. *Forms of Intellectual and Ethical Development in the College Years*. New York: Holt, Rinehart, and Winston, 1970.

Bibliographic Instruction:
Building the Librarian/Faculty
Partnership

Betsy Baker

SUMMARY. The intent of this paper is to reinforce and demonstrate the necessity for: (1) integrating instruction into the research process; (2) achieving a balance between faculty, students, and the library to meet that goal. This goal can only be met by addressing a number of issues that have traditionally been associated with the instrinsic value of BI integration into a curriculum, the institution's support for this move, and the attitudes of faculty and librarians toward BI, and the strengths which each can bring to the research process to benefit students.

INTRODUCTION

Many of us who have used libraries through the years may have fond memories of "simpler times," when collections were smaller and more manageable, resources for locating information were fewer, and the card catalog was a very tangible representation of a library's holdings. For some, such a time may have seemed a "golden age" for libraries. Now, however, the rapid changes taking place as a result of increased publication activity and technological developments may be overwhelming. Paradoxically, the more complex world of the library today may in reality be closer to a "golden age." New tools and new approaches are emerging that greatly facilitate library research. To increase the visibility of these

Betsy Baker is Head, Reference Department, 1935 Sheridan Rd., Northwestern University, Evanston, IL.

An earlier version of this paper was presented at the Iowa ACRL Chapter's Spring Conference, Cedar Rapids, IA, April 25, 1986.

311

tools and to help make the library less overwhelming to students, public service librarians at all types of institutions are striving to create a bridge between the information needs of individuals and information sources. One of the most effective ways to do this is by providing bibliographic instruction.

Bibliographic instruction (BI) has enjoyed a rapid, almost whirlwind period of development and growth in academic libraries during the past two decades. A number of pioneers in the library field during the late 1960s and early 1970s, who recognized a need and had a commitment to education, brought tremendous energy to the instruction issue.[1] Due to these efforts, many have come to view instructional services as being at the heart of library service. During the early years of development, some introduction to the library and its resources emerged not only as a constant in basic composition classes, but also in a variety of other courses and programs in academic settings throughout the country. Subsequently, we have witnessed an impressive growth of instructional principles, concepts, and practices. Accompanying this growth have been innovative approaches to design of instruction. The role of the public service librarian continues to evolve into one which includes both individualized consulting and group instruction.

Although instruction has become well integrated into the academic library profession, questions still remain about how well it is integrated into curriculum development throughout higher education. With the exception of institutions such as Earlham College, where BI integration into the academic curriculum throughout the campus has become a model for other libraries, most BI development still takes place within the library setting, often in isolation of an institution's broader educational goals and philosophies. As is well documented in the literature, instruction that takes place without strong links to academic coursework can impart little knowledge of lasting significance to students.[2] Teaching that takes place within disciplines such as mathematics or biology always includes coursework that is linked directly to the subject, such as a research paper that forces a student to analyze the information that he or she is using. While the focus of BI does not demand that students become experts on the subject of research skills, it can give them an opportunity to accomplish three goals: subject-related research skills, analysis of the way in which they conduct research, and a greater awareness about the value of substantiating their own ideas with published data.

In order to reach students through BI, however, librarians must actively pursue a delicate balance involving interaction and cooperation among faculty as course planners, librarians as facilitators of research objectives, and students as learners. The tenuousness of this interplay may be illustrated by using a model of an equilateral triangle, which includes librarians, faculty, and students all equally participating in the education process. In such a model, the role of each is clearly defined and understood. Ideally, each apex will support its own weight within that structure if the triangle is to be truly equilateral. If the angles become unbalanced, the changes in the relationships can clearly be seen. For example, if we change one of the angles to 90 degrees, we have a right triangle, which indicates that one group would be contributing a considerable amount, while the other groups would be contributing lesser and unequal amounts. Such an imbalance occurs when faculty plan a research oriented course without some librarian involvement. The result in this case goes beyond poor research papers, to a more fundamental problem—students do not have the chance to cultivate anything but poor research skills. Each institution must determine what constitutes appropriate levels of involvement by each of the three groups in the academic learning process. Ideally, equal amounts are something we should strive for—it is not a question of whether we as librarians can contribute equally, but rather, whether we share the same commitment to supporting the educational process as do our faculty colleagues. Poor research papers are also a symptom that communication between faculty and librarian is not occurring. The efforts of the early instruction pioneers have moved into a new phase—one that necessitates making a commitment to establishing BI as an ongoing institutional priority.

The intent of this paper is to reinforce and demonstrate the necessity for: (1) integrating instruction into the research process; (2) achieving a balance between faculty, students, and the library to meet that goal. This goal can only be met by addressing a number of issues that have traditionally been associated with the instrinsic value of BI integration into a curriculum, the institution's support for this move, and the attitudes of faculty and librarians toward BI, and the strengths which each can bring to the research process to benefit students. The paper is divided into seven sections. The first section is a review of the recent developments in libraries and in society at large that are shaping bibliographic instruction efforts in libraries. Within this background, the second section presents re- search findings that shed some light on how undergraduates seek information — what are their sources of choice? Section three then examines differing perspectives on the need for bibliographic in- struction. This is followed in section four by a review of the un- derlying philosophies of bibliographic instruction. Section five ex- amines attitudes of faculty toward libraries and librarians. An awareness of these attitudes can serve as a useful insight, since faculty practices strongly influence student library practices. A look at attitudes, however, is not complete without looking at the librari- an's attitude toward faculty members. Particularly important is the treatment in section six of our attitudes toward and interaction with faculty, which in turn affect faculty perceptions regarding the use- fulness of integrating library research into course assignments. The paper closes with some suggestions for enhancing the faculty/librar- ian partnership. This discussion, it is hoped, will serve as a founda- tion for identifying those barriers and challenges associated with involving faculty in bibliographic instruction endeavors. Of course, such initiative will only be taken if we share with our colleagues the perception of the value and need for bibliographic instruction within the institution. We cannot assume, even within librarianship, that all share the same philosophical values about library services.

DEWEY, THE MODERN LIBRARY, AND INSTRUCTION

As a matter of course, academic education has always included a commitment to a strong library collection and some instruction in its use. The teaching function has complemented reference services since Dewey introduced the "reference department" as part of his "modern library idea" at Columbia University in the late 1800s.[3] However, over the past twenty years a number of changes have occurred that pose considerable challenges to integrating the library into the core of educational services: (1) the quality and complexity of information sources has grown; (2) subject-matter has become more diversified and interdisciplinary with the growth in publishing activity; (3) formats of information sources are changing rapidly; (4) media bombardment has highlighted society's awareness of the power of information and need to obtain current information quickly, values which are becoming pervasive in every human endeavor. These developments have certainly brought instruction issues into sharper focus. The current challenge we face, however, is implementing our instructional goals in this changing environment.

While we have a clear perspective of instructional issues, we face working with a diverse and continually changing user community which has a variety of motivations for using the library. In order to develop meaningful instruction, it is important to consider how the personal goals and priorities of individuals determine the approaches used to pursue research in the library. Motivations for using the library can be traced to two broad areas for discussion purposes: (1) library users typically do not share with librarians the same level of dedication to knowing or learning the many facets of using the library; (2) library users' perceptions of the approachability and expertise of library staff are often, unfortunately, less than positive.

VALUES AND MOTIVATIONS: PERSPECTIVES ON THE NEED FOR INFORMATION

The ways in which values toward research differ is discussed at length by David King and Betsy Baker, who use the concepts of "law of least effort" and "law of time management" to describe the different approaches employed by librarians and users for conducting research. The concept of "law of least effort" questions the motivations, priorities, and values of those users who limit their searching to certain tools, who settle for items which are easily accessible, or who terminate their searches at a stage librarians consider premature. In fact, many library users, perhaps most of them, hold different values than librarians and have their own purpose for using or not the library. Their priorities often conflict with the ideals of comprehensive searching. The degree of effort a user will put in a search is less than what we would consider optimal because the search for the user is not the final goal, but only an interim goal. What is to librarians a "law of least effort" may be to the efficiency-minded user a "law of effective time management."[4] The library is of a more peripheral value even as it is related to research.

In addition to varying degrees of motivation and incentives to use the library for research purposes, studies have shown that a silent majority of students exist who, for a variety of reasons, are reticent to ask reference questions. While reference desks are often extraordinarily busy, our own observations confirm that many users are not apt to seek assistance in the research process. This can be seen on several levels. Many students hesitate to use the library because they are unfamiliar with basic information sources. Unfortunately, they feel they do not need the library until they are faced with writing a "research paper," an exercise where some familiarity with basic information sources becomes essential. Even for such assignments, they are afraid of becoming involved in library research because it is perceived as too time consuming. Consequently, our service commitments are difficult to implement. Our objective is to help users' perspectives grow to encompass a positive image of the library as being an accessible and valuable resource rather than the more commonly held negative perspective, fraught as it is with the imagery of excruciating research papers. It is only by demystifying the intricacies of gathering information, while developing a realistic outlook on library users' goals and priorities, that we will help them develop this image and pursue effective research. Within this context of disparate perspectives on the need for library information, it is important that librarians be able to educate their clientele in the most efficient methods of acquiring, assessing, and interpreting information. Instruction is one of the most effective ways we can formally reach users and educate them about seeking assistance and using a library on their own.

PERSPECTIVES ON THE NEED FOR INSTRUCTION

The growth of BI has not been without its critics. However, a healthy dose of skepticism has only served to strengthen its focus and clarify its purpose. Early writing by Wilson points to the need for ego recognition as being behind the impetus for librarians to adopt more of a teaching role.[5] Recognition, in and of itself, is somewhat useful. However, the most important component of recognition is respect by faculty for the role librarians can play in helping students meet research objectives. The label "teacher" is irrelevant to this role.

Other critics focus on this label as well in their discussions of BI. A recent article by Connie Miller and Patricia Tegler entitled "In Pursuit of Windmills: Librarians and the Determination to Instruct" provides not only a summary of the fundamental issues involved in assessing the value of BI but also raises valid questions about the motivations of librarians for seeking instructional opportunities. Miller and Tegler contend that librarians should focus their energies and attention on providing information rather than instructing users to locate information — the age old information or instruction question. They say, that like poor, elderly Alonzo, who calls himself Don Quixote and rides out into the world for adventure, many librarians are approaching instructional services filled with similar heroic visions. And, like Alonzo, these librarians are calling themselves by a new name — teachers — and have ridden out to practice their profession in order to seek recognition. Miller and Tegler see such recognition as being like Don Quixote's windmill, since — in their opinion — the circling arm of bibliographic instruction has time and again lifted librarian-teachers high into the air only to then drop them to the ground. And yet, they say, much like Quixote, they press on undaunted.[6] Miller and Tegler seem to feel that in many cases bibliographic instruction efforts simply provide too little too late. As such, they suggest that our energies would be better spent on meeting the immediate information needs of users. Many of us have encountered at least one situation where we might be inclined to share these sentiments.

The painful reality of many instructional programs is that, indeed, they offer "too little." Many are directed exclusively to incoming freshmen, occur during one class period, and offer little in the way of follow-up. Furthermore, in many situations, the faculty member does not provide useful reinforcement for the value of the instruction, and therefore, it is not seen as a common thread in the educational process. Even when instruction is directed to graduate students or faculty, we often feel compelled to force onto these individuals highly structured research processes. We try to teach them the science of information, an overall methodology for doing library research. These methods may be completely alien to the way professionals conduct their own research within specific disciplines. So why do we persevere?

While I appreciate the Miller/Tegler perception of the "too little, too late" problem, providing information on demand does not seem to offer an acceptable solution to meeting the information needs of large groups of students and other library users. Perhaps by examining the value of BI as an aspect of the liberal arts education, it may become clearer why it should be one of the central dimensions of the educational triangle. Concentrating on the value of bibliographic instruction as an aspect of the liberal arts education program, not on the specific problems associated with particular instructional methods, clarifies the motivations and efforts surrounding bibliographic instruction. The involvement of the faculty in our library instruction is the crucial link to realizing this value.

WHAT THEN IS THE VALUE OF INSTRUCTION?

The philosophy behind bibliographic instructional efforts is that the development of a critical and informed use of information is a key part of a liberal education. Bibliographic instruction aims to do more than simply provide directions on how to use particular library resources to complete a specific assignment or research project. Indeed, the concepts and models used in bibliographic instruction make a significant contribution to the aims of a liberal education itself. An important facet of such an education is the opportunity it affords to develop the special qualities of a rational mind, including the ability to solve problems by asking informed questions, critically analyzing pertinent information, and then answering the questions. It may be possible for students to learn these skills without using library resources, however, students will be able to realize the full potential of these skills only if they learn how to gain access to a rich array of information. With the ability to use bibliographic sources effectively, students are able to collect the relevant, timely, and authoritative information needed for problem solving. This ability is critical to more fully enhancing students' quality of life after their formal education has been completed.[7]

Without bibliographic instruction, most beginning students are poorly equipped to conduct research necessary for college-level papers. As Thomas Kirk notes, at best students graduate from high school with a working knowledge of a high school library; they know how to use a card catalog for a small collection of books, and are somewhat familiar with the *Readers' Guide*, and other general reference tools such as an encyclopedia and almanac. At worst students graduate from high school without ever having used a library. When they enter college, they are expected to know how to use the vast array of specialized bibliographies and indexes, a card catalog and an online catalog, and, of course, much larger collections. So how do students learn or even come to care about using these tools?

Unfortunately, without bibliographic instruction most students do not learn. Too many students will continue to use the tried and true methods learned in a high school library: the card catalog and the *Readers' Guide*. Others learn by trial and error, expending hours in frustrating attempts to make the library "work." Some will be bold enough to ask a reference librarian for help and will receive specific guidance. However, the reference librarian at a busy reference desk can provide only a solution to an immediate problem. In all of these situations, the expanded array of information sources will likely remain untapped by students, thus limiting the sources of information to a fraction of what the library has to offer.

Bibliographic instruction can help students move beyond these behavior patterns by providing them with new techniques in research and in the use of information sources. Such instruction is most effective if it is provided as an integral part of individual courses. This instruction, while not meant to eliminate fully the methods of trial and error or the expertise of reference librarians, helps to eliminate useless frustration and inconsistency. Perhaps most importantly, bibliographic instruction as a component of formal coursework delivers a message to students that their faculty believes that learning to use libraries efficiently and effectively is an important part of education. Experience has shown us that most students will use library resources in their courses only if encouraged to do so by their instructors and will care about learning how to use the library if they see how it can enhance their studies. Bibliographic instruction that takes place without involving the faculty too frequently amounts to a guided tour of the collection and imparts little knowledge that is of lasting significance to students.[8]

If we agree that the underlying philosophy behind our instructional programs is to promote the development of critical and informed users of information as a key component of a liberal arts education, how can we better speak to these information needs? Our attention turns to the faculty, since we both share a concern for furthering educated inquiry. And as Kirk noted, the trial and error method of accessing that information may still serve as a learning method, but our overall goal should be to perpetuate the process of inquiry.

FACULTY IN THE INFORMATION CHAIN

Success in furthering the inquisitive process seems likely only if library instruction can be integrated into the regular teaching programs and can incorporate the teaching faculty. Most students will use library materials in their courses only if professors require them to. Kathleen Dunn spoke to this issue in a paper presented at the 1986 ACRL Conference in Baltimore.[9] Specifically, Dunn was interested in exploring the psychological needs motivating undergraduates to seek information and in determining what types of information sources (not simply reference sources, but information sources such as teachers, experts in the field, friends, the library, etc.) are used to satisfy these information needs.

Dunn found that different types of psychological needs directly influence the type of information source sought. Not surprisingly, it was discovered that many students do not use the library as a primary information source. A variety of sources is available to them; the library is only one of these, and, for psychological reasons, it often is not their first choice. In her study, Dunn found that teachers were considered the most important source of information since the faculty play such an important role in the chain of information delivery. This further supports the importance of building a librarian/faculty connection in the education process.

HOW DO FACULTY FEEL ABOUT THE LIBRARY?

Since faculty use of the library can be a major factor affecting library use by students, the teaching faculty's perceptions and use of their libraries must be of primary concern to bibliographic instruction librarians. In fact, a study conducted in the late 1960s by Kenneth Allen showed that the attitude of individual instructors is the most notable factor influencing student use of the library.[10]

More recently, Jinnie Davis and Stella Bentley from Indiana University explored factors affecting faculty perceptions of academic libraries. They conducted a survey of the teaching faculty at three institutions to determine the effect of institutional affiliation, subject area, academic rank, and length of time at the institution on attitudes toward the library. Three conclusions of the project are noteworthy. First, for most of the survey questions dealing with satisfaction or adequacy of the library collection, policies, and staff of the library, there were no significant differences in the responses by school, field, or rank.

Second, significant differences by subject field, rank, and length of time at the institution were found in expected satisfaction rate for a known item search. Faculty in the sciences exhibited the highest satisfaction of expectations, which may reflect the more compact nature of scientific literature. Circulation policies may also have a bearing on the matter—material of greatest use for scientists tends to be current periodical literature, usually not circulating and therefore more readily available. Third, and perhaps most interesting, is that faculty members with less time at an institution are the most dissatisfied members. The authors suggest several possible reasons for this: newer faculty are less familiar with the library and its services, they may use the library more due to their perceived need to publish or perish, and they may come from institutions with stronger collections. In their study, these dissatisfied faculty members were also the group that ascribed a lesser importance to the helpfulness of the library staff. This suggests that librarians should focus upon new faculty members as a target for concentrated public relations and public service efforts.[11] How do many faculty view library instruction? A passage from an essay written by William

Stephenson, Professor of Biology at Earlham College provides an insightful response to this question.

> What are faculty persons really like? I suggest three character-istics relevant to a discussion of library instruction; faculty members are disciplinary chauvinists. We faculty don't want to give up the time our students spend on subject matter for training in literature-accessing skills. We don't want to learn from librarians. We feel that the most effective learning is learning in our narrow subject matter disciplines. I don't want to give up time in biology for "less important things."[12]

However, since Professor Stephenson is associated with Earlham College, we might expect a positive attitude toward library instruc-tion. He goes on to say that faculty members need what librarians have to offer.

> As a faculty person who has used library instruction for almost a decade, I know this. The problem is that most faculty mem-bers don't yet know that they need librarians. Since faculty members are disciplinary chauvinists, we need librarians to help us grow beyond that chauvinism by leading us to utilize library instruction.[13]

A certain amount of what Stephenson terms chauvinism exists in each discipline. In librarianship, that chauvinism is often mani-fested in our attitudes about the "right ways" to do research. Clearly, there is no one right way to do research in the library, but there do exist certain concepts, principles, and techniques, which can greatly facilitate research endeavors.

WHAT DO LIBRARIANS FEEL ABOUT FACULTY?

There seems to be a general consensus among librarians that fac-ulty are not good library users — but according to whose standards? Are the expectations we have for them in this area unrealistic? Should all research begin with a strategy? In an article entitled "The Faculty Problem," Connie McCarthy explains why she feels the lack of library skills in teaching faculty to be a major problem for bibliographic instruction programs.

It is true, says McCarthy, that most library faculty can do perfectly splendid research without ever using a library-owned reference book (and, in some cases, without even coming near the library). But it was not for their everyday use that the great complex of bibliographies, indexes and catalogs was created. It was created, of course, as an indispensable means of access to the record of our civilization; also, for the use of the sizable minority of scholars to whom it is essential; and, not least, for the use of students. For it is the students who need to do basic library research — to pass their courses, to write their term papers, to satisfy their curiosity, follow their investigations, find their inspiration. Unfortunately, without the active encouragement of faculty, their incentives to do so are seldom sufficient.[14]

This then, is the faculty problem: Faculty members do not feel the need to use the library, thus, depriving their students of the opportunity to learn how to use the library. In addition to this honest naivete about methods of bibliographic research, McCarthy describes faculty as being reluctant to relinquish their ancient image as bookish savants, even if books have only played a minimal role in their own scholarly accomplishments. She calls this the myth of the bookish professor.[15] We are guilty of holding other stereotypes of faculty. Daniel Gore, in his well publicized article "Something There is That Doesn't Love: A Professor," further elaborates on the conflicts that can arise between librarians and faculty members. He speaks of the faculty perception of mismanagement of libraries, the inevitable clashes this creates between faculty and librarians, and the resulting animosity which thoroughly inhibits any concerted efforts to assist students in the research process.[16]

BUILDING THE LIBRARIAN/FACULTY CONNECTION

Although there is no established formula for changing stereotypes and overcoming some of the barriers to faculty/librarian partnership, there are some basic approaches for building partnerships. Before we can begin building a solid faculty/librarian relationship, however, we must first make the effort to minimize our own stereotypes of faculty. By and large these are just that. Once initial contacts are made, it is surprising how faculty members become less bookish savants. They are generally friendly and interested in individuals, and they share our aim to help students learn and to pursue research in an effective manner (although their concept of effective use of library resources may initially be different from ours). Seen from this viewpoint, one of the most general courses of action is for librarians to seek out faculty to discuss library services and materials and how they may be improved, as well as to communicate a genuine interest in and concern for faculty research and teaching needs. Simply put, librarians can assist in the promotion of library instruction by being thorough and persistent communicators.[17] In addition, librarians should identify those faculty who are most likely to be open to library involvement in their courses, and concentrate their efforts where they are most likely to be productive. Responsive faculty are most likely to be those who are teaching courses with research components, who are just beginning to develop their course syllabi, or who are in the midst of revising the curriculum for their discipline. And as seen from the research referred to above, the most receptive may not be the new faculty, although librarians tend to think they will be.

A variety of techniques should be considered for diminishing dissatisfaction of new faculty. Faculty orientation sessions are useful. At Northwestern University, a faculty open house is held at the beginning of each Fall term. Although especially directed to new faculty members, established faculty are also encouraged to attend. It has been found useful to contact department chairs and ask them to personally escort their new faculty to the library. During the course of the day, special library tours are offered, demonstrations of online and CD-ROM services are provided, special introductions to the online catalog take place, and a chance to mingle and meet library staff is interwoven with the other activities. Each reference librarian and subject bibliographer personally telephones new faculty members from their respective departments to encourage them to come to the library for a special day to meet their librarian colleagues. Other institutions have had success with special workshops for faculty members, either focusing upon general library resources or upon specific areas of library service.[18] The structuring of formal channels of communication can be achieved by means of membership on library liaison committees, and where appropriate, by librarians' attendance at departmental meetings. Useful printed communication can include the dissemination by librarians of library handbooks, newsletters and individualized letters. In many situations, informal, personal notes are particularly effective. Catherine E. Pasterczyk provides an extremely useful checklist for finding out about a department's collection development needs in a recent issue of *C&RL News*. Although intended primarily as an aid to bibliographers, much of the advice offered is of equal value to a reference librarian who is building a liaison relationship with a particular department. The suggestions for questions to ask departmental liaisons include issues concerning the faculty, the staff and students, the department, the curriculum, and departmental publications.[19]

CONCLUSION: SHEDDING INSECURITIES AND BUILDING ENTHUSIASM

In closing, I wish to once again refer to Professor Stephenson's essay and review another passage—one that I feel offers some thoughtful advice.

Faculty members are insecure in at least two major dimensions. We are insecure as scholars. As teachers, we are expected to know everything in our fields, and of course we fall short in this. Therefore we are defensive about being challenged on points of knowledge and authority in our subject matter specialities.

Faculty members are also insecure as teachers. Most faculty have personal histories of having been good students. Through grade school, junior high, and high school, we were the achievers. We earned good grades, awards, and honors of academic achievement. We have been evaluated highly as scholars, and we are not accustomed to receiving low marks.

Library educators must be sensitive to these insecurities in their faculty members. They need to be sensitive to them and still have the maturity to put up with overbearing academic-intellectual egos and with the attitudes of superiority that many faculty members exhibit. I know this is difficult, but to be effective it is essential that librarians tolerate the disciplinary chauvinism and the facade of super-competence that faculty persons attempt to present.[20]

Professor Stephenson goes on to suggest three areas for personal changes in librarians: leadership, assertiveness and enthusiasm. The role of librarians has changed from the stereotypical curator image to one of partner with faculty in the education process. Librarians must become more assertive in order to deliver the leadership that is essential for the extension and success of library user education programs. Faculty members are very aggressive within the academic setting. Librarians would do well to adopt similar assertive behavior in representing our interests and objectives in the education process.

Librarians also need to develop and to project a greater level of enthusiasm about their work. The effective teacher projects enthusiasm about the subject matter and instills students with enthusiasm for the material. If we do not examine what led us to view as necessary the integration of user education into the broader education policy of the University, we will continually perpetuate the "too little, too late" phenomenon. Only by working in tandem with faculty to ultimately changing education policy will we be able to have a little more a little sooner. What Miller and Tegler are finding fault with by their Don Quixote analogy is misdirected idealism. By trying to understand faculty, as opposed to perpetuating the stereotypes each might have of the other, we can assume a more positive direction for our idealism. After all, education and the spirit of inquiry certainly provide a place in society where idealism has purpose and high value.

REFERENCES

1. See for example, "Toward Guidelines for Bibliographic Instruction," *College and Research Library News* (May 1975): 137-139, 169-71; Carolyn A. Kirkendall and Carla J. Stoffle "Instruction," in *The Service Imperative*, ed. Gail A. Schlacter (Colorado: Libraries Unlimited, 1982), pp. 42-67; Larry Hardesty, "Instructional Development in Library Use Education," in *Improving Library Instruction: How to Teach and How to Evaluate*, ed. Carolyn A. Kirkendall (Ann Arbor, MI: Pierian, 1980), pp. 73-87; John Mark Tucker, "User Education in Academic Libraries: A Century in Retrospect," *Library Trends* 29 (Summer 1980): 9-27.

2. David King, "Evaluation and Its Uses," in *Evaluating Bibliographic In-*

struction: A Handbook,'' (Chicago: American Library Association, 1983), 5-21; David N. King and John C. Ory, "Effects of Library Instruction on Student Research: A Case Study," *College and Research Libraries,* 40 (1981): 31-36; Roland Person, "Long-Term Evaluation of Bibliographic Instruction: Lasting Encouragement," *College and Research Libraries,* 40 (1981): 19-25.

3. See for example, Samuel Rothstein. "Reference Service: The New Dimension in Librarianship," *College & Research Libraries* 22: 14 (January, 1961). Hannelore B. Rader, "Reference Services as a Teaching Function," *Library Trends* 29 (Summer 1980), pp. 95-103; Mimi Dudley, "A Philosophy of Library Instruction," *Research Strategies* 1(2) (Spring 1983): 58-63.

4. David King and Betsy Baker, "Human Aspects of Library Technology: Implications for Bibliographic Instruction," in *Bibliographic Instruction: The Second Generation,* ed. Connie Mellon (Littleton, CO: Libraries Unlimited, 1987): 85-107.

5. Pauline Wilson. "Librarians as Teachers: The Study of an Organizational Fiction," *Library Quarterly* 49:146-162.

6. Connie Miller and Patricia Tegler. "In Pursuit of Windmills: Librarians and the Determination to Instruct," *Reference Librarian,* Winter 1987, 119-134.

7. Patricia B. Knapp. "A Suggested Program of College Instruction in the Use of the Library," *Library Quarterly,* 224-231.

8. Thomas Kirk. "Concluding Comments," *Increasing the Teaching Role of Academic Libraries.* San Francisco: Jossey-Bass, 1984, 95-97.

9. Kathleen Dunn. "Psychological Needs and Source Linkages in Undergraduate Information-Seeking Behavior," *Proceedings of the 1986 ACRL National Conference,* Chicago: American Library Association, 172-178.

10. Kenneth Allen. "Student and Faculty Attitudes," *Library College Journal* 3:29 (Fall, 1970): 28-36.

11. Jinnie Y. Davis and Stella Bentley. "Factors Affecting Perceptions of Academic Libraries," *College & Research Libraries* 40 (November 1979): 527-32.

12. William K. Stephenson. "Library Instruction: The Best Road to Development for Faculty, Librarians and Students," *Library Instruction and Faculty Development: Growth Opportunities in the Academic Community.* Ed. Nyal Z. Williams and Jack T. Tsukamoto. Ann Arbor, MI: Pierian, 1980, p. 81.

13. Stephenson, p. 81.

14. Constance McCarthy. "The Faculty Problem," *Journal of Academic Librarianship,* 11 (July 1985): 142-145.

15. McCarthy, p. 144.

16. Daniel Gore. "Something There is that Doesn't Love: A Professor," *Library Journal* 104 (April 1982): 686-691.

17. Nancy Gwinn. "The Faculty-Library Connection," *Change* 10 (September 1978): 19-21. Evan Ira Farber. "Librarian-Faculty Communication Techniques," *Proceedings of the Southeastern Conference on Approaches to Bibliographic Instruction,* edited by Cerise Oberman-Soroka. Charleston, SC: College of Charleston, 1978.

18. Anne Grodzins Lipow. "Teaching Faculty to Use the Library: A Success-

ful Program for University of California, Berkeley, Faculty," In *New Horizons for Academic Libraries*, edited by Robert D. Stueart and Richard D. Johnson. New York: K. G. Saur, 1979.

19. Catherine E. Pasterczyk. "Checklist for the New Selector," *C&RL News*, July/August 1988, 434-435.

20. Stephenson, p. 82.

PART VIII:
THE PAST AND THE FUTURE

Conclusion

James Billington, the recently appointed Librarian of Congress, stated in an interview published in the *Princeton Alumni Weekly* (March 23, 1988, page 21):

> I am now presiding over the world's largest library, with 85 million items and three quarters of its books in foreign languages. There are vast quantities of knowable things that we don't know in this country because nobody can read those books. As we enter the information age, this is a major national need and an area in which, at the present, there is no real leadership.

Dr. Billington is right that few people in the United States have the foreign language competencies to read non-English language books. However, an even more serious concern is that only a small percentage of our U.S. population uses libraries and many who do are not very successful in using them effectively and efficiently. This volume of *The Reference Librarian* has been devoted to describing some of the library instruction programs available in our nation's higher education institutions and in providing areas for future development of our academic library instruction programs. From perusal of these articles, one can gain great insights into progress librarians have made from the traditional focus on library orientation tours to a more encompassing and sophisticated approach to library instruction. Several of the articles define methods of offering basic library skills instruction via new technologies such as online computer-assisted instruction, CD-ROM (computer disc-read only memory), and innovative microcomputer applications. Some of these newer methods of instruction can relieve librarians of more labor-intensive personal contact instruction, thus freeing up time from lower division instruction to devote to upper division and graduate courses, special groups, or preparation of other alternative modes of instruction (e.g., video or slide tape instruction). In addition, some libraries have been able to redirect time and level of staffing devoted to reference desk assistance to increased levels of professional librarian instruction via in-depth assistance by appointment or via term paper counseling services.

A major focus in library instruction today is on programs that build on progressively more sophisticated library expertise and advanced research strategies unique to a particular discipline or needed to conduct interdisciplinary research. Instead of emphasizing types and specific titles of reference sources, library instruction today is geared towards question analysis as it relates to information generation in a field, structure of published knowledge in that field, dissemination of the literature of a discipline, and retrieval of information by discipline or among interrelated subject fields. The articles published here demonstrate some real leadership and innovation in library instruction since the 1960s and 1970s. But, it is also clearly evident that few programs address all of the library instructional needs of an institution of higher education.

As documented by the authors of the articles herein, a fully integrative library user education program needs visionary leaders and highly competent, well-organized administrators and professional staff. The growing complexity of library collections, services, operations, and new technologies requires a myriad of expertise never before required of library users, librarians, and other educators. In addition, it is becoming even more important to establish greater cooperative efforts among school, public, special, academic libraries, other information agencies, computer center personnel, online database vendors, other faculty, administrators, and the like. Greater emphasis needs to be placed on librarian visibility and contacts outside of the libraries, political and public relations issues, alternative and supplementary funding sources, teaching faculty/librarian liaison, extended library services to off-campus and on-campus users utilizing online remote access capabilities, and increased focus on meeting the needs of widely divergent library user populations.

Contributors to this volume of *The Reference Librarian* have raised some important questions, offered some creative ideas, and provided insight into many of the improved and enhanced library instruction programs available. Dr. Patricia Breivik points out the need for library user education program heads and staff to gain a greater understanding of course content in order to redirect classroom faculty to build courses around the existing literature of their fields rather than on lectures and textbooks, to redirect faculty's reliance on "reserve room reading" for student educational experiences to a more active participation by students in identifying, locating, and retrieving information on their own. As teaching faculty and university administrators move towards a renewed emphasis on critical thinking and reasoning skills, improved question analysis and inquiry abilities, ability to evaluate what one reads, librarians need to accommodate these skills in library instruction programs and integrate library user education skills as closely as possible to what is taught in the classroom and to assignments given requiring library use.

Administrators of library user education programs and librarian-teachers in these programs must work together to ensure a directed, but visionary library instruction program. As mentioned by Mary Nofsinger, academic library instruction programs need to be coordinated with elementary and high schools in the state to ensure that entering college and university freshmen have mastered basic library competencies/performance standards. The same coordination is needed between colleges and universities and community colleges to ensure that transfer students have mastered the level of library skills needed upon entering a more advanced academic institution. Only through such cooperation and coordination can academic libraries hope to gain the time needed to devote to more sophisticated library instruction needed by their students.

New technologies, particularly computer-based online searching, have forced radical changes in the way literature searches are conducted, in speeding up retrieval and delivery of information, and in provision of library instruction. Judith M. Pask, Dana Smith, Mary Huston, Cerise Oberman, and Nancy Allen provide specific examples in their articles, demonstrating that online instruction and computer-assisted tutorials can provide alternative modes of instruction that are just as effective as the more traditional one-hour library presentation. These modes of instruction can release librarians from time devoted to lower level basic instruction and allow more time for upper division and graduate level library instruction. These computer-based instruction programs allow for more advanced evaluation methodologies and speedier statistical analysis of teaching effectiveness, leading to additional revisions and enhancements in user education programs.

Rao Aluri's article demonstrates that software programs are available that can greatly enhance manipulation of data information retrieved via "downloading." He also points out the added problems in teaching library skills and research strategies that such microcomputer hardware and software can create.

All of these articles offer creative and innovative methods to enhance and develop library use instruction. They also provide insights into the problems, challenges, and frustrations faced by teaching faculty and students in gaining life-long learning skills and by instructional librarians in defining, developing, improving and enhancing library instruction to the library user populations served.

From reading these thought-provoking essays, it is apparent that any integration of library use skills into the general education curriculum will require a carefully planned, well-organized, and comprehensive library user education program with highly motivated, competent administrators and professional staff, with expertise in a wide variety of areas.

The following recommendations are provided to those who are building an initial program or revamping an existing one:

A. Begin your integrative library user education program by targeting individuals and groups with whom cooperation must be gained.
B. Target user populations to be served and course curriculum areas for instruction to determine the objectives and competencies to be expected from groups and individuals reached.
C. Build a progressively sophisticated program from basic skills needed to advanced strategies to be used in the students' majors and through life-long learning needs.
D. Develop relevant assessment and evaluation methodologies for all modes of instruction to test effectiveness of teaching and learning.
E. Plan for professional development and education retraining needs of staff involved in provision of instruction.
F. Investigate alternative sources for supplementary funding of the library user education program.
G. Determine promotional efforts needed to ensure a successful, visible, and politically viable program.
H. Realize the impact of a successful program on other library units, other libraries, and staffing/service priorities.
I. Be prepared to adjust library service priorities and budget allocations when necessary, but don't allow the library instruction program to adversely impact other user needs such as collection development and interlibrary loan.
J. Budget time devoted to library user instruction activities carefully so that the demand doesn't overrun resources and staff's ability to meet the demands in a positive, constructive manner.
K. Determine how staff initiative, innovation, motivation, and excellence will be rewarded.
L. Allow for flexibility and change but realize that consistency in content and objectives for learning is necessary.
M. Consider provision of a variety of instructional modes and teaching methodologies. Prepare for different learning styles. But don't try to do too much. "Burn out" is a risk.

N. Leave adequate time for planning interaction and cooperation with student groups, faculty, administrators, other library staff, other libraries, information agencies and brokers.

It is apparent that library instruction has developed rapidly in the last 2-3 decades and that the renewed emphasis on general education curricular reform, changing technologies, and increasing financial constraints will require greater leadership, increasing levels of knowledge and expertise on the part of all librarians, greater visibility and political savvy, and revised service priorities and staffing/budget/resource reallocations. It is also apparent from these articles that the creativity, willingness to accept new and changing challenges, and the expertise to carry it out is being developed.

Maureen Pastine